NATIVE LINKS

The Surprising History of Our First People in Golf

Mark Wagner

BACK NINE PRESS

Back Nine Press
Chicago, Illinois
www.back9press.com
@backninepress

9 8 7 6 5 4 3 2 1

First Edition

Library of Congress Cataloging-in-Publication Data:
2024940565

ISBN 978-1-956237-22-1 (hardcover)
ISBN 978-1-956237-23-8 (e-book)

For Monica, Myles, and my loving family

CONTENTS

FOREWORD

BY STEVE McDONALD

In *Native Links: The Surprising History of Our First People in Golf*, Mark Wagner takes you on an enlightened, historical trail of Native golf's many stories, the game's unsung heroes, and the many emotions raised by this journey. His ability to compare the cosmos of golf to making a way home, from tee to green, and in dealing with all the difficult lies, the undulating bounces of the ball in these closely held stories, the author keeps one from placing this amazing book down once you've tee'ed it up.

We as Indigenous people, trusted keepers of the land, water, wind, fire, sky, and every direction, celebrate being brought home and being recognized as contributors in the game we all love. And as someone who has spent his life making these pilgrimages from tee to green and green to tee, this book also has a deeper connection to Native Americans.

Native Links' celebrates and tells the histories of the Native-owned golf courses, from the sacrifice of tribal members who built Shinnecock Hills to the excitement of the Native American Open at Santa Ana Pueblo. There are many great Native-owned golf courses across the country.

As Native Americans, golf is a way to play a sport that puts us in touch with our lands, lands our ancestors walked and cared for, so we can be here today. The game allows us to maintain Native traditions of respect and awareness. *Native Links* demonstrates how we have been and are successful at the ancient stick-and-ball game.

From Oscar Smith Bunn and the 1896 U.S. Open to Gabby Lemieux and the new generation of great Native golfers like Gene Webster, Jr. who now have access to courses and instruction, *Native Links* tells this compelling story both about the land and about the people.

As an enrolled member of the Prairie Band Potawatomi Nation, and through my journey to becoming a Life Member of the PGA of America, I celebrate this lineage and welcome this foundational history of contributions to American golf by Native Americans.

Just as the architect routs the path, and the golfer becomes the pathfinder on those routings, Wagner's *Native Links* finds a home in both golf and Indian Country . . .

—Steve McDonald
Devoted loving M-Sho
Tribal Member, Prairie Band Potawatomi Nation
PGA Life Member
North American Indigenous
Athletic Hall of Fame Member
Haskell Four-Sport Letterman

A Note on Terms and Language

Golfing on Turtle Island could have been an alternate title of this book. In many Native oral histories, from Back-Then-Time into Right-Now-Time, it's common for communities to call the North American continent Turtle Island. Notable origin stories include Sky Woman building the earth on the back of the turtle that emerged after the great flood which was caused when the lake at the top of the world overflowed. Some Native cultures do not use the term Native Americans for this reason: they've been here since the earth sat on the back of the great turtle, long before Columbus drifted in, and long before Amerigo Vespucci drew his first maps.

Native Links uses the terms First People and Indigenous People (literally, "of the land") whenever possible and refers to members belonging to a community—a tribe, or nation, or band. The term Indian has also been regarded in some communities as inaccurate, as it is based on Columbus' reports from when he arrived in the Caribbean and thought he'd found Southeast Asia.

Native Links acknowledges these historical inaccuracies and attempts to make tribal affiliations wherever possible, though acknowledges that, in telling history, some terms are "baked in" and cannot be avoided.

As for golf tours on Turtle Island, stay tuned.

TABUTNE/ MIIGWECH / THANK YOU

You don't have anything
if you don't have the stories.
—Leslie Marmon Silko, "Ceremony"

Of all the fancy, ancient, vulgar and comic vernacular we use for golf, the hole as "getting home" surrounds the themes of *Native Links*. Making the tiny pilgrimage from the green to the next tee, we have temporarily arrived in a place of satisfaction and return. For a short while anyway, we have made it home.

There's a Scottish word—*Hiraeth*—defined as a longing for a place that we can't return to. The Welsh spell it slightly differently—*Hireath*—and claim the word has no specific translation in English. This may or may not be the case, though it's safe to point out the root *hir* can be found in a lot of languages' words for home. *Hir. Here. Hier.* This must be the place. It makes sense that the least violent, most difficult game in human history would have finding home, as opposed to victory, as the goal. The literature of the game at its finest speaks to this idyllic world, a nostalgia for an ancient place to which we want to return and forever want to remain.

Bernard Darwin expressed this same Mecca-like longing for a simpler Yesterday when he lamented how numbers were replacing the more poetic names for clubs. What unimaginative cad would call the stick a 9-iron for what we used to call a niblick? Is a number word like *five* better than *cleek*? Wherefore the baffie? This romantic longing, the backward glance for the lost, the hope for the ancient, peaceable homeland: these sentiments of the game drive the sweet labor of this book, but also set up a more difficult task.

Gathering the stories and oral histories, and researching the achievements of our First People in the game of golf, many spoke to this idea of return, a longing for some unsullied paradise that may exist only in our collective imaginations. A new history of golf with our First People as part of the central cast won't solve climate change or discover the unified field, and it won't resolve past injustices that number as many as the stars. *Native Links* simply acknowledges that in the DNA of American history, Indigenous history is a leading strand and that is true for golf as well. While our civilization of productivity has brought us unparalleled levels of comfort and wealth and fun, we've also grown apart from the land, from the natural world. There's a growing sense we've been removed from a place where the ancient wisdom is real, where we can rediscover connection with the earth, a connection with the "we're still here" logic of the elders of our tribes and nations and bands.

As Cassie Prue, Lakota and a PGA professional, has it: "We come from the earth and belong to the earth, so we see ourselves as related to everything and everyone." Some golfers go back to Scotland or Ireland for that sense of belonging, to explore whether that longing is abated, swimming upstream to the seaside hills where the game was codified. We golf aficionados and historians like to think our DNA evolved from that place, one of unending belonging, if only for a few hours on a beautiful afternoon.

While many in the golf industry are plateauing and in a "hold" pattern, even after the surge in outdoor activity during the Covid pandemic, according to *Golfweek*, "there is one group of builders as bullish as ever on course construction: Native Americans." With Fee to Trust programs, in successful advocacy, litigation, and lawsuits, with #LandBack, and aided by the revenues from gaming, many tribes have built museums, archives, government centers and—surprise—golf courses. Artful and challenging layouts, designed by the finest of architects, now populate some reservations and homelands, and through this window we have pulled back the curtain on a long history of players and teachers for whom the ancient stick-and-ball game has been a way of finding home.

The new history is multifaceted, layered, and spoken here by those who were there in the right-now-time, or knew someone who was there in the back-then-time, or knew someone who knew someone who was there. Oral traditions are able to get at a layering of truth, to participate in the story in a way that resists the tropes and stereotypes of "accepted history." A golf instructor from the Potawatomi, Emily McDonald put this to me plainly as well: "We hold the stories of our elders high. They are here with us when we walk the land. They are the ones who persevered so we can be here."

Finding those elders, playing a match with them, getting a lesson from them, winning their trust: well, it was all the sweet will a Jersey Boy could muster. I would be smudged, taken for a rat, taught (Arnold Palmer's) perfect grip, and lose matches to Rod Curl and Steve McDonald among others—(I went 0-for in all matches over a two-year span)—still the goal remained to find a home in these shared stories.

While asking for forgiveness for those I've overlooked, here are the folks of the right-now-time who helped and gave that special taste to this traveler as he listened to and walked The Red Road alongside the First of the Firsts.

Mike Smith, Shinnecock; David Bunn Martine, Shinnecock, Apache; JC Wright, Lakota, Poston Butte Golf Course; Cal Nez, Dine, Roy Smith, Talking Stick; Blessing McAnlis-Vasquez, Salt River; Steve McDonald, Potawatomie; Richard Humphreys, Golf Course Architecture; Diane Fraher, American Indian Artists; Maggie Lagle, Veronica Nenno, and Rosemary Maravetz, USGA Museum and Library; Chuck Olson Wawashkamo; Dianna Hunt and Kevin Abourezk, ICT; Karen Moraghan, Hunter PR; Margaret Morrissey, Southbridge Public Library ; Arthur Lussi, Lake Placid Golf Club; Bambi Pedu, Librarian, Lake Placid Library; Jennifer Ambrose, the Adirondack Museum at Blue Mountain; Lori Potter, Mashantucket Pequot Tribal Council; Rees Jones, The Open Doctor; Robert Trent Jones Jr. Golf Course Architect; Jay Garcia, Chairman, Tamaya Tribe, Santa Ana Pueblo; Derek Gutierrez, Santa Ana Golf Club; Rod Curl Sr and Rod Curl Jr., Wintu; Tom Lovell, Diné; Curtis Osceola, Miccosukee Tribal Chief; Jack Dempsey, Historian; Fran and Pate Hudson; Tom Coyne, Writer and Historian; Micah Hummingbird Jones, Santa Ana Golf Club; Jason Montoya, Santa Ana Pueblo, Player Development at Santa Ana Golf Club; Adrian Hopper, Osage Golf Pro; Anthony Shackleford, Osage Nation; Clint Begay, Diné; Robin Herrington, Nike; Sam McCracken, Sioux and Assiniboine; Johnny and Linda Miller; Paul Reams and the Utah Food Industry; and Dr. Gerald Bagley.

Part 1

Before and After Back-Then-Time

Back-Then-Time in Native languages and ideas refers to the time before the Era of "Contact and Discovery," before what would be centuries of struggle and suffering for our First People brought on by colonialism. Before and After Back-Then-Time is this book's term for when golf informed a shared history, and "contact and discovery" did not take the form of murderous or disease-ridden interactions. Golf—with its focus on being part of and hugging the land, requiring the most amount of land of any game played—has many surprising overlaps with Our First People's history, and these confluences give us cause for hope and optimism. And Surprise.

Surprise is said to be one of the six universal human expressions—an emotion all people in all cultures are said to be able to understand—and it's this sense of surprise that has guided this research into Native Americans' place in a game generally thought to primarily be elitist and white. The phrase "a struggle within a struggle" might be one way to articulate this surprise: The accomplishments of Native Americans in golf are enduring and inspiring, as well as a way to tell history. To know these stories helps us to enjoy what many of us know to be a sublime experience—the game of golf and all that it entails—the challenge, mental tenacity, and comradery; being with nature, being with the land.

Being with the land—the sensuous appeal of the earth herself—is not the least of the reasons why Native cultures continue to grow into the ancient club-and-ball game. Whether on the sheep-designed terrain of the old links, or the naturally rolling hills among the native trees of a woodlands course, we return to reclaim a balance with nature and with each other, and with how an architect's vision of 9 or 18 holes sculpts itself into a natural order of things. As Robert Trent Jones II says about his routing at Cochiti, one of the first Native-owned courses, "Great golf courses are collaborative: the land, the golfer's eye, the designer. A composition and collaboration, like an orchestra that is playing the land." This connection to Land with a capital "L," to our collaborative music-making with the land, makes for a natural bridge between the game and our First People, though the story takes at times amazing turns and hardly goes in a straight line.

Chapter 1

PUTTING FEATHERS ON THE GOLF BALL

"If you want to hear a good story, ask a caddie," Mike Smith says with a smile. This idea might be as old as civilization itself: who holds the talking stick (or the story lance) is the privileged one, given to speak. A longtime resident of the Shinnecock reservation, Mike followed his brother, father, and grandfather onto Shinnecock Hills and started looping when he was 11 (in 1960, for $2.50 a loop). His smile seems to be one of both wisdom and preparation when he talks about a good story. As in: This might take a while. He is up to the task.

On the eve of the 1986 U.S. Open at Shinnecock Hills Golf Club, Smith—a Native and pastor, a golfer, groundskeeper, a father and son, grandson and brother, husband and father—stood on the 9th green looking over the sandy hills of one of the world's finest links. He'd worked alongside his brother in prepping the course for The Open. In the calm of a Wednesday night, not a creature was stirring, and these storied sand bumps rose gently between Peconic and Shinnecock Bays. All competetitors were level, as the salt air flowed from the ocean to the bay, carrying the expectations of the best golfers in the world, who were all in town to try to win the hardest one to win.

It was a calm before a storm.

"No one was there," Mike Smith recalls. "It was quiet, and

there was this sunset over the ocean. Purples and reds and oranges painting the sky. And I looked over and saw my father and Charlie Thom standing like they always do. They had cigars in their mouths. My father had his arms crossed, and Charlie had his hands in his pockets. They had cigars and looks of satisfaction on their faces. They knew the course would defend itself."

If these links have known the robber barons and families of presidents, if the clubhouse had a who's-who of champions on the walls, if the soul of the Shinnecock Nation and First People guard the land, then the presiding spirits of Smith and Thom had made this place about relationships—human to human, earth to sky, ocean to land, land to golf, all born of a desire for excellence. By 1986, Elmer Smith, Mike's father, a Shinnecock Native and the first full-time superintendent of Shinnecock, had been gone five years. Charlie Thom—a Scotsman, the first full-time golf pro on these hallowed grounds—started in 1906 and held court for 54 years. Thom's legend includes a hole here in his name: Thom's Elbow. That's golf immortality that will last as long as the earth circles the sun.

"They knew no one was going to burn the course," Mike continued, still wearing his knowing smile. "The predictions were saying the pros were going to go low. Six under. Eight under." Bets were placed, bragging rights ventured, and the subtle rolls and treacheries of the course laid in wait. And the thin veil that separates our world from the rest of the universe pressed down on the links as a nor'easter began to gather in the not-so-distant Atlantic. Beach plums and laurel and holly that lined the spirited fairways began to wave, and ancient spirits and the weather became players.

"Ray Floyd won at one under," Mike recalls. "In 1995, when The Open returned again, Corey Pavin won on even par." It's worth noting that in '04, Retief Goosen's winning score was four under, and in '18, Brooks Koepka got home in plus one. Mike notes all this with a tone of pride and foreboding: In those last two U.S. Opens, when no Smith was on the course, controversary ensued. He doesn't like to go into details, and won't label it a curse. He only offers, "It's ancient, tribal land."

Mike Smith is 75 and the retired pastor at the Shinnecock Presbyterian Church, the same church where John Shippen's father had brought the Living Word to save the souls of a tribe that didn't need saving. His early life included some of the trappings that come with the least violent and most difficult of all human games. Booze and women? Check. Performance versus potential? Like most of us, a thousand times he performed under potential. And how about a story of being saved and returning to the spiritual through a higher power? That too.

Mike Smith's ties to Shinnecock Hills—beginning with his grandfather Tom, and his great grandfather on his maternal side—capture the irony and humor and beauty of the game we all love. The family name turns up in the minutes of the club from when there was a chairman of the Grass Committee. His father had one job in his life. Even the *New York Times* took note: "Smith is a legendary figure, famous for his grass-growing genius, his probity, his decency, his way of treating everyone, caddies and members, with the same respect." When that respectful spirit presides, there are no curses, and the course shines.

"They did things in the old way when they built it, with the road plows that the oxen had to pull. Our ancestors, yes. We manually built that course." Mike is proud of the tribe's heritage, which goes far back before the club, with a history—not of war—but of whaling and wood and ivory carving. Shinnecock rituals celebrate love and parenting. Their wood crafts and baskets line the Americana shelves of our finest museums. Shinnecock and Peconic Bays had the best oysters in the hemisphere. And while the golf club and its history make up a sliver of Shinnecock Time on Mother Earth, here's the rub: The course came to be a central part of the tribe's life, and the people on both sides of Montauk Highway mixed, married, and mated.

David Bunn Martine remembers when Elmer Smith

brought Charlie Thom by the house to pay respects to his grandmother, Alice Osceola Bunn Martinez. “He bought her a bottle of wine,” Martine recalls (though Thom was reported to be a tea drinker). Dave’s grandfather, Charles Martine, worked as a foreman on the ground crews at both The National Golf Links and Shinnecock. From Charlie Thom’s visit, he remembers that the Scotsman had a big, dark mustache and was quite personable. And true to form, Elmer Smith widened the circle by introducing the tribe to the pro. The golf course was the engine driving economic and social integration.

“We were able to play there growing up. And in the 1960s and ‘70s, growing up and as a teenager, we were afforded that privilege, to caddie and play. ... I’m trying to restore those relationships,” Mike Smith says, “It’s what my father taught me.” Mike’s son Matthew is now the assistant superintendent, the first recipient of the Elmer and Peter Smith Scholarship, which was set up by the club to honor the past and prepare for the future.

“My father and brother were all about relationships and integrity,” Mike recalls. The combined years of the Smith family on the sandy hills of the stony shore called Shinnecock Hills is well into the triple digits. His family’s history—like the tribe’s history—is now tied to these links in a weave of tournaments and rounds, injustices and prayers, stories that celebrate a history distinct from “Out East,” as New Yorkers call this area. And that same tradition of integrity and relationship building continues with Mike’s son Matthew, who followed his uncle in the turf management program at Rutgers. Matt has returned to tend the course his great grandfather, grandfather, father, and uncle tended. He will be here when the Open returns in 2026, when again the White Tribe and the Red Tribe will discuss who gets what of the $85 million windfall brought in by the tournament.

This interplay of the trappings of wealth and the desire for human excellence is not new here. “Out East” is the place of the Springs and Jackson Pollack, of Jay Gatsby and parties gone out of bounds in fictitious East Egg and West Egg, but for golfers and the Shinnecock Nation, these are the links Johnny Miller called "the best in the world." Contemporary golf course architect Christine Fraser used the word "sublime," a word that seems to surround both the highest and simplest compliment that can be had. If you asked Tiger Woods or Jack Nicklaus to pick the perfect spot for a golf course, they might well have selected these sandy hills. What causes this greatness, this sublimity?

"You're talking to a preacher," Mike Smith warns, then adds after a pause, "Look. It's as if God dropped it in place. I mean, the flow of the holes is organic, as if it were dropped from the skies." How else to explain the beauty and the integrity of the place standing after five or six of history's great [golf course] architects had a go at it? He adds again, as if this needs repeating, "It's on ancient, tribal lands."

Ronald Eleazer Jr. is also one of Shinnecock Nation's legendary golfers; his father and brother had also worked for decades on the grounds alongside the Smith family. He has spoken to the same point: "To Whites, Shinnecock Hills is just a golf course, but the course sits on our ancestral land. God entrusted us to take care of it."

Dondi Williams Jr. is the former Sachem of the Shinnecock Tribe, a former Marine who lost a foot in service, and a lifelong golfer. He's also the son of Dondi Williams Sr., one of the legendary Shinnecock golfers who founded the Shinnecock Golfers Association of Native golfers in the 1960s. The organization formalized in 1974 as a 501(c)(3) for scholarships for the tribe's folk. Dondi Sr. played—and won—regularly at Shinnecock Hills, and any other local course that got in his way.

"I listened to the stories growing up," Dondi Jr. says from his hospital bed where he's just received a new knee. "I always heard all the names of the golfers on Shinnecock. Mr. Eleazer. He was a real good golfer … the Bunns … Shippen … my father! These are the very beginnings."

The stories bend time. One of the shared human desires—

to go back and forth in time. Hell, space can be bent, so time can be bent as well. The mathematician Kurt Gödel imagined we'd be able to get outside the bubble of space time—through wormholes—and come back in at another (earlier or later) time. While we haven't quite reached a wormhole yet, if we reach back—through stories and listening—there is the possibility of redeeming time, fixing the past: not only through the long memory of our tribes, but of our actions as well. For if that relationship between Shinnecock Hills and the tribe went through troubled times—a relationship rich in both history and ironies—it's a relationship worth redeeming.

"There's a new generation there," Dondi Jr. tells me. "They reached out to us and our leaders, and they are starting to do clinics with us and our children. They want a relationship with us because now they know the history."

No other course has held the U.S. Open in all three centuries. And where many of the hole names speak to Scottish traditions—including Redan and Eden and Ben Nevis, named for the highest hill in the Old Country—it's worth noting that the one hole named for the tribe—the 17th, Shinnecock—is uphill and into changeable winds. The Smiths, who have lived and played through this history, could easily see how the universal forces and golf combine to create the Shinnecock mystique. If the creator landed the finest links in the world on the narrowest expanse of land on Long Island, some well-spring of life force ebbs up from the soft flow of the hills, from the bones in the ancient burial grounds, in the airflow from Great Peconic Bay to Shinnecock Bay, in the drift of Atlantic blue and grey mist. It's a rare day that the full sun doesn't honor these hills. The spirits of the elders are happy here, where human labor, and vision, and a creator's handiwork have combined to make a delightful and difficult dance among golf links.

The courts have used the phrases *estoppel* and *laches* to settle any of the legal challenges to the land. *Laches* is legalese for: too much time has passed to get this right. For this and a thousand other reasons, some here don't even like the term Native American. The tribe was here before there was even a concept of America. *Shinnecock* is preferred, and their traditions, like most of Native American history, are carried down by recipes and songs and stories, the tribal wisdom passed on through the words that carry the truth—and the ironies—of generations.

These shores were once part of a vast and relatively peaceful confederation of whalers and water men and women, who raised their families over generations that go back well before Latin was even spoken. It's a story that requires an understanding of considerable ironies: generations of Shinnecock worked alongside Meads and Whites, Vanderbilts and Roosevelts, Fords and Ten Eckts, and the Havemeyers.

"He only called that in once," Mike Smith recalls a story his father passed down.

Elmer Smith had a green Ford pickup, Mike recalls, an infamous ride used to ferry the many Shinnecock men and women who worked at the club. The reservation's West Gate is a short drive to Tuckahoe Road, which bisects the course, and sometimes Elmer Smith's green chariot would sway from

Elmer Smith. Behind him: Charlie Thom, Oscar Bunn, and Willie Dunn. By David Bunn Martine.

the folks in the back. One season, Elmer Smith's green ride broke down. He tried to get it fixed once, and it came back broken. So, he sent it back in. When it wasn't right, he talked to Henry Ford II. Ford contacted the dealership. He told them to fix it right and send the bill to him.

"For the rest of my father's life, the bills for his repairs went to Henry Ford himself." Mike chuckles telling the story, but the meaning speaks to the high-wire act his Shinnecock relatives strung between The People of the Stony Shore and the White people that came looking for a place to play. There is an unstated acknowledgement that the tribe had selected the best place on the universe to live, and the White folks could summer there, but had to buck up.

These complexities and complicities—these relationships—bring us one of the great ironies of the game: How do we explain that in this supposed "White man's game," this "rich man's game," that the first golf pro and teacher born on the continent was Native?

Long memories and satisfied spirits stand guard over the ancient, tribal lands: Elmer Smith and Charlie Thom continue to take all comers. The ghosts of Willie Dunn and Seymour, whose Golf *Fundamentals* (1922) is the real secret behind Ben Hogan's *The Modern Fundamentals of Golf*. It's only a long-flushed drive from Shinnecock Hills to the town cemetery where C.B. Macdonald and Seth Raynor watch over their masterpiece. Toomey and Flynn, all the winners, along with hundreds of the unnamed and restless dead, their biographies erased.

"If you want to hear a good story, ask a caddie." Yes. Leave it to a caddie and golfer and retired pastor to lead the way: Mike Smith knows where the golf course and the tribe's spirits live. He'll be the one with the courage to take us to the reservation burial grounds, where we will find distant relatives, the Shinnecock golfers and, yes, the one who—with all the irony and surprise—could be said to be the first golf pro born on this continent: a Shinnecock Montauk Native. His name is Oscar Smith Bunn, and that story begins with a shipwreck.

Chapter 2

AN ORIGIN STORY OF GOLF IN AMERICA

On the evening of December 11, 1876, nine months after Oscar Smith Bunn was born, The Circassian—a large trading vessel with a damaged rudder—ran aground on the outer bar off Mecox Bay of the South Fork. The ship had picked up a pilot in Sandy Hook, the spit of land in New Jersey 50 miles across the New York Bight, but had been unable to negotiate the coastal bend and drifted north in a nor'easter. Was her compass off? The pilot incompetent? Whatever part cruelty or carelessness plays in what follows, the ship could not negotiate the currents and winds of a storm blowing snow and sleet. The loaded vessel wound up on the sand bars off the South Fork of Long Island. The Captain—Richard Williams of Liverpool—called for aid, and ten Shinnecock men answered that call. After all, the Shinnecock were whalers and watermen and knew the currents and bar better than anyone. Among the four members of the Bunn family that responded, David Waikus Bunn—the father of a nine-month-old Oscar and five other children, a celebrated whaler and waterman—fought his way out to The Circassian. Over the course of ten days, all efforts to dislodge the ship failed. Breacher buoys fell into the surf, and on December 29th, as the people on the shore could hear the Natives praying and singing on the bow, the storm proved too fierce. The ship broke apart, and all were lost.

As the Shinnecock tribe hovered around 200 in number at the time, losing ten watermen, whalers, and fathers was a devastating blow. The men were buried in a horseshoe-shaped mound in the tribe's burial grounds. "Circassian widow and orphan" became a social category after the tragedy. And while there is, we can be sure, a Mount Olympus of literature on how an absent father drives the ambitions and insecurities of young men, what we know is this: Whatever the psychological and familial consequences the shipwreck had for the tribe and its young, Oscar Bunn would become the country's first golf pro, clubmaker, and teacher born on the continent. He learned to untie the Gordian Knots of the family and tribe's losses enough to set course records, to teach on two continents, to take down the great Harry Vardon in a nine-hole match. Perhaps most surprising of all, he would—as a brown-skinned Shinnecock—represent a golf club that had no ethnic members in the 1896 U.S. Open.

Whatever days and weeks and months and years are erased by time, we know Oscar's mother, Mary Emma Bunn, raised her six children and made the best clam chowder in the world from the mollusk jewels plucked from Shinnecock Bay. We know Oscar learned wood and ivory carving alongside his brother Charles, who would grow up to be a hunting guide for the New York set. (Charles' hand-carved decoys are valued as among the finest in history.) And where Charles became a guide to Roosevelts, Vanderbilts, Walkers, and others who came to hunt fowl "Out East," teen-aged Oscar fell under the tutelage of Willie and Seymour Dunn: two of the many Scotsmen who came to this country to spread the gospel of golf. He would have had a hand in taming the oxen that pulled the road scrapers that finished the first edition of Shinnecock Hills' famed golf holes.

David Bunn Martine, Oscar's great grandnephew—an artist who has completed a portrait of his distant uncle Oscar for the USGA Museum—notes,

> "The early days of the 20th century when Oscar Bunn

> lived was a very harsh time in the United States for most Native Americans. This was the time of the boarding schools, when Native children were removed from the home and forced to go to the boarding schools. Tribal nations did what they had do to survive, in many cases continuing their traditions secretly. Some of our people, who made their living from the natural out-of-doors environment, came to know many of the wealthier people who had come to live all around on the remaining lands of the Shinnecock and Montauk. So Oscar would have intermingled with many of the people who originated the game of golf on Shinnecock land, and he excelled at the sport. He became well respected as a player and a teacher, not just in New England, but also in South America. He blazed a trail that today can serve as an inspiration to other Native Americans who want to play the game of golf, and also for anyone to attempt to achieve something even though the expectations for them may be very low."

Some Shinnecock would go on whalers, or to work in the big city, or would marry into the diverse population of opportunists and colonists making up 19th-century Long Island. One group followed the circus up to Wisconsin, and there's a story about a letter coming back from a whaler who settled, married, and mated in Papau New Guinea. Oscar was not one to take to the far and wide, at least not early in life. He not only stayed, but thrived on tribal lands and found a niche in what was known as a "White man's game." Whether a missing father played a role in this accomplished life is a matter of pure speculation. In fact, we have only one eyewitness account of Oscar. Bunn's niece—a daughter of Oscar's brother Charles Sumner Bunn—recounts, "Uncle Oscar took me to a fair more than once when I was a kid. It was just an ordinary fair. He gave me everything to eat that I saw. ... The fairs used to be down to the eastern end of Southampton. Later they were at the Southampton Golf Club. Whatever there was to eat, Uncle Oscar got it for me. Hot dogs. Lemonade. I had a wonderful time with him. He was jolly and good natured. I don't remember anything but a merry-go-round and a Ferris wheel at those fairs long ago."

We could just as easily submit to the stereotypes, much like the ones in Edith Wharton's *The Age of Innocence*, in which only wealthy New Yorkers travelled by train Out East to summer and play tennis and golf and watch polo, but Oscar's story puts the lie to those simpler histories. And the undoing of the simple history would all begin when Oscar—alongside dozens of unnamed tribesmen, men and women—led the oxen that pulled the road scrapers that shaped the land where the finest links sits on the narrowest spit of land on Long Island. Whatever ambition was driven by the loss of his father, his good nature, his skill with wood and ivory, his physical stature and courage: all of these traits would put Uncle Oscar in the company of two of golf's most noted names—Willie Dunn Jr. and Seymour Dunn—whose familial ties go back to Musselburgh, the city in the Scottish hill country where golf was first and famously codified.

And while the Dunn family's history in golf is celebrated, it's critical not to sugarcoat the reality of contact. Willie Dunn, speaking of the efforts to build the course, recorded a note that is still being debated today: "The place was dotted with Indian burial mounds, and we left some of these as bunkers in front of the holes. Others we scooped out and made into yawning bunkers, and sand-traps. We did not find out this until later when playing the course. One never knew what an explosion shot out of the sand trap would bring out a couple of fire-water flasks, or perhaps a bone or two."

To this day, the tribe views the golf-course land as sacred, for reasons other than the least violent and most difficult game in human history. Despite this, and with complicities in tow, Oscar would learn his swing and clubmaking and instruction alongside Willie. With good intentions, we can imagine he helped carve some of the early clubs, some of which sit in the Southampton Historical Museum. And through Willie, Oscar Bunn would meet and mingle and play beside the giants of the "build up" era of golf in America.

The so-called humbling game did not humble Oscar. While he continued to teach and play at Shinnecock, he would also leave to teach at Lake Placid Golf Club in the Adirondacks where he would have worked alongside Willie Dunn's nephew Seymour.

A Shining Moment in Golf History

But first, the second U.S. Open came. As is well known, the fledgling USGA had five clubs as founding members. The overseers included folks who would shape both golf and U.S. history in profound and multitudinous ways—George Herbert Walker, the Vanderbilts, William Whitney, C.B. Macdonald—the names ring with influence, and all were being led by sugar magnate, Theodore Augustus Havemeyer, who had helped to establish the USGA and one of its founding clubs: Newport Country Club. An industrialist who had developed and cornered the sugar market with his brother, H.O. Havemeyer, Theodore played a principle role in founding the USGA in 1894, and—in a famous moment in 1896—secured that this new game would be an inclusive operation, despite the challenges that lay ahead.

According to his great grandson, Frederick Christin Havemeyer, Theodore Havemeyer's legacy is manifold: "It's amazing that golf has become such a principled sport. And that began in part with our family. If he was on Earth today, and he saw what the game had become, he would be flabbergasted. He would be very proud. We're very proud of him, and extremely happy that our family played a part in bringing this to the United States."

The source of that pride begins on Saturday, July 18, 1896, a beautiful day in Southampton. The field for the second U.S. Open counted 35 players, including John Shippen and Bunn. Like Shippen, Bunn had been a caddie at the club, as had many other members of the reservation. Shippen's father had established the Presbyterian Church on the reservation, the same pulpit that Mike Smith would eventually preach from. And that Shippen and Bunn were both dark-skinned would come in for considerable conflagration and protest ... from the English and Scottish golfers.

The New Jersey sportswriter Arthur "Red" Hoffman reported in the *New York Sun* a conversation with Shippen from the mid-1960s. Seems the English and Scottish golfers had objections to the non-White players. Here is Shippen's first-hand account: "The professional golfers objected to colored boys meeting them on equal terms, and they held a meeting on Thursday night to protest against it." Hoffman reported that Shippen, over 65 years later, could recall "in a distinctly understated way" that there was "some slight objection by the field of Scottish and English pros" to he and Bunn playing. A meeting did take place, but Theodore Havemeyer "told the other pros he was going to run the tournament as he saw fit, and he didn't care if they played in it or not, and furthermore, the tournament would be played if only Oscar and me were in it." In effect, he told 'em to go to hell."

According to Bayliss Green, in *The Southampton Review*, "Their [Bunn and Shippen's] presence caused a protest among the white golfers at the Open—mostly Scots and Englishmen —a revolt that was famously put down by Theodore Augustus Havemeyer, the first head of the United States Golfers Association, who decreed if they didn't take up their irons, he'd simply run Bunn and Shippen out there to play by themselves."

"This was a watershed moment," said Victoria Nenno, the senior historian at the USGA Golf Museum. "The participation of Bunn and Shippen set a precedent that the U.S. Open would remain an *open* championship. The competitors would be the best in the world, regardless of background, nationality, or social standing." While golf would be tainted by the PGA's Caucasians-only rule (1916-1961), the separate USGA—from its inception—saw things differently.

"Perhaps the easier decision would have been to give in to the protests," the USGA historian said, who considers this to be a shining moment in golf history. "Rather, Havemeyer sent a powerful message that Bunn and Shippen were supported by their club and its membership, and they were going to compete."

About that moment in 1896, Fred Havemeyer notes that these events are part of their family history and passed on at the dinner table:

> "My great grandfather travelled extensively and had a broad mind. He was extremely intellectual and was up on things. When the other players threatened not to play, he wasn't going to put up with that nonsense. My great grandfather was making an example to the sports community and the rest of the world by amplifying, 'what's right is right.' If you have any brains, and you like a sport, you won't restrict it to a race or religion to qualify to play the game. The game was the game. If you're good at it, you play it and let the best man win."

At that championship, among 35 entrees, James Foulis bested the first U.S. Open Champion, Howard Rawlins, by three strokes. Shippen, who led after the first round, would receive $25 for his fifth-place finish, and famously would have competed for the top spot but for one bad hole. Oscar played alongside James Park and finished 21st, while his mentor Willie Dunn came in at 12th.

What slings and arrows of golfing prejudice attended Oscar's life, we do know the legacy of Bunn at the 1896 U.S. Open is only part of his influence in early golf. As noted in a recent interview by David Bunn Martine, the great grandnephew of Oscar Bunn, "Oscar is in the Caddie Hall of Fame, but there really is no record of him caddying. While he most definitely did caddie, as a lot of the Shinnecock Tribe did, the record is he is the only one of them to become a golf professional."

Oscar Bunn was inducted in 2009, posthumously. In their description, the Western Golf Association states, "A former caddie at Shinnecock Hills Golf Club in Southampton, NY, Oscar Bunn was a pioneering Native American golfer who competed in the U.S. Open at Shinnecock in 1896, where he was introduced to the game of golf as a young caddie. Bunn was taught the game by the club's Scottish professional, Willie Dunn, and, at the age of 19, competed in the 1896 U.S. Open there as well.

But in those early days of golf—years before he would even be able to be considered a U.S. citizen—as the game gained traction in the country, Oscar Bunn was a marquee name as a player. Take, for example, the July 15, 1905 edition of the *New York Times*. The headline reads: "Indian Contestant Holds His Own Well Against Scotch Rivals." Bunn is listed as representing Shinnecock Hills Golf Club at an event at Van Cortlandt Park. More than half the article is devoted to describing Mr. Bunn's physical characteristics, in a rather unseemly manner, but his golfing aptitude was why he was there. A review of the literature finds him listed as a professional representing these clubs in his career: Shinnecock Hills, NY; Lake Placid, NY; New Britain, CT; Jacksonville, FL; and Ampersand in Saranac Lake, NY.

In 1901, he set the course record at Quananapoxet, Connecticut at age 72, "beating the mythical opponent, who makes no mistakes." In *Golf, By Appointment*, the official bulletin of the USGA, June 1899 issue, we find: "The professional record of 36 plus 39 equals 75 is held by Oscar Bunn, the club instructor who, although young, has proved himself to be a first-rate golfer as well as a capital instructor and clubmaker. His teaching has given the game a greater interest than any it has received during the four years of the clubs' existence." And as the golfing boom swept through America in the late 19th and early 20th century, Oscar Bunn was a key figure and marquee name, so much so that he was hand-picked to meet the titan Harry Vardon at Lake Placid, when the "Vardon Invasion" came to spread the gospel of golf—and the Vardon Flyer golf ball—in America. Bunn and Vardon would link up twice (more on that later), but first we should hear the story of Frank Dufina (Chippewa), who would become the longest serving golf instructor in our nation's history.

Chapter 3

WHERE IT'S NEVER NOT BEAUTIFUL

In 1898, another Scotsman, a Carnoustie boy named Alex Smith, about 700 miles from Shinnecock, landed on Mackinac Island—Mikinaak to the local tribes. Smith had travelled there as the guest of a Chicago physician by the name of McArthur, who hired Smith to build a nine-hole course, Wawashkamo, which would become the home of Frank Dufina (Chippewa, Anishinnabek), the longest serving golf instructor in history.

"The First Hundred years are the hardest."
—Frank Dufina on learning golf.

By October, the boy knew the steamships were coming first from the crooked needle of black and gray smoke rising above the red flares and the south wall of green pines. Then, trailing smoke, a white sliver of the prow would crawl into view. If coming to town by the western road, if it were the big-city ship, the great white axe would appear, breaking the green-gray waves, lifting and heaving across the big water, coming toward the wharf.

September could stay warm, but by October the long coats attended the town's folk, sliding down the hill toward harbor. If it was a Chicago boat, everyone would turn out to watch the hull huff and puff to a slow crawl in the harbor, rocking front to back, then the purring groan along the pine-tarred piers of the dock. Everyone would be there. Whether you had a relative or mail on the boat, whether you wore some fineries or just had a welcome for the new charges.

On that October day, the young islander slid down the western road—his legs were the fleetest on the island. Quicksmart and savvy, he could outrun Gillespie's cab by ten minutes and earn good money running bags up to the Grand Hotel. That day, he copped one run from Mrs. Amberg, fighting a strong westerly up to the Grand, but on his second trip, after the crowds had died down, he passed the two well-dressed men in Jay's cab, not heading toward the hotel or Sunset Rock, but past the hotel, up to the interior.

"Muskie!," his mother Ursula called to him from across the pier, where his father had brought in another haul.

"Gigoohn!" She yelled again.

"It's pike," Frank yelled back. The wind and whirr of the crowd swallowed their calls. Pike now, he knew. The old words were fading. The Ojibwe didn't even have a word for golf. Whatever the catch, that could wait. His father was the best in the world and would bring more tomorrow.

The boy heard about this stranger's visit, and that meant more to him than all the fish in the lake. He followed behind Jay's cab, up toward Fort Holmes. Up where the young boy spent his summer chasing gutties in the meadow behind Hubbard's Annex. He tried to keep the clatter of his shoe soles at bay, even though there was no need to hide. He knew the driver to be his mother's uncle, and anyway Dr. McArthur was fond of the boy, always tipped him plenty. Sure enough, they turned inward at Devil's Kitchen. He knew it! The rattle box of Jay's carriage was drawing toward Early's Farm!

Through the summer at The Meadows behind Hubbard's Annex, everyone talked about the Doctor buying Early's Farm and making "a real golf course." The boy wanted nothing more than a real course, a full course. More gutties to shag, more patrons to pay him for hoisting their bags. The thrill of it ran through him like soft lightning. He had begun to swing as well. When no one was looking, he had made himself a mashie and had begun to launch lost gutties into the evening sky—old featheries and gutties scraping the clouds, landing among the stubble brush.

And now, the doctor and the foreigner walked Early's Farm, as if nothing could dent their fine threads. Drawing, making shapes out of the land, their heads nodding, their long arms pointing across the high ground the young one loved. Quick as a lynx, he darted into a clearing between hemlocks to wave. Dr. McArthur waved back, pointed and laughed. Everyone loved the boy, especially Doc. This was the boy's island. The doctor, he only came and went. The boy's eyes and legs were the very warmth of the land. And as the foreigner walked the old battlefield with the doctor, the young one watched until the sunset turned red. *A full course, yes.* He ran home with tomorrow's weather and carried with him—as young men do—the sense of a new beginning.

The Center of All Things for All Time

The year is 1898. We're on Mackinac Island, in the Straights of Mackinac, the confluence of waters between Lake Huron and Lake Michigan. Mackinac is the shortened version of the Anishinaab word, *Michilimackinac*. The young boy is the fleet-footed 13-year-old Frank Dufina, of French Canadian and Anishinabek heritage, who over 68 years will teach thousands—including three generations of professionals—the Scottish game on his people's island. The doctor is a wealthy cottager, L.L. McArthur, who has brought a young Scotsman, Alex Smith, to design a course on the place of the great turtle—that is the name given to the island by the Anishinaab, the group of Great Lakes tribes that includes the Ojibwe/Chippewa, Odawa, and Potawatomi, folks who would have called this island home since before the Great Flood.

Four seasons turned around the Big Turtle's back, where the Anishinaabe peoples considered it to be home of the Gitche Manitou, created by the Great Hare, Michabou, the first land to appear after the Great Flood receded. The wind, the waters, the sun, the moon, and the clouds: all things kissed the scarp of this protected and protecting place, leading some to call these waters and their islands, "where it is never not beautiful." *Apane miikawaadad.*

"It's a different kind of beauty," Phil Porter agrees. "It's dramatically beautiful. Even in winter. The summer is, well, it's one of the nicest places in the country to be."

Porter is the emeritus director of Mackinac State Historic Parks and now serves as the historian at Wawashkamo Golf Club. He notes that in archeological time, the First People have been here since "around 1000 AD," but for the tribes, the island has a spiritual connection that is timeless.

"For about 20 years now," he recalls, "we've hosted a group of Native American women from the Upper Peninsula who come—grandmothers, mothers, and granddaughters—and they come, they stay here, to pass along female lines the traditions of the tribe. I once asked them, 'why don't you go to Mackinac City or St Ignace?' 'No!,' they tell me. 'No! We come home. We go to the center. We go to the place of worship.' It's like going to Rome for a Catholic. And that's exactly how they feel about Mackinac. That is an unbroken tradition that goes back, you know, into the early mists of time. Mackinac Island is the spiritual center of their tribe."

Having a state historian and third-generation islander to connect us with Wawashkamo Golf Club, and Frank Dufina spares us from having to imagine what time has moved on from: Dr. McArthur was a wealthy vacationer, a Chicago man whom everyone knew to be generous. His work life was in the Windy City, and in the Fall of 1898 at Washington Park Golf Club he convinced Scotsman Alex Smith to take the day-long ferry ride up the big waters. Smith was keeping the greens and a champion player. Golf fever had gripped America, and Scotsmen were in demand. The Dunns and Bendelows and Campbells and Smiths were hard at work making the grounds for the game in the States, while winning the early (but small) purses. McArthur gathered the 24-year-old

Alex Smith and dogged him into a trip up to Mackinac. A full day's trip each way, and a couple to mark out the course. A week was a lot of time to a young man, but McArthur had places to stay, and the means to make it worth it.

Early's Farm

Early's Farm had seen a battle in the war of 1812. In 1814, the British and a troop of Great Lakes Indians had defeated the U.S. Forces on what had been Dousman's land, well-cleared land, surrounded by bushy hemlock and white pine and overseen by Fort Holmes (later Fort Mackinac). The British would hold the island until the end of the war, when terms called for its surrender. As far as the trees and the islanders could tell, not much changed, or not much until a young man from a vaunted Scottish family—near Carnoustie, near the very origins of golf itself, at the doctor's invitation—made out a plan of what to do with the cleared acres. McArthur and the summering families—Cochran and Gillespie, and Tuley and Amberg—they put up the means to bring the young Scotsman around. The new game had brought their community together: men and women, boys and girls. One size fits all. Morning, noon, and night. The cottagers gathered outdoors in the field behind Hubbard's Annex, which had grown too small. Six short holes would never do.

So it began. The 24-year-old Alex Smith, greenskeeper at Washington Park, second-place finisher at the U.S. Open that June at Myopia Hunt Club, walked the 57 acres of Early's Farm with the benevolent Dr. McArthur. Smith would spend his days pounding stakes, in some places into welcoming limestone, in other spots ledge and granite. He would have worked quick, as the golf writer Herbert Warren Wind had observed about young Alex Smith: "He never took his golf too seriously, never dawdled over a putt. His motto was, 'Miss 'Em Quick.'" He wouldn't have had much of a day to work with in October anyway. Whatever else we know about his visit can be found in the links of Wawashkamo Golf Club: you play the lay of the land. No need to improve on nature.

Phil Porter suggests there was a bit of Native American humor in the naming of Wawa, as it's known. The early founders of the club—who were all wealthy and White—asked the Native Americans on the island to suggest a name.

"It wasn't something they these White guys from Chicago came up with," Porter recounts. "And I actually think it carries a sense of humor. The name means 'a wandering trail.' 'Crooked.' And it's the way we who are golfers walk—who hit right and left, you know, down the golf course—and I think that it was sort of not-uncommon type of humor about the cottagers that they would have had at that time." In particular, two Native Americans—Moses and Mike Nauwegesic—suggested the name: *Wawashkamo* means to walk a crooked trail. No straight shooters in the early days at Wawa, and it took the Native islanders to point it out.

Once the stakes had been laid, the Good Doc hired a local contractor named Rounds to build the nine, cut out of horse sweat and road scrapers. Dr. McArthur and Judge Tuley and the Ambergs would put up the money. Rounds would bring his horses and scrapers and sleds, and he would work through a snowless winter. By August 1899, the crooked trail would be bringing the golf fever to the center of all things, and the young Native boy would be there at the start.

Alex Smith was part of a wave, a great gaggle of Scotsmen—a rag-tag group of golf fanatics and entrepreneurs, clubmakers and shot-makers—with names like Findlay and Dunn—who had come to sooth the golf fever in America. Would he have met a young local boy, one who would return the next summer to shag balls, beginning a lifelong vocation, first caddie, then golf professional and teacher, the very spirit of the Wawa? We only know what the game of golf reveals: Alex laid a Scottish mask over Early's Farm and established a new meaning on an old land: a battlefield, the back of a big turtle.

And now cometh the hour, the teacher: Frank Dufina.

Full Blooded Indian or Thoroughbred Frenchman?

The issue of tribal affiliation was a complicated one for Frank Dufina. When speaking with a tribal council today—such as Martin Reinhardt, an Anishinaabe Ojibwe scholar at the Center for Native American Studies, or in speaking with the many chairmen and archivists visiting upon this history—pride in one's tribal association may be stated loud and proud. There is pride in tracing associations back to the great men of Native American history: to Geronimo, to Blackbird, to Sitting Bull. But at that time, tribal association was not an easy matter. After all, the 1890s marked a transition from the "Era of Termination," called for by the U.S. Government, to the rise of the failures of the "Era of Assimilation." Frank and Helen's own three daughters, given different circumstances, could have been removed for schooling.

To illustrate this shifting ground of identities, Phil Porter recounts a moment in Frank Dufina's career, playing the Western Open in Grand Rapids in 1911 at the Kent Country Club. The *Grand Rapids Herald* had a headline that read, "Noble Red Man Golfer." The article described Dufina as "the most interesting player ... a full-blooded Indian ... and has picked the game up from just watching others."

Porter says, "Like many mixed-blood Native people at the time, Frank was acutely aware of the prevailing prejudices. It's not uncommon." Regarding the article, Porter surmises that Dufina, or someone close to him, contacted the paper. Phil continues: "Two days later, another article appeared with a two-column photo of Frank with the caption, 'French Expert at Scotch Game, Frank Dufina, Mackinac Island Professional, who is Thoroughbred Frenchman.'"

The truth lies somewhere in between. Frank's grandmother was an islander, an Anishinabek named Shinsia Josette Okademank Desjardinas Henry. She married Francois Dufinais at the Presbyterian mission in 1823. In 1835, they brought forth Alexander, who married Ursula, whose biological background we don't know much about. Frank was born in the house his father built in 1884. About the difficulties of being mixed race in 1897? One can only imagine the inner confliction—full-blooded Indian versus thoroughbred Frenchman? Long memories of the "Patriot War" and the French and Indian Wars would have continued to bring pressure not to celebrate blood lines and Indigenous histories.

We do know that the shifting spelling of the family's last name stopped with Frank. There were various spellings over time: Daufinais, Dufinais, Daphiny, and Duffine. Family members recounted that once Frank had established his career at Wawa, he took the lead in settling the matter once and for all: Frank made the correct and only spelling: *Dufina*. Phil Porter points out that the meaning hadn't changed. Literally *du* (of the) *fina* (finest). The name, in French, means "prince."

Good Golfer, Great Teacher

Some sources list Frank Dufina as the first Native American to play on the professional circuit. As we know, in 1899, the year Frank began to caddy at the newly opened Wawashkamo, Oscar Bunn would have represented Shinnecock Hills at the U.S. Open at Roland Park in Baltimore and would have already set the early mark for Native Americans on the professional circuit at the U.S. Open at Shinnecock Hills in 1896. But this is a minor point, and falls to the fact that both Bunn and Dufina would shape a living out of golf, not as tournament players; as far as this researcher can tell, neither finished in the money in a tournament. No, but long before the USGA or the PGA had codified any principles in relation to teaching this fickle game, Bunn and Dufina made livings as clubmakers and course designers, and—primarily—as teachers. While Bunn travelled the world to spread the gospel of the new Scottish game—more than a bit of his father's whalers' blood in his bones—Frank Dufina stayed put. As a Native grandmother will teach you: The stars return to the same place each year, that is how you know you are home.

At Wawa, Dufina quickly rose from caddie to golf pro, becoming known as The Professor for his skill at teaching, while never losing his humor that so many enjoyed. As to the question, "How long does it take to learn the game of golf?," Dufina routinely replied, "The first hundred years are the hardest."

And if Dufina wasn't the first Native American on the professional circuit, the research shows fairly clearly he was the first Native American to design golf courses. In 1918, two years before Dr. Alister MacKenzie published his book *Golf Architecture*, Dufina advertised his services as a "golf course architect." Four years later, in 1922, he was hired to design a course for the Cheboygan Golf and Country Club. Three years after that, the St. Ignace Lions Club hired Dufina and Prentiss M. Brown Sr. to mark out a course along the shores of Lake Michigan. Both courses are still open, and they stand alongside Dufina's redesign and expansions—the new back tees and rearranged routing—that he oversaw at Wawashkamo beginning in 1911. All of this happened before Dufina—or any of our First People—would have been legally considered a U.S. citizen.

"My mother took lessons from him," Mr. Porter recalls. "I have a photograph that shows my mom and her sister with their clubs in front of their cottage—their father's cottage on the West Bluff. They are on their way out for lessons. All the young people and the young cottagers took him for lessons. And again, his real strength was as a teacher. Apparently, he was a very, very effective teacher of the game of golf."

His classroom at Wawa fell in the green space between the 9th green and the 1st tee, where he developed his "shadow lessons." Because learning golf is inherent learning, implicit learning—because one can only learn by observing themselves—Dufina would have his students watch their own shadows, their own motions, in order to improve. He could teach them the principles, but it was up to them to perform them, over and over. And in parallel with a couple of other great teachers—Socrates, ho hum, and Jesus, sure—Frank never wrote things down. The stories about him come by word of mouth: Dufina's family and friends have long noted a golf version of a biblical genealogy: Frank Dufina taught his nephews Phil and Jim, who taught Dennis Dufina, who taught Jack Parel, who taught his son Scott, who has won more than $7 million on the PGA Champions Tour.

"Scott came last year," Phil Porter enthuses. "He did a pro-am exhibition with our pro and our men's and women's champs. We had a wonderful scramble, closed the course. Really fun to watch him play. You know, Scott's got Native American heritage from here. He's related to a Fort Mackinac soldier and several families on the island, through blood and through different relations. His dad grew up here and was taught by the Dufinas. It was thrilling to have him, but I think he was also thrilled to come back and be part of the event. This is a kind of home for him as well. He knows he has an ancestor that served at Fort Mac and all. He's certainly aware, because we talked about it."

Frank Dufina had retired by the time the professional ranks codified instruction in any way. Seems fitting in a strange way. He'd trained professionals, sectional winners, tour champions, but—as witnessed by Phil Porter and many others—Frank's genteel nature, humor, and worth ethic endure through the oral stories of in the island's history. For someone from the center of all things, on Mackinac Island, to be educated in golf means to be self-reflecting, to be kind and exacting, to have a good humor, as much as to have a good swing.

Time and Memory

The philosophers tell us to ask our children questions to expand their thought. Two of them are: What exists before time? What comes after time? When we talk to someone who remembers their grandmother telling stories of Uncle Oscar taking them to get an ice cream and ride a Ferris wheel, or when talking to someone whose mother took a golf lesson from a man who appears to be one of the great teachers and solid characters of the game, memory appears in some ways stronger than time. Like the way light bends around a gravitational field, time seems to bend around memory. Memory seems to stop or bend time. Through its magic we are transported. 20 years. 50 years. 100 years. More. Until no time gets in the way. Memory invites us to an Absolute Now that includes something irrepressible, includes things we need to know and preserve. Such is the case with the memories others have of Frank Dufina.

One can imagine a final tribute dinner, where both the old and the young gathered to honor a man retiring at just the right time. It's 1967, and Wawa remains as he has cared for it. The island still doesn't allow the iron horses, and The Professor is still effective and willing to teach the next one, but ready to rest on heady laurels. His old friends, like Walter Hagen, are gone; the Professor had born his coffin. It was time, and he had to make plans for his daughters. Time.

After the lights have gone down, and the bar is locked up, after the last clip-clop of the one-horse carriages turn into the dark, the moment arrives only when the kitchen lights are left on, The Professor walks the well-worn edges of that crooked trail, perhaps still in touch with the same awe he felt as a

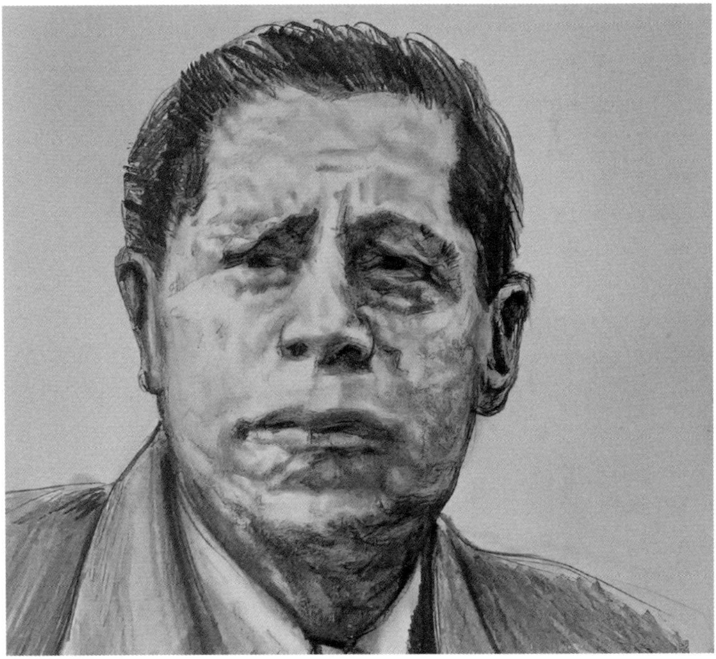

Portrait of Frank Dufina by David Bunn Martine

young boy in chasing gutties behind Hubbard's Annex. He might remember watching the good doctor and the foreigner lay out the course that would be—along with Helen and his three daughters, along with Phil and Jim and Dennis and Jim and Scott and countless others—the focal point of his life. Maybe he would sense again what he was too busy to write down: Of the many things that lay beyond us, of the eternal rules and fates that turn with the stars, of the things we don't control, golf is just one way to make peace with them, or at least have good company as we try.

Chapter 4

PANTHER. THUNDERSTORM.

In the year 1900, Harry Vardon, 30 years old and already twice crowned Champion Golfer of the Year, comes to America and Canada and, between March and November, plays 90 exhibition matches. Sponsored by Spalding, the tour is seen as the start of an extended golf boom and meant to sell the public on the new "Vardon Flyer" gutta. What began in Virginia, and after stops in Colorado and Cleveland, the tour reaches the Adirondacks that August, where he plays not one but two matches against a local amateur named George Stevens and Oscar Smith Bunn, a clubmaker and teaching pro at Lake Placid, New York. Oscar spent many summers in the Adirondacks where he followed Seymour Dunn to make clubs and teach and where, as a 25-year-old, his fate included two goes against "the best golfer in the world."

Seymour Dunn, an apostle of golf, jumps up onto a step in front of the Stevens House. Slight of frame, knickers to his knees, he could be taken for a horse jockey. He raises his arm, opens his palm and announces, "Lassies and good fellas, we've got a special guest. Champion golfer, Harry Vardon."

Vardon takes a weary bow. It's the second half of a nine-month tour; from Cleveland, the Erie Rail got them to Old Forge. From Old Forge the new train line, the Raquette, splendid for speed, got them to Lake Placid where Mr. Colgate met them with his new gas buggy and brought them to The Stevens House: a wooden mansion that seems to have fallen from a giant's imagination. Like at every stop, going back to March, Vardon would play a local pro and an amateur, for $250 and a bottle of scotch. His handlers would sell the Vardon Flyer; then, like a golfing circus, they'd be off to the next show. For reasons we shall see, at Lake Placid they would play twice. This mountain match came with an interesting twist: Among all the possible competitors, and the curious, barking spectators, there stood a tall Indian: the first American-born pro, a clubmaker who could carve persimmon like potatoes. Oscar Bunn, a Shinnecock Native with a swing like the breeze. He'd been working with Seymour's uncle Willie Dunn for nearly a decade, building Shinnecock Hills together. The Dunns had taught Oscar to be a teacher, a fine clubmaker, and an even better player.

"They call 'im 'The Indian,'" Seymour would tell Harry. "Can truly Skelp that Bawl. Truly."

"They" was the press, who showed up to report on Vardon's strange tour—a strong man, a giant, and a fortune teller all rolled into one. Vardon's handlers would corral the growing crowds around a table where they had the Vardon Flyer golf balls for sale. *Even got his name on it, look.* There's a hubbub, handshakes among a small gathering, the men in Jim Dandies, and some of the women, looking swell in "gym suits," all gathered round the spectacle of Harry Vardon. Paid to play golf? Like a fire-eater or the tattooed lady!

Oscar Bunn would not have been totally unknown to Vardon. Oscar was paired with James Park in the 1896 U.S. Open. The Park family knew Vardon enough to ask for his recommendation for jobs in the states. All of them could play. And Harry would have heard the ruckus about the dark-skinned ones in 1896 at Shinnecock. After he withdrew, Park had kept the card for that Black fellow John Shippen, when Shippen had put a scare in the whole United Kingdom by nearly capturing the trophy. But Harry hadn't expected Bunn to be so young, and as fine a player, either.

"Sure," Seymour would assure him. "After the mist's off, you'll face 'em in the morning?" In his Scottish heart, Dunn would want nothing more than for his friend and clubmaker—"The Indian," as the press called him—to find the grace in his game and knock the Brit off the throne. Seymour and his family had been preaching golf in America for near ten years. Now Vardon shows up like he owns the place? Let 'im miss short putts!

Some will say Vardon's tour is the beginning of America's love affair with golf, in years also called The Age of Hope. From 1900 to the sinking of the Titanic, Americans would bring forth *The Wizard of Oz*, *The Souls of Black Folk*, *Pragmatism*; years that also saw the birth of Walt Disney, Louis Armstrong, and Rachel Carson. Between 1900 and 1914, over 13 million people left Europe in search of the American promise of creating one nation, one family of humanity, joined by ideas of freedom rather than flag or race or blood. Is it any wonder that these years saw the birth of a golf boom? Between March and November 1900, Vardon toured New England, Chicago, Florida, and Colorado, playing matches for a curious public and to sell this new golf ball. Harry also had an eye on the U.S. Open in Chicago in October. What better practice could there be? Two rounds a day with lunch included. They'd laughed at him in the elementary, but here he was getting rich doing the thing he loved. But this match, with this Indian, Vardon felt as uneasy as he ever had.

And as evening settled in, Seymour Dunn would add to the intrigue.

"You should see th' faces!" Dunn reaches up and grabs Vardon by the shoulder as they walk toward the big house. Vanderbilts and Roosevelts? The Meads and Whites? "They'd think bein' rich's e'nuff. Oscar learned th' game as if he was born in a feckin' kilt. Him and his friend Shippen. Aye, help me, naturals both. Very good motions."

"And he followed ya into these woods?," Vardon asks with the hint of a snicker. Even in Colorado, he had never seen woods this thick.

"The woods? Aye." Seymour leans in and looks both ways. "Keep to the open. They've caught a panther in thar, just last week."

"A panther? Blimey." And that much was true. *The Argus* had first reported it. The last of the forest beasts! Vardon would never see a panther, and didn't want to. The island of Jersey, where Vardon was from, had cows and not much else. Not even snakes and trees. Indians? Panthers? Vardon thought he had seen it all, but the next morning, as the golfers rode a wagon up the road to Eagle's Nest, all his nerves had softened. He would take all comers. And if he'd seen worse courses, he'd seen no one as bad as this hillbilly Stevens, a flatlander who couldn't hit a straight ball. The Indian? He was the mark, to be sure.

Oscar was at the 1st tee when Seymour and Vardon arrived, his head stuffed into a floppy fedora. Mr. Colgate had given him a ride, along with a photographer from the Brooklyn paper who had set up an apparatus in the field. *This way, this way.* Before the round, Harry posed on the tee like some ambassador from the future. For the folks who couldn't make the trip, yes, and for history. To *oohs* and *ahhs*, and *would you look at that*, Vardon drove a few of his Flyers into the clear, morning, mountain air. Seymour tracked them down and ran them back to the tee with the enthusiasm of a fresh pup.

Oscar waited in the wings. Wearing his fedora pulled low, he was brawny with big hands. Vardon would take a liking to him. He could appreciate a Native teaching golf to city slickers. Color of the skin mattered nothing to Harry. He was only looking to get under it. And that August morning, Harry felt cool as the other side of the pillow. He had seen crowds this size at morning tea. Only two from the press?

As the photographer broke down his little tower, Seymour Dunn jumped up onto that raised square of mud and grass and set of rules: he would forecaddie, then meet the teams at each tee to record the score—Harry's and the best of the other two, until there was a clear winner.

And then they were off. *Thwack. Whiff. Thwack.* The diminutive Seymour ran around the fairways marking balls, while Oscar—his hands shaking straight away—had a few good drives. The muddy earth was no bother if you could lift that little sphere into the sky. He drove one or two onto the green early. Only problem? Three putts. And Stevens was no help: He was busy chatting with the Spalding men and the ladies on the sidelines. And Seymour met them at each tee, and after each big number from Oscar, his smile turned down another cubit.

Vardon was happy winning and happy to see women line the fairways. Vardon would write about this trip to America: "Golf is a game of freedom. I like to see a lady go out on the links, and they can wear whatever costume she thinks fit to wear." He'd heard a local preacher say the ladies on the links "swore like troopers." All to the good.

When Seymour met them on the 5th tee. He whispered to Oscar.

"T'is nerves. He's goot in yer 'ed." He had seen Oscar Bunn play better golf in his sleep, and his high Scottish hopes drooped like a muffed chip.

"I think the panther's got his mate," Vardon smiled. "Aye? Yay."

"Keep to the open," Seymour replied dully and pointed at the woods. "The panther."

Oscar thought the trapped beast might have been an old, black dog, but didn't venture a guess.

At another turn, Vardon asked Oscar about Uncle Willie and Shinnecock. The Vardon Tour had begun with Willie's assistance—in Richmond, yes—though his tour would not make it to Shinnecock. Ever. No bother that August morning. Harry would have his eyes on Chicago, and he inquired if Oscar was playing come October.

"No. Shinnecock would be shutting down," Oscar replied. He would be advertising for winter engagements, in Florida or beyond. He didn't want Vardon to know he had to work, even though—truth be told—Vardon might have put up the dough. Being a native of the Island of Jersey, Harry would've been called a grockle, a bean, and worse. He could appreciate a local boy slipping the noose of fate with his hickory sticks.

"And Willie's taught ya to carve and swing, aye?" Vardon spoke not needing an answer. "You can't get any closer to the bone of the game than that."

By the 10th Vardon had the match in hand. He could see Oscar could hit a long ball, but he just couldn't score. No shame in that. But Seymour had given up, and he was trying to make hay with some of the spectators. They could find their own bloody balls. Besides, Vardon had plenty. In fact, when they reached the 10th, he reached into his pocket and produced the finest sphere Oscar had ever seen. A Vardon gutta.

"I'm bringing this to Chicago," Vardon smiled, handing one to Oscar, who tried to put it right to work, like a set of extra legs. Anyway, hard to golf when you're trying to learn new equipment. Vardon made a hip turn deeper than the lake, and Oscar watched. And Vardon had his right hand turned up on the club. *Thwack. Whack. Whiff. Thwack. Whack. Whiff.* Stevens went on a safari again, looking for a lost ball, as Vardon asked Oscar about his plans.

"Chicago?"

"Not this year, no."

"Next year's Open? You'll have 'a come for it," Vardon told him. "The ways you hit long, you'd be fine. The balls roll a bit, unlike 'n this bloody mud."

Oscar could see Vardon liked golf more than home, was home in his swing, home in his head. At 30, had already won the British Open twice, while Oscar, at 25, needed help getting from Shinnecock to the hills for a month in the summer. In August 1900? To cross the ocean hadn't even entered his mind. And though Harry would never get to Shinnecock, Oscar assured him it was much, much finer than Eagle's Nest. Which was barely golf, in Vardon's view.

"It's why I've played so poorly," Oscar says, and the two share a laugh. The result? Reported on in a number of places including *The Brooklyn Eagle*, Oscar was quoted: "I was nervous, of course, meeting the player ranked best in the world, and I am sure only for that I would have won." The newsmen had a story at every stop—free advertising for the Vardon Flyer, and a tease for the American public with a sudden interest in golf. The Spalding men knew what they were doing. Newsmen and crowds at every summer stop. The mountain towns boomed when the stone streets of Boston and New York got hot.

And Harry did what Harry does. In his 90-match tour that year, he'd claim to be beat but two times, and that morning at Eagle's Nest was another win.

But then, out of the blue, when the golfing party got back to the shop, Seymour announced that Mr. Colgate would put up another $250 if he and his friends—Dexter Hunter and Doctor Gorham—could play the Champ. Vardon had an appointment at Saranac, but agreed to return. Why not? The following week, he'd play four nines. Good practice. Another stay at that magnificent house on the lake? Not a bother. And this time they'd play the "home course": a short nine, wrapped around the lake house like a primitive shawl. Seven par threes and two par fours—what would later become the Pristine Nine at Lake Placid.

So, on Saturday, August 18, 1900, a day of shifting weather, Vardon returned from the Grand Hotel and Ampersand at Saranac. That morning broke a blue sky protecting the woods and lakes and streams, but with a wind high in the trees, coming from the south. After the Spalding crew laid out boxes of the glorious new guttas, Harry made it no secret he was happy to see "The Indian" again, wanting to know straight off if he'd dropped the Hillbilly from his team. Oscar hadn't, but was hungry to play Vardon again. The first round had been a mess, and he was hitting better now with a new ball, turning his hip deeper, like Vardon, and he hadn't lost that Flyer ball.

There was a buzz in the crowd gathering in the morning mist outside the shop.

"Paid to play golf!" Someone yelled. Vardon stalked

the crowd: an anomaly, like a hunger artist or human pin cushion. Speaking of which, Doctor Gorham, Dexter Hunter, and Sutherland Colgate had all checked in. Vardon had committed to four nine-hole rounds, and the Stevens links were short. Vardon imagined he'd make short work of it all, and the morning was bright. Doctor Gorham—reputed to be a good golfer—was making his way forward to the tee.

"Thunderstorms this afternoon," The good doc noted. He would go first, followed by Hunter and Colgate. Oscar and Vardon, with Stevens in tow, would play the last nine of the day. Seymour would again forecaddie and record scores at the tees. And Oscar manned the shop that morning, keeping a keen eye out for Gorham first, then Hunter, and then Colgate. They all slaked back to deliver the news to loved ones and friends: Not by tight margins, Vardon prevailed. But no big thing. Even in defeat, August at the lake was a glimpse of heaven on earth. Golfing was a fine affair, but not a career. Their offices and banks and printing houses were back in Manhattan and Boston, waiting for school and work to begin again.

Meanwhile, Seymour stewed. He thought Doctor Gorham might keep it close and had the words of a telegram to his father Tom all laid out in his head: *Brits Lose the New World Once Again*. He'd longed for at least one of the locals to make a dent in the inimitable Vardon.

Oscar Bunn in 1899.

"Ya goot to git to his 'ed," Seymour pleaded. "Talk with 'em about anything. The panther! Thunderstorm!"

Vardon was not to be bothered. Money, golf, and lunch on the porch. Just getting ready for Chicago. His mind was elsewhere. Vardon had taken an extra helping at lunch and was 27 holes into his day, while Oscar carved out an hour before the match to settle his nerves and take a few putts. Chamomile tea does the trick for the stomach and shakes. And only a slight bit of food. Don't need a stomach getting in the way of golf.

And this day there was no extra trip to Eagle's Nest. The 1st tee was just behind the porch, and, as they stepped to the level little field they called the 1st tee, Oscar knew what he could do. Vardon had played all day, played first, and was in a groove. Bang.

"What do you want to talk about now, Mr. Bunn? Have you changed your grip?"

By now Oscar knew Vardon played the head game, and Oscar would need three holes to get straight, but Bunn had only given up one stroke. When Seymour caught up to them, he asked Harry about Ampersand, at Saranac. On Thursday last, Vardon had won all his matches there.

"Did ya knows Oscar's got the record there?," Seymour asks.

"At Ampersand?"

Harry nodded as he made the tiny pilgrimage from the green—such as it was—to the 4th tee. He was not surprised. Oscar Bunn hit a long ball, and even longer now with his unlost Flyer.

"Could be the Panther goot 'em," Seymour said when Stevens didn't report for the 4th. He'd been off on a goose chase all morning—clearly a flirt, chatting up the females.

"I'll be up a 'ed. I'll be look'n for it!"

With Seymour in place up the fairway, Vardon missed on his drive! Following that, Oscar laced a good one, 250 yards. He could even feel the ball when he hit it—this Flyer—and when he was on, he could outhit anyone, including the Champ. In the week since Vardon had been at the lake, he had turned his right hand up on the club and begun to kick his left heel up. With a good 4th hole, and Vardon short, Oscar was a stroke ahead on Hole 5.

Seymour was shouting incomprehensible things whenever Oscar did anything good. Meeting on the 5th tee, he gave

Oscar a wink and pointed at his temple. *Git in' h's ed.* Vardon griped about stroke play.

"In a match, I'd be dormie four," he moaned. Stroke play gave Oscar a chance. And what about the crowd? Harry played better under pressure. The crowd had thinned out, now the course looped up above the lake house by the tree line.

And a storm was coming.

The wind swirled in the tall pines, and the lake had a chop. The only crowd now was the diminutive Seymour in his knickers, dancing up and down the fairway, and on the sidelines, only the newspaper man and one from the Spalding clan. The people watching people playing golf had all found something else to do. In these hills, by these trees along the backside of the hotel, an early dark brewed. The shadows had come up, cooled things down. Seymour could say something about the panther, but now a thunderstorm was a more likely foe. The wind swirled. Vardon had never seen the likes of an Adirondack thunderstorm over the lake. With a distant boom, the crowd had scattered in fear, and Oscar had begun to play like he could. *Thwack. Thwack.*

Just the three of them now. Seymour patting Oscar at each tee. Vardon had grown quieter each time Oscar made a putt. When Oscar went two strokes up on 6, Seymour put on a mug and hummed a line from "Rule Britannia."

The 7th was a Redan set on a slope with a pothole bunker on the right to keep the ball from rolling off the earth. If you could carry that or stay left and get on in two, you'd be lucky. Sure enough, Vardon found the road. Oscar stayed left, up the slope. His beautiful new ball ran down to the fringe.

Seymour cried out, "goot bawl."

Vardon thought he might have even bet against him. The fool. He'd show 'em, given the chance, but the sky had begun to spit, the pothole was wet, and we were decades from having a proper spoon. Oscar took another hole!

On the 8th—another par three, downhill and over a creek—Oscar had the honors and planted one off the back fringe. He was a long hitter, sure enough, and this new gutta ball had seemingly been sent by his happy ancestors. Seymour planted a flag at it, waving back at the duo with a grin the size of Old Baldy. Vardon would have liked to knock one off his Scottish head, but he had to go for it. He took out a mashie and tried to sculpt one over the creek, and did, but for what reason, the golf gods had put a rock where grass should be.

"Bloody 'ell, 'en," Vardon cried. His Flyer flew all right, off the rock and well past the green. Oscar two-putted for par. Vardon was four strokes behind with one to play, the short par-four 9th. Seymour met them at the tee and was quietly gloating. They'd play the last, sure, fair was fair, but under the cloud of Harry Vardon's furious mug.

In an article titled "Vardon's Waterloo," from *The New York Argus*, August 20, 1900, we find written, "Harry Vardon was defeated by Oscar Bunn, 'The Indian' ... the other day ... in a fashion Vardon is not likely to forget—33—38."

It's quaint, yes, like Waterloo. The 1900 tour would have landed Vardon on a very high hog. $6,750 was a conservative estimate of Vardon's earnings: an enormous sum at the time, and there was no income tax. And there was no tanking. When the tour ended at Van Cortlandt Park that November, a month after he'd won the U.S. Open in Chicago, Vardon won the morning and the evening match. There were an estimated 2,500 in attendance and the *New York Times* reported, "The throng followed the players behind a long rope, but the mob of urchins who were allowed to roam at will along the links, yelling at every stroke, made the game the noisiest in which Vardon has ever been seen."

Golf had begun in America for real. People would watch people who got paid to play the least violent and most difficult game in human history. This was human pin cushions, fire-eaters, and tattooed ladies all rolled into one, and the golfing giant Harry Vardon would return to England to his Alice, have six kids, win four more Open Championships and 40 some-odd titles.

None of that could have been known that August Saturday beside the mirror of the lake. Harry had played 36 holes and was in no mood for a party. Oscar walked with him back to the porch.

"You'll win in Chicago," Oscar offered. It was true. Mr. Vardon had some business in Chicago, and, after getting his schedule from the Spalding men, he retreated to his room, but not before a strong handshake with Oscar, who again invited him to Shinnecock.

"I hope."

"Ya will."

"Give my best to Willie. And all."

"I will."

Then Oscar, once he'd doffed his fedora and wrapped his big, brown hand around Vardon's, ran to the back of the house and uphill a short bit to find Seymour Dunn taking the flags in from the rain. His boss, his friend, the keeper of the till, Seymour Dunn looked up to see Oscar skipping off the porch. The tall, brawny man took a few quick steps and picked up the little Dunn by the arms. In a fit of joy, a state of pure golfing grace, he swung him around like a top as Seymour cried, "Ya beat 'im, mate. Ya dun it. I seen it me-self."

Seymour would telegraph his father in the morning: *Brits*

Harry Vardon teeing off at Eagle's Nest, 1900. Bunn with fedora.

lose new world again.

Oscar's smile was as warm as the summer rain that began to fall. Yes, 33—38. Della and his brother Charles would hear about it first: Oscar Smith Bunn—"The Indian"—had beaten the best in the world.

Postscripts

Oscar would continue to teach and play, and he would follow Mungo Park II to Argentina. On January 6, 1917, from the port of New York, aboard the S.S. Vauban, Oscar set sail to help build a golf course and teach. Some of the living believe he went with a crew of Shinnecock tribesmen to build a new course, but we can only guess.

What we do know is that 1917 saw ocean passages rife with soldiers and equipment heading to the deadliest war in human history. Influenza infections accompanied with high mortality in the winter of 1916–17 was only the beginning. By 1918, the Spanish flu would kill 50 million people worldwide.

In this setting, returning from South America, *The Southampton Press* reported, Oscar Bunn "was apparently unprepared for the cold weather and caught pneumonia ... from which he never recovered." He fell ill in October 1917, and died at the age of 42 on January 24, 1918.

Seymour Dunn would teach at Shinnecock and in summer at Lake Placid for many years. In 1922 he would publish the influential book *Golf Fundamentals*, which includes among the first considerations of the mental aspect of the game of golf. In the book's summary on the chapter "The Psychology of Golf," there is only this on a large, otherwise blank page:

> *Perseverance: Continue in a state of grace,*
> *until it is succeeded by a state of glory.*

Chapter 5

GRANDMOTHER EARTH

"The point is we wanted to hug and embrace the earth."
—Dr. John Low, Pokagon Band of Potawatomi Indians

A professor used to tell his class that the sinking of the Titanic in April 1912 was the beginning of the Modern era. He meant *Modern* both in the sense of great technological feats, such as the mighty ship, but also of the perils that attend those feats—world war, the nuclear age, the space race, and so on. Putting aside for a moment the fictional story of Jack and Rose, the Titanic as an historic marker is a compelling one. While there were none of our First People on that boat, Mark Ford and others have noted that—but for a bad case of the flu—Harry Vardon was scheduled to sail on the doomed liner. Seems his British sponsors were aghast that an American had won the U.S. Open, and they wanted Vardon to return and take the upstart's flag. Harry's bad cold saved his life.

There is one other golf connection to history's infamous sinking: Joseph Bruce Ismay, an avid golfer, was the chairman of the White Star Line, the Liverpool shipping company. Ismay was a long-time member of Formby Golf Club and—in 1909, on the club's 25th anniversary—gifted Formby with a stately clock that still stands, perhaps as notice that Bruce's time on earth is still kept. The connection between Formby, the gifted clock, and the fate of Ismay is not forgotten. Ismay was aboard the Titanic when it sunk, but was not one of the some odd 1,500 who lost their lives. Some have suggested he dressed in women's clothing and boarded a lifeboat 20 minutes before the ship went down. He survived, yes, but was called the "Coward of the Titanic" and received a plethora of criticism for deserting the ship, particularly given the number of women and children who had perished. (This tainted legacy is depicted in a number of movies about the tragedy.) Where Vardon went on to play The Greatest Match Ever Played, Ismay's fate became one of depression and solitude. One imagines not too many satisfying rounds of golf.

If golfers are known for valor and excellence, like Vardon, the game is also known for louts and loafers, sandbaggers and boozers. One could say that this tie to the Titanic exposes the Janus-faced nature of the the game—the vaunted and stalwart hero in Vardon stands alongside a hiding coward. One is the game's great and principled son, the other is his evil twin.

All of this is a way of saying, if we put a marker down on April 1912 as the start of what would be a complicated modern episteme, let's also put a marker down on the year prior—the proverbial and clichéd "simpler time" of 1911, a critical year for our purposes here, for reasons other than imagining how golf would be without Harry Vardon.

There are two reasons the year 1911 resonates. For one, 1911 marked the opening of Moundbuilders Golf Course in Newton, Ohio, just outside of Columbus: a course that sits on 2,000-year-old earthworks named a UNESCO World Heritage site in 2023. It's also the same year when—just a drive down the road—Ohio State University hosted the Society of American Indians, the first national conference of Indigenous people.

Headlining this curious confluence of events, Moundbuilders is a course designed by Tom Bendelow (1868–1936), a man nicknamed "The Johnny Appleseed of American Golf." Moundbuilders was one of some 600 courses Bendelow designed in his 35-year career, including the original layouts at East Lake, Medinah, and Van Cortlandt. What makes this particular plot of land different is that it already contained massive, man-made features.

Bendelow laid Moundbuilders into an Octagon Earthworks that consists of a 50-acre, 8-sided enclosure with earthen walls measuring about 550 feet long and 5 to 6 feet in height. Built by the Hopewell People between 1 and 400 A.D., it was part of a four-square-mile complex now known as the Newark Earthworks, which was part cathedral, part cemetery, and part astronomical observatory. In building a course on top of the Octagonal Earthworks of the Hopewell people, Bendelow and his benefactors preserved a work of great genius and creativity from the sprawl of Newark, Ohio, while at the same time laying a golf course on what is now equated with the pyramids in Egypt and the Taj Mahal.

"We wouldn't want a country club on the Acropolis," Dr. John N. Low noted in a recent interview. Low is a citizen of the Pokagon Band of Potawatomi Indians and the director of the Newark Earthworks Center. As we walked through the Earthworks, he argues for his heritage. "We don't want a country club on the Octagon."

Like many battles over land and old and broken treaties, the negotiations about The Octagon and Moundbuilders are complicated. The Ohio History Connection has owned the site since 1933 and leases it to the Moundbuilders Country Club. The lease was renewed in 1997—when the Ohio History Connection was known as the Ohio Historical Society—for an additional 50 years, until 2078. But given the importance of the site, and the work of Dr. Ray Hively and Dr. Low and others, Ohio History Connection began negotiating in January 2013 to provide full public access to the site and break the lease. The Ohio Supreme Court in December 2022 decided in favor of breaking the lease and removing the golf course. Arguments about the monetary value of the club are in appeal.

Glenna Wallace, the first female chief of the Eastern Shawnee Tribe of Oklahoma, considers the Hopewell People her ancestors: their culture gave rise to the language, ceremonies, and rituals of the Potawatomi, the Shawnee, and dozens of other tribes who were forced to the plains of Kansas and Oklahoma. She sees the dispute as going beyond monetary value. The UNESCO recognition for the Earthworks—and the demand for full, public access—would play a crucial role in reframing the way visitors think about Native Americans.

"The sophistication required to create this shows our ancestors weren't savages," she said. "This needs to be open to people every single day of the week, every single day of the year. The Hopewell People built an engineering marvel of earthworks and mounds that are enduring examples of the genius of our people. My people."

The Titanic sank in a matter of hours. The Newark Earthworks have been orienting ancient and modern people to the moon and the stars for millennia.

Dr. Low agrees. The Great Circle and The Octagon, on which Moundbuilders Country Club sits, are among the greatest works of human history in terms of science, technology, architecture, and creativity. That the golf course saved the Octagon from residential or commercial building is ironic, yes, though returning the Octagon to the public realm would complete the restoration of two reimagined Earthworks.

"The Octagon traces the moon rise," Low recounts. "Along the eastern embankments, The Octagon traces the moon rises in an 18-year cycle. Most people in human history never celebrated that, and that is its creative genius, and why it's a UNESCO World Heritage site. More importantly, I believe the Hopewell community wanted to confirm the stability of the universe, to confirm that their ceremonies were working and their lives had stability and meaning. That is the beauty of the site, and why it should be returned to the public."

Low asks rhetorically, Why did they use dirt? Why didn't they use stone? Hopewell could have used stone, but Mother Earth was the most sacred material we could have used.

"It's entirely appropriate that we used ... Grandmother Earth." Created one basketful of earth at a time, using pointed sticks and clamshell hoes, the mounds at the golf course are just part of the broader Newark Earthworks and widely embraced as an astronomical and geometric marvel. Professor Low rejects questions about whether size matters.

"Would it be more impressive if they were bigger? This is misleading," Low argues. "They are built horizontally. The octagon has the golf course on it. The Great Circle once had an amusement park on it. They are enormous. Tipped on their side, they are taller than the pyramids at Giza. The point is, we wanted to hug and embrace the earth."

The Octagon is aligned to the four moonrises and moonsets that mark a complicated 18.6-year-long lunar cycle. For Native historians and experts, the alignments are no less sophisticated than the arranged stones at Stonehenge. Ray Hively, who researched these alignments with a philosophy professor, Robert Horn, in the 1980s, has suggested the effort might have been an attempt to connect with or communicate with the powers that appeared to control the larger universe. The Hopewell culture likely intended the earthworks, which can now be fully appreciated from above, to show their moon and sun gods that they understood their movements.

At the same time—and regardless of just how sacrilegious or offensive a golf course on these mounds is—the course and its architect come into play for two reasons: Bendelow's legacy is celebrated by some. His design principles were steeped in the Scottish Highlands of his youth, where he became acquainted with other golfers of the period, some of whom, like Willie Dunn, John D. Duncan, Seymour Dunn, and Alexander Findlay, have already been woven into our story. To Bendelow's credit, with the design and completion of Van Cortlandt Park in New York City, he established a number of new practices: supervised construction and maintenance of a course, directed play (including the introduction of reserved play tee times), organized tournaments and players associations, and sites for instruction.

The Society of American Golf Course Architects notes that Bendelow used a "naturalist's approach," in that he strove to use the natural features of the chosen site to maximum advantage. His courses have often been called Olmstedian, contending that his naturalist design was greatly influenced by the work of prominent landscape architects Frederick Law Olmsted Sr. and Jr. If a site had an especially unique feature—rock outcrop, stream, grove of trees, scenic view—Bendelow would work his hole placements in such a way as to take full advantage of the features, even if that meant working his layout from the middle out. In the case of Moundbuilders, Bendelow's use of unique features included tee boxes made from 2,000-year-old Indian mounds used as burial grounds and ceremonial sites. Of course, moving early in the early 1900s was very difficult work. But just imagine doing it 1500+ years prior to that.

Yet whatever Bendelow's place in history, Moundbuilders will be a shady legacy, in part because just down the road at Ohio State University, the first National Conference on Indian Affairs was held by the Society of American Indians, led by Laura Cornelius Kellogg (Oneida) and Henry Roe Cloud (Winnebago), among others. We can be sure they did not plan a golf outing to break the tension. The organizers chose Columbus Day for the opening of the founding conference of the Indian reformers—October 12, 1911. While still not afforded U.S. citizenry (this would come in 1924), the society's members were educated professionals from the fields of medicine, nursing, law, government, education, anthropology, ethnology, and clergy. These attendees—and Kellogg and Roe Cloud, in particular—would begin to articulate the need for the Native Americans to have land that would generate an economy, what could be said to echo the cry for food grown on our own land and in the promised land. As Bendelow dropped a private golf club atop the earthworks of the ancient Hopewell culture, a key finding of the plenary of the SAI conference was a vision of a return of lands, so that Indigenous people could use that land as a means to generate economy.

What was clear to Indian and Native scholars and leaders—if not to the White leaders—was that assimilation of Native cultures into "the grand republic"—the goal of the Age of Assimilation (1880-1920)—was not going well. In what would later turn into decades of advocacy, Kellogg envisioned a re-flowering of her own Haudenosaunee culture through a return to tradition, not assimilation into White American culture, and this would be led by a restored and powerful Haudenosaunee Confederacy. She worked for the return of 6 million acres of Haudenosaunee lands that would be valued at $2 billion. (It's worth noting that a very small portion of the land that Kellogg fought to restore today includes Thornberry Golf Course, one of the most economically successful Native-owned tracts.)

Kellogg's economic thinking can be seen in the paper she delivered at the first annual conference of the Society of American Indians (1911), and which later formed part of The Lomoli Plan: a visionary proposal for the recovery of our First People, which she circulated through the 1920s:

> "So interdependent are the business and social problems of the Red man, they cannot be separated in his life. Lacking a stable income or credit on the business side, the task of the social survey is to see how these things affect his health, his psychology, his morals, his efficiency, his opportunities. Securing ties to the land, or at a minimum collecting damages for illegal treaties, would provide a way for Oneidas and other Haudenosaunee people to become self-supported."

The economy as *land* is the central theme of Kellogg's efforts. Any proposal to create "a social order which intends to build a broken people ... must have business." Kellogg encouraged Native people to refuse demeaning representations, and began advocating for a branch of Indian Affairs to span the bridge between Christian missionaries and forced education, to resist the Bureau of Indians Affairs and the goal of genocidal termination of Native cultures. More than any other figure, she was the founding eyes and ears and voice of our current Age of Self-Determination, which we are in today. In addition to advocacy, she wrote stories and poetry. "A Tribute to the Future of My Race" is her only known surviving poem.

Ned Blackhawk, in his study *The Rediscovery of America* (2023), writes, "Kellogg did not consider herself a Red Progressive." At that first conference, where she was the only female, she proclaimed, "I am not the new Indian; I am the old Indian adjusted to new conditions." Cultural continuity, not assimilation, would be essential for survival of Indigenous cultures, and this political adaptation would include legal battles, such as the one that has forced Moundbuilders Country Club to extinction, and legal battles that would result in Indian gaming and golf resorts. More readily, Kellogg and Roe Cloud's work would bring about the Indian Citizenship Act in 1924, granting birthright citizenship to American Indians.

While this is notable, in Blackhawk's view, the major breakthrough would come in 1941 when the Supreme Court, in the case of United States v. Santa Fe Pacific Railway Co., issued "the first major articulation" of Native American land rights. The decision was written by William O. Douglas, the longest serving justice, who believed a judge's role was "not neutral ... as the Constitution is not neutral." In Douglas' view, the Constitution was designed to take the government off the backs of the people. In this case, Douglas was lifting a long and heavy hand off the backs of Native Americans, and though their cultures were decimated, the ruling can be seen as the culmination of the work of the 1911 conference. Of historical note, the decision was handed down on December 8, 1941, a day following the Japanese attack on Pearl Harbor, so it did not garner much attention. No major news media covered the event, but it would become the foundation of land-right cases that would—for this book's purposes—make possible the mixing of the Scottish game with Indigenous recovery. Douglas' opinion concluded: "Aboriginal possession is a question of fact." Our First People owned the land, and this "fact" would manifest in many ways in the ensuing century of legal battles. Despite the complexities that came before and after the ruling—and the forced removals, broken treatises, and betrayals—the ruling will generate cases involving claims to lands for decades.

Only a few of the participants of that first Native conference would live to see the 1941 ruling. Kellogg is thought to have died in 1949, though the details of her passing are unknown. While she and Henry Roe Cloud and Elizabeth Bender Cloud (Ojibwe) had railed against ideas of Native peoples as a "vanishing race" through the 1920s, the Great Depression would in some ways halt their progress. Nevertheless, United States v. Santa Fe Pacific Railway Co. may be seen as the culmination of the work of Kellogg and her associates, which had begun a day's walk from Moundbuilders on Columbus Day, 1911.

In 1919, this advocacy would find Kellogg before the League of Nations calling for justice for American Indians. She pleaded, "You Americans have rescued distracted Belgium from the atrocity of the Hun, you have poured money and sympathy into starving Poland, you have sent your

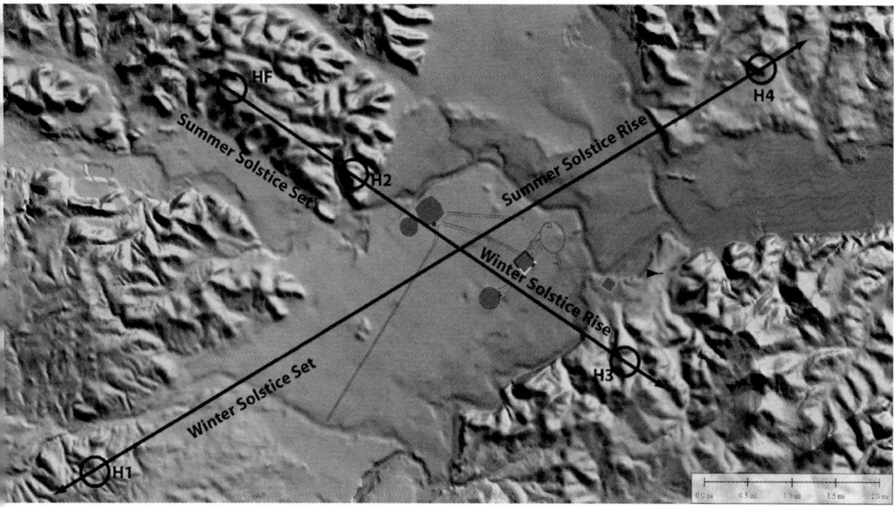

Alignments from prominent hilltops H1 and H2 through the centers of major earthworks to the northern maximum moonrise (North Max Rise) and northern minimum moonrise (North Min Rise). Image courtesy of Robert Horn and Ray Hively.

armies into riotous Russia. Through all the world you are a mighty righter of wrongs, the savior of oppressed peoples. And in your midst a people have cried in vain."

Susan Sontag once wrote that remembering is an ethical act, that it has ethical value in and of itself. This goes not only for our dead. Remembering cherishes and preserves their hardships and achievements, while forgetting their human failings. Grandparents, parents, teachers, and older friends, the wisdom of the elders—all of it expressed in memory. Elders' memories that lead to action is the story of the struggle against injustice.

While UNESCO's naming the Hopewell Earthworks as a World Heritage Site in 2023 has not righted all the wrongs, in the year prior, the Ohio Supreme Court did side with the Ohio History Connection in demanding the mounds be returned to the public domain. Ohio History Connection would like to convert the site into a public park and submit it for recognition as a World Heritage site, as a place of "outstanding value to humanity ... like the Taj Mahal and the Grand Canyon." Neil Thompson of the Ohio History Connection is also looking to the future, when the golf course is gone. "We feel an obligation on behalf of Ohio taxpayers to responsibly protect and interpret the site's historic value. And we hope we'll finally be able to do that soon."

For a golf historian, finding the first Society of American Indian's Conference was held the same year and in the same locale that Tom Bendelow landed a course on an ancient site is a curious coincidence of events. One might even allow for some of the ancestral spirits to be at work here. In the words of Professor Low, "It's time for the golf course to go." The Newark Earthworks, including the Octagon, represent an older and more enduring technology than, say, an industrial-age marvel like the Titanic. The value of the Earthworks is priceless to our understanding of Native Americans, while golf—to mash up C.K. Chesterton—remains just an expensive way to play marbles on the generous back of Grandmother Earth. There are plenty of courses to go around.

Part 2

No Way Back, Only Through: 1911–1952

In the Build Up era of golf, there were some individuals and courses claiming Native heritage. These "Pretendians" were part and parcel of the "Indianization" of places and—as pertains to golf—include tournaments and course names. One of the more popular of the early invitations was Ray McCarthy's Seminole Pro-Amateur event in Miami, which ran from the early 1930s to 1959. McCarthy was a newspaper man turned golf promoter, who was clever in bringing in big names such as Jock Hutchinson and Gene Sarazen and in having guests of resorts put up money for the ever-growing purses. (Notice that the year the Seminole ended was the year that a handsome fellow and gifted golfer by the name of Arnold Palmer started appearing on television.) This Indianization of a golf tournament should be seen as obscuring rather than honoring the Seminoles, the tribe that "never signed a treaty" with the U.S. Government. The tournament also would took place during the years when Laura Kellogg, Henry Roe Cloud, and Elizbeth Bender Cloud—among others—made slow but steady progress on Native American concerns.

As Kellogg would lament, the policies that shaped the previous Eras of Removal and Assimilation left little for the U.S. Government and the expanding empire to take any more from our First People. Many tribes, bands, and nations faced staggering levels of poverty and dissimulation. The rise of the Society of American Indians (SAI) and their advocates would begin to create the means needed to begin to address Native issues. (Citizenship rights would be won in 1924.) And with the aid of John Collier at the Bureau of Indian Affairs, Congress did approve new regulations for taking fee lands into trust. The Fee-to-Trust regulations in the 1934 Indian Reorganization Act (IRA) will continue to be critical to any progress tribes, bands, and nations make. Other positive actions came in the form of land claims, which required—as many historians point out—lawyers and time and money, and most of all judges who would begin to see the "rightness" of Indigenous claims to their aboriginal lands. But then the Great Depression and war years would set many organizations and individuals back in many ways.

With respect to golf, Native athletic cultures, unlike the United Golfers Association (UGA), did not organize around the game in a similar way. Individual athletes would emerge from these years, when tribes and bands and nations began to organize their own schools and win back land. Nevertheless, as far as the least violent, most difficult game in human history was concerned, athletes such as Althea Gibson (Black American and Lumbee) and Joe Louis (Black and Cherokee) would move the needle in indomitable ways.

Following the integration of the PGA and PGA Tour, not only Black Americans but Native Americans like Rod Curl, Tom Lovell, and Orville Moody—some for love and some for love of family and the game—begin to realize the promise that Oscar Bunn and Frank Dufina had defined in those early days of golf in the country.

Chapter 6

LEGENDS, IN A WEAVE OF BLOOD

1911–1952

In a 1997 television interview with Oprah Winfrey, Tiger Woods showed an uncharacteristic flash of humor when he said, "Growing up, I came up with this name: I'm Cablinasian. I'm half Asian and half-Black from my dad's side, and I'm half-White from my mom's side. People see me as Black, but I'm not just Black."

"We're all mixed."
—Henry Louis Gates Jr.

At Myopia Hunt Club in Hamilton, Massachusetts, the apron to the 10th green is guarded by a deep bunker, one supposedly taking its shape from military trench work: long, deep, and narrow. Tradition has it that President William Howard Taft—a man rather large of frame and who notoriously preferred golf to politics—while trying to hit his ball out of the sand, toppled over. And if you thought your troubles in sand were tragic, President Taft required draft horses and caddies with ropes to get out of that abyss. The club has since renamed it the Taft Bunker and mercifully installed steps.

Like many golfers, even though he was far from scratch

(he could not regularly break 100), Taft was often accused of golfing too much, often by his friend-turned-enemy, Theodore Roosevelt. In fact, their friendship turned so foul that Roosevelt ran against the incumbent in 1912 in a third-party effort that split the Republican Party. Democrat Woodrow Wilson was elected president on November 5, 1912. Roosevelt finished second. Taft came in third, winning just two states (Utah and Vermont). Non-plussed, the next morning, the lame-duck president got up, ate a hefty breakfast that could reportedly include 12 eggs, and went golfing.

If we can imagine the leader of the free world on his fat tush in a sand trap, needing horses and caddies to get him out, as far as this golf historian is concerned, we might make the case that Roosevelt, Wilson, and Taft were suitably preoccupied. Serious efforts at politics—at least as far as this book is concerned—were happening elsewhere.

As we've seen, from their first SAI conference in 1911, through the 1920s, Laura Cornelius Kellogg, Henry Roe Cloud, and Elizabeth Bender Cloud, among others, steered Indigenous cultures and official government policy away from the idea of assimilation. Their calls—for land reforms, for industries on Native territory, and for legislation against forced education and other oppressive policies—were in the long run prescient. In the short term, history interfered with these efforts in a number of ways. From World War I through the Great Depression until 1934 and the Indian New Deal, the U.S. Government did little in the way of policies to improve the lives of our First People. (Taft, as we know, was golfing.)

During these same years, the golf world was engaged in politics in a way that informs our history as well. Following the boom years lit by the Vardon Invasion, and the build-up years that saw more than 1,000 golf courses carved into the earth, professional golf began to evolve, and not in the best way. For one, the PGA established an unwritten, Caucasians-only rule in 1916. This rule would become written into the rules in 1934, and not officially removed until 1961.

In response, the United Golfers Association (UGA) formed

in 1925 and would begin to operate golf courses and run a series of golf tournaments for Black golfers. Their first national championship—the Negro National Open—was held in 1926 in Stow, Massachusetts, at Mapledale Country Club. All Black courses would follow, and the UGA would nurture the enormous talents of folks such as Ted Rhodes, Bill Spiller, Pete Brown, Lee Elder, Willie Brown Jr., and Charlie Sifford (the man Tiger named his son after).

While the history of the UGA and its golfers have been explored, a number of Native Americans of mixed race—including Jim Thorpe, Dewey Brown, Althea Gibson, and Joe Louis—all will play a role in growing the game, in reversing archaic policies, in integrating golf, and in bringing the wonders and frustration of the so-called humbling game into a new and enlightened era.

The Indian boarding schools during the Age of Assimilation (1790-1920) were deadly. The list of Native Americans who resisted or ran away from Indian boarding schools due to their policies of forced education reads like a who's-who of our American history: Sitting Bull (Tatanka Iyotake), Geronimo (Goyaałé), Black Elk (Heȟáka Sápa), Zitkala-Ša (Gertrude Simmons Bonnin), Chief Joseph (Heinmot Tooyalakekt), and Sarah Winnemucca (Paiute).

These individuals and leaders—who were also runaways—include Jim Thorpe. In fact, Thorpe might have been lost to history, lost to the byways of America—riding the rails and finding a way among the Jack Straws and Mr. Bojangles of our songs and stories—if not for his twin brother Charlie, who convinced Jim to return to Carlisle School. And for that, we have the following bit of irreplaceable history.

In a photograph from July 1929, Jim Thorpe is standing on a green with Barton Millard at Rancho Santa Ana Golf Course, well-known at the time as Bing Crosby's home course. Here was the site of Crosby's Clambake, that would decades later become the celebrated AT&T Pebble Beach Pro-Am. The photograph comes from the collection of Charles Schneider, who photographed celebrities and golf courses. In the photo, both Millard and Thorpe are well dressed. It's not for nothing to note this is a few shorts months before the October crash and ten years of economic depression, years during which Jim Thorpe—once touted as the greatest athlete of all time—will have to hustle for both money and his reputation. For Thorpe, it was "a cycle of loss and recovery," his biographer David Maraniss would write. What we might call a "support network," the cultural and professional organizations that nurtured talent were not a thing for Native Americans at that time. Thorpe had to stand on his own.

And in the photo at Rancho Santa Ana, Thorpe is in fact rigidly upright and sartorially splendid. He holds a putter stiff across his waist and is looking toward the camera. At the time, he would have been consulting on casting Native Americans in Hollywood pictures. He counted Bing Crosby among his friends. Bob Hope would later loan him a few bucks, and there is some indication that he had helped Millard lay out the course at Rancho Santa Fe.

But to our point here: There's a note from this period that indicates that a Native American golfer named Charlie "The Chief" Thorpe had played in some local events. Could it be that Jim Thorpe played under an alias for the Barton Millard Bowl at Rancho Santa Fe?

Thorpe biographer David Maraniss told me, "I don't doubt it. Thorpe reached California in 1929. He was often called Chief. His twin brother, who died at age nine, was Charlie. Jim was inspired to play golf by his New York Giants [baseball] teammate, the great Christy Mathewson, who said it would improve his hand-eye coordination. He golfed off and on the rest of his life."

Using that alias would be an inside joke from Thorpe. If he had used an alias—like most other amateur athletes in Baseball's minor leagues had—his two Olympic medals would be on his trophy shelf, and he would have been celebrated in his lifetime as being the greatest athlete of all time. No doubt, a lot of people had it bad in these years, but Thorpe, stripped of his Olympic medals because of a media hit-piece (*The Worcester Telegram* in January 1913) would see his fortunes decline. That alias would also be a way to honor his late brother. As he stands with Millard, that injustice of being stripped of his titles would have still been the wound that would begin to infect his life in many ways. No longer the gold-medaled "greatest athlete in the world," the unending hustle for a living was on. Thorpe—having been shamed out of his Olympic medals—would spend a good deal of the rest of his life looking to strike oil, as he once did as a child in Oklahoma, to fall into a wheelbarrow full of money

Millard and Thorpe (courtesy San Diego Historical Society)

somewhere, somehow. Wasn't his greatness worth something?

It's difficult to speculate, but what we know is this: Whether playing as the Great Jim Thorpe, or Charlie the Chief Thorpe—one Saturday morning in early September 1929, aided by Millard at the Rancho—Thorpe had a made a little walking around money by giving a punting and drop-kicking exhibition at the Rancho, before a golf match between Cyril Tolley and three other amateur golfers.

Jim Thorpe was given the birth name Wa-Tho-Huk, which translates to "Bright Path" or "Path Lighted by a Great Flash of Lightning" in the Sac and Fox language. He had a direct native bloodline of Sac and Fox to chief Black Hawk, who disputed the treaty signed between his tribe and the U.S. Government to cede all land east of the Mississippi River, and was the chief who spurred and led the 15-week long Black Hawk War in 1832.

James Francis Thorpe—Jim—was born a twin on May 22, 1887, and he and his brother Charles were a mix of Sac and Fox, Potawatomie, Kickapoo, Irish, and French. As is well-documented, Charlie, who helped Jim through school, died of pneumonia at the age of nine. What's curious is that we find a golfer in the early 1920s named Charlie "The Chief" Thorpe who apparently competed in a number of events, and who helped to design a course in San Diego, though there are no solid records. Numerous sites of the Sac and Fox Archives and the USGA could not confirm the golfer Charlie "The Chief" Thorpe, and those who would know, particularly Thorpe's daughter Grace (No-Ten-o Quah—"Wind Woman"), an American environmentalist and Native rights activist has "gone to the great spirit." The trail of the golfing exploits of Charlie "The Chief" Thorpe may be cold, but at the time, in the early 1920s, Jim Thorpe would have still been playing professional football and soon became the first president of the league. As Grace has it: "Later in his life, Jim said that no one had ever replaced the role that his twin had played in his life."

Thorpe would have started into the Scottish stick-and-ball game in 1915. After football season, Iva and Jim Jr.

returned to Oklahoma from Indiana. As recounted by Maraniss, "During a warm February, taking advise of his baseball teammate, Christy Mathewson, Jim spent his afternoons at the Oklahoma City Golf and Country Club hacking away at a dimpled little ball. The Big Six, still rooting for Jim to make it in the big leagues, told him that golf could improve his hand-eye coordination, and help him hit a baseball, a skill he was still determined to master."

There's yet another incident that demonstrates that Thorpe had learned the game of golf well. In early 1946, with his third wife, Patsy, Thorpe had bought a trailer and traveled to Florida. Though Thorpe, like other Native American heroes who had fought in the war, found that the racism at home interfered with the trappings of a normal life: a life where service should have been respected and honored. He was hustling to earn a living. He and Patsy planned to open a sports camp in Miami, where Jim could train young athleteS: in football, track and field, and golf. According to Maraniss, "He told one reporter that in golf ... he was now shooting in the mid-70s. 'I've had a lot of fun,' he said. 'Now I'd like to teach.'"

Despite military service, despite being the finest athlete in the world, Thorpe was struggling for a decent living by this time, and still looking to have his 1912 Olympic honors restored. Bob Hope would lend Thorpe money ($500) in a particularly rough year (1946), but Jim would never get to teach golf, and his last years were made difficult by "the forces" and his personal demons. The terrible injustice that he suffered, like his people suffered, would only be righted after his death.

A Weave of Bloodlines

There's an interesting contrast to be drawn between Thorpe and the professional golfer Dewey Brown. Both knew Bing Crosby and counted Bob Hope among friends. Dewey Brown kept a far lower profile than Thorpe, even if the struggle for both Native Americans and African Americans in golf cannot be easily separated.

Golf history parallels race history in many ways, and the story of race in golf is not only a fraught subject, but also one that reveals many characters and survivors, not to mention early social justice warriors. The “original sin of slavery” and the genocide of Native cultures ensures that at the heart of the heart of the country, race is a Gordian Knot snarling the blood flow of our country’s veins.

As one example, describing his mixed racial and ethnic background at a 2012 campaign rally in Virginia, president Barack Obama said, “My mother was from Kansas. My father was from Kenya. I was born in Hawaii. I’ve got a sister who’s half-Indonesian, and who’s married to a Chinese-Canadian. My brother-in-law is Canadian, my niece is half-Mexican. And we have Blacks and Whites, and—what was I talking about? —I’ve got a lot of mutts in my family.”

Tiger Woods would also make a point of stepping away from the classification as “Black” or the “first African American” to win a major in golf. As witnessed by Obama, Woods, Thorpe, and countless others, this history of races mixing is at the heart of the links between golf and Native American culture. There is perhaps no better examples than Thorpe and Dewey Brown, who is called “the First African American in the PGA.” Where Thorpe fought to stand on his own, Brown had advantages that make clear how race and professional support play a critical role in golf and life.

Regarding Brown, the question is: How is it that a Black man was a member during the years when Caucasians-only was an unwritten rule? Quite simply, Dewey Brown could pass for being White. When the PGA institutionalized the Caucasians-only rule in 1934, a rat tipped the PGA off that Brown was African American, in part because Brown’s son, Roland Brown Sr.—a man who would go on to become a war hero in World War II—had a darker complexion. His fair skinned father, Dewey Brown, had his membership revoked “without explanation.”

Brown’s story is beautifully told in Calvin Sinnette’s book *Forbidden Fairways* (1998), and it comes with other notable tales. Dewey Brown is listed as the first African American to be a member of the PGA, but the story is a bit more complicated, as he was thought to be White. On September 1, 1928, he became a member of the PGA while working at the Shawnee Country Club in Pennsylvania. He was also a renowned golf clubmaker, and golf teacher during the 1920s and '30s, and made clubs for a number of the nation's leading professionals and statesmen, including President Warren G. Harding.

And there may have been other reasons for Brown's inclusion in the PGA other than his fair skin. He studied caddying and gamesmanship with George Low, at Baltusrol, who was of the school of thought that golf "came down to a matter of good manners as the crowning feature of showmanship." It seems Mr. Brown never forgot the lessons of George Low on matters of high emotional ratings: If you could play with charm, winning and money were more about luck.

Brown's genteel nature may also have played a role in his success after the insult of having his PGA membership revoked without explanation. It may not have been as symbolic and devastating as having one's Olympic medals taken away. Brown lost his PGA membership in 1947, a year when Jim Thorpe's prospects would have begun a precipitous decline, prospects that did not turn around even with the 1951 release of the film *Jim Thorpe—All American*, starring Burt Lancaster as The Chief. Undaunted by the PGA's slight, in 1947 Dewey Brown purchased the Cedar River Golf Course on Indian Lake in the Adirondacks, where he continued teaching and clubmaking, and where he raised a family of three boys. He led what he called "a blessed life" at Cedar River, commanding a great deal of respect, joining and becoming a leading figure in the Golf Course Superintendents of America.

Two years after formally removing the Caucasians-only rule—in 1961, the PGA was right to reinstate Dewey Brown, "re-elected to a class A membership." But our story does not end with that injustice corrected. And the role of Native Americans in the integration of the PGA brings us another athlete considered “the greatest of all time”: Joe Louis.

It was the Brown Bomber, also known as the Sepia Slugger, who—along with the likes of Althea Gibson, Charlie Sifford, Bill Spiller, and Calvin Peete—would soon begin to ring the bell at the top of golf’s leaderboards.

Chapter 7

A FEW POWERFUL INDIANS

> "We come from big people, mostly Blacks, some Whites, and a few powerful Indians; put that all together and I guess you got something."
> —Joe Louis, boxing champion and pro golfer

Walking across the matted grass to the ring, the blue-gray evening twilight created a halo above The House That Ruth Built, the old Yankee Stadium on the first day of summer sky. Professional boxer Max Schmeling covered his head with towels and tried to hide behind a phalanx of New York's finest. Not rain, but cigarette packs, paper cups bearing beer, and cigar stubs cut through the humid air. The Big House? Michigan be damned. This was Louis's Lion's Den, the decibels louder than a hungry lion's roar. This fight was bigger than Green Bay-Dallas. Bigger than Frazier-Ali, Celtics-Lakers, or Red Sox-Yankees combined. This was Us versus Them, and as Schmeling stepped inside the ropes, already in his corner, the Brown Bomber bounced on his powerful Indian feet with the fate of the free world on the tip of his leathers.

Schmeling's card carried the unfortunate symbolism of Nazi Germany. This is June 1938, just 12 months before Hitler's invasion of Poland, and 15 months short of Kristallnacht. And though Schmeling did not support Hitler, he was made into the symbol of every bad thing in this world and the next. While

Schemling was an extraordinary boxer and knew right from wrong, Schmeling attended lunch with Hitler, and a Nazi Party publicist travelled with Schmeling and his team. Someone put out stories that Schmeling's purse would "help build German tanks" and that "a Black man could not beat Max Schmeling." The story was that Hitler's heavyweight strode through the early evening blue twilight of Bronx, New York to face a rabid 70,000 polis that included Gary Cooper riding the fame of *High Noon.*

Louis had not only the fate of the free world, but his own personal dignity was at stake. Two years earlier, in 1936, Schmeling had scouted the Bomber, and he dropped the cocky young Louis to the canvas for the first time. Schmeling beat him in 12 tough rounds. The German fighter had perceived a weakness. When Louis had overwhelmed Paulino Uzcudun six months prior, Schmeling, who was in the audience at ringside, said, "I saw something which made me think I had a chance. Joe had a wonderful straight hand, but he'd punch and then sometimes drop it."

And he spent "a lot of time on the golf course," his son Joe Louis Barrow Jr. recalls. "I don't doubt it. He loved golf like he loved boxing: because it was an individual sport, a sport of self-reliance. The dedication that he gave to boxing he gave to golf as well. He spent many hours on the course."

In Joe Jr.'s estimation of that first fight, "No question he took Max for granted. There is some truth to that. He didn't train." The Champ was 21 at the first go, but by the age of 24, older and wiser, he also had learned not to drop the right.

When 1938 rolled around, despite the fact that the German boxer did not support the dictator, Schmeling had become associated with Hitler and the Nazi Movement. By that time, Louis' "weakness" had been resolved. The Brown Bomber was smart enough to switch things up. It's the first principle of warfare. When Schmeling stepped onto the canvas in Yankee Stadium, it wasn't a dropped right that gave an opening, but a left uppercut and a right hook that closed the doors and turned out the lights.

"He gave up the golf for that one," Joe Jr. recalls with a smile in his voice. Louis had focused, had trained, knew the stakes, and knew he had to get to Schmeling early. Was 124 seconds early enough? Louis pounded. A body blow snapped a vertebra in Schmeling's back. He wailed loudly in the second round before a right hook heard round the world brought the German to his knees, and then his back. Just over two minutes into the round, Schmeling was on the canvas, and a white towel was pitched into the darkening ring to help with the mop up.

In Maya Angelou's *I Know Why the Caged Bird Sings*, in a chapter called "Champion of the World," Angelou recounts her community gathered around a radio in Stamps, Arkansas. There, they listened to a boxing match in which Joe Louis carried the hopes and dreams of an entire people—the African Americans who had endured slavery and Jim Crow, economic poverty, and the legacy of lynching and the Ku Klux Klan. As to their June 1938 bout at Yankee Stadium, promoters estimated over 100 million people around the world were listening to radio coverage.

"Here I was, a Black man," Louis Sr. said. "I had the burden of representing all America. They tell me I was responsible for a lot of change in race relations in America. ... White Americans—even while some of them were still lynching Black people in the South—were depending on me to K.O. Germany."

So much so that President Roosevelt famously met with Louis before the fight and said the country "needed muscles like his to defeat Germany." We are only two years on from Jesse Owens' feats at the 1936 Berlin Olympics. Hitler's fascist ideology had been embarrassed by another Alabamian. Black Athlete Owens became the first athlete at any Olympics to win four gold medals—in the long jump, the 100- and 200-meter dashes, and the 4 x 100-meter relay.

As far as Joe Louis was concerned, Roosevelt's coaching worked. Joe Louis reportedly told a friend before the fight, "Yeah, I'm scared. I'm scared I might kill Schmeling ... I knew

I had to get Schmeling good. I had my own personal reasons and the whole damned country was depending on me."

In his own autobiography, Max Schmeling recounted the trip to the hospital after the fight: "As we drove through Harlem, there were noisy, dancing crowds. Bands had left the nightclubs and bars and were playing and dancing on the sidewalks and streets. The whole area was filled with celebration, noise, and saxophones, continuously punctuated by the calling of Joe Louis' name." That iconic popularity would carry The Champ into the war years and beyond. When he had nothing to prove as a boxer, he turned to golf. Through all of this fanfare, the build-up and aftermath of the fight, Louis was identified as Black, not Black Indian.

"He didn't talk about his Native heritage," Joe Jr. says, "but they both had Native blood. My mother as well. She [Marva] was from Boley, Oklahoma. Her parents were members of a ... " Joe Jr. wasn't entirely sure. His mother Marva was a talented beauty, like his father and his sister. She was so beautiful Joe Louis married her twice. She modelled and sang with Duke Ellington, among others. If Joe Louis was headstrong, Marva would have given it right back at him.

Marva Louis was "more than likely Creek," Joe Jr. continues. "She was very proud of that heritage. She was a very proud woman." Marva's parents were John Trotter and Viola Trowell Trotter, and all we know is—in the era of Indian removal and later settlement—they moved out of Boley for Chicago. If only to get their talented beauty a shot at a life other than stenographer.

In June 1938, the state of Native American culture was still not in a place of social or political status, still native but foreign. In the largest nationalist sports narrative of its day—in the history of boxing—no one included Louis' Native heritage. Is this at all a matter of cultural disownment? "Our family knew of our Indian heritage," Joe Louis Jr. says. "My mother wouldn't hide any of that."

When first Louis met Schmeling in 1936, the country was only two years on from The Indian Reorganization Act (IRA) of 1934, which had been brought forward by the sociologist and social reformer John Collier. Collier had studied the Taos Pueblo in New Mexico and saw firsthand how the loss of tribal lands had decimated the rich cultures of our First People. Education was a high priority for Collier, who focused on ending boarding schools and transitioning to community day schools and public schools. Collier authored the IRA—known as the Indian New Deal—as an attempt to reverse the Dawes Act, which had effectively continued the legal absconding of tribal lands. The Indian New Deal can be seen as just a first-legislative step in reversing the assimilation policies and providing recognition of tribal cultures.

Joe Jr. notes again that his family was very aware of their Native heritage, but after his father began to focus more on golf than boxing, becoming the first Black man to play in a PGA sanctioned event, The Brown Bomber had a different focus: "If you talk to Lee Elder and Jim Dent and Calvin Peete and others, they will say that Joe Louis opened the door for them to succeed. My father had Native American heritage, but the discrimination was focused on Black golfers. There was no emphasis on Native American golfers at the time. If there were, that focus could shift today, but at the time the fight was to have Black golfers play the best in the game."

Bill Black is the general manager of NDN All-Stars, which honors Native American athletes. A descendent of the Okanogan Band of Indians, part of the Confederated Tribes of the Colville Reservation, Black's father "made a point of raising my brother and me to be proud of our Native American heritage." He says, "Growing up in and around 'Indian Country' I noticed something. Why are there no 'Indian guys'? Were they not good enough? Or did they hide their cultural background? We had Chief Joseph, Sitting Bull, Crazy Horse. Are there no Native American heroes that were great outside of the context of war?"

In Bill Black's view, Joe Louis represents a kind of second wave of Native American athletes. He explains, "In the early 1900s, initially the path to getting off the res for Native athletes was baseball. Vast number of Native athletes played baseball and football. After that era of an easy way for fast money, boxing and fighting became prominent."

Black sees this as a cultural development. Growing up as part of the Colville people, Black recalls, "On the res, there's a lot of fights. When I was a kid I got into a fight every day—not because I was a good fighter, by the way. Take, Jack Dempsey—Cherokee—he was getting into fights, and no doubt thought, I might as well make some money at it. When he became the most famous athlete in the world, that became a way for other Native athletes."

As to boxing and golf being uniquely individual sports, Black suggests that the bi-racial nature of many of our Native American athletes plays a part. He explains, "Being a bi-racial minority, Jack Dempsey, Joe Louis, they don't fit in in any tribe. Out of that loner and individual status, I can't say that's an umbrella situation, but ... maybe they were in a different cultural or social environment. Once boxing is seen as a way out, they started their own gyms and started training."

The story doesn't end there.

In 1952, Louis was invited to play in the San Diego Open, but the PGA's Caucasian-only membership clause in its bylaws prevented such an entry. Louis wasn't the only Black golfer attempting to enter that week. His then friend, professional Bill Spiller had qualified as well. For Spiller, it was a matter of "may the best run out there with their irons" and show their stuff. For Louis, it was about integration, and the popular Brown Bomber made plans to go to San Diego to confront the tournament officials.

"I want people to know what the PGA is," Louis told the *New York Times* on Jan. 14, 1952. "We've got another Hitler to get by." He also told the *Los Angeles Sentinel*, "This is the last major sport in America in which Negroes are barred. It's about time that it is brought into the San Diego Open."

There are a lot of accounts of what followed, but perhaps the best is from Joe Louis himself. In his autobiography, he wrote, "All that was alright until I heard from my friends Ted Rhodes, my pro, Bill Spiller, and Charles Sifford. They said that the all-White PGA decided they couldn't play in the San Diego Open. Then they gave a message from Horton Smith ... telling me not to show up either. Well, the funny thing is I hadn't thought about playing until then. But all this made me mad as hell."

Louis thought the PGA should tell him he couldn't play to his face. He confronted tournament officials and, after an emergency meeting, Louis was allowed to compete as an exempt amateur. PGA President Horton Smith paired himself with Louis and, lo and behold, even in practice, Louis drew a crowd. The waitresses and caddies and bell hops at the course would greet them at every turn. Louis was their hero. Horton Smith allowed the Champ Joe Louis to play. The Champ would write, "That was a breakthrough I was proud to be part of."

When the dust settled, Spiller wasn't as happy; he was still pissed off. Here is Joe Jr. on these matters: "From my perspective, my father was invited by the Chevy dealers to play in the San Diego Open not knowing there was a Caucasians-only rule. He was very excited to play in that tournament, from his perspective. If you want to be the best, you had to play the best. If the Black players wanted to be the best, they had to play the best on the tour. He was excited in opening that avenue. When he was disinvited. He was upset and he felt it was his duty. He flew out to San Diego. This was a very important entry point to him. There was no discrimination in boxing. But Ted Rhodes? Bill Spiller? They were getting on in years and felt it. He didn't like it. That's why he went out to San Diego. He said if they were going to bar him, they would have to tell it to his face."

One can only imagine having the Boxing Champion of the World talking to the press about a face-to-face meeting about why he couldn't play in a tournament he had both qualified for and was being sponsored for. Lucky for all involved, no blood was spilled, and Horton Smith had the presence of mind to allow Joe Louis to play as an amateur. While neither made the cut, the door was open, however, at a high price: Louis had lost his friend Spiller, despite the wisdom of telling him, "Bill, you crawl before you walk."

Spiller was not placated. He was in his prime and didn't have much more time to compete against the best. Anyone who got in his way was no longer considered a friend. As much as that must have hurt both of those proud men, Joe Jr.'s role in this relationship creates a fine epilogue to this troubled history.

"When he agreed to play, it created animosity with Bill Spiller. Spiller had qualified as well, along with Ted Rhodes and Charlie Sifford. But they were [still] barred because they were professionals."

We could argue whether Horton Smith parsed out these qualifications out of fear or fairness, a compromise that did not actually compromise the Caucasian-only professionals clause. Either way, Spiller did not forgive Joe Louis for playing. The need for forgiveness would be passed on to their sons.

"My father told Bill, it's going to take time, but we're going to push ahead. He understood it. He also understood the impatience that Spiller had. There was animosity between the two of them because of that."

While Spiller and Rhodes and Sifford would all play professionally the next weekend in Arizona, there is a wonderful denouement to any bad blood between The Champ and Bill Spiller. When Sifford, Spiller, and Rhodes, along with John Shippen and Joe Louis, were posthumously inducted into the PGA as full members, Joe Jr. was there. He recalls, "It was in New Orleans in 2009. They were all given membership. Posthumously. There were some unfortunate consequences at the time of the San Diego Open. ... I was at that meeting and Bill Spiller's son came up to me. He told me, 'Everything was right by his father and my father.'"

In the induction ceremony, then PGA President Jim Remy had said at that meeting, "They say that you can't turn back time, but you can do your very best to make it right." Stories that are untold or that need to be told again can reshape the past, can acknowledge the ancestors who paved the way for us, and may make a new and better way for those who are to come.

Joe Louis Sr. had called integrating the PGA "the fight of my life," and he won that one, too. On November 10, 1961, at the Diplomat Hotel in Hollywood, Florida, the PGA Annual Meeting's agenda became historic. The Georgia-Alabama delegation co-sponsored the amendment, adopted by a vote of 87-0, to remove the discriminatory bylaw that had existed in writing since 1934, and in unspoken codes since 1916.

When Tiger Woods won the Masters Tournament in 1997 to become the first Black man and mixed-race minority to win a major golf championship, he was quoted as saying, "I wasn't the pioneer. Charlie Sifford, Lee Elder, Ted Rhodes, those are the guys who paved the way." He forgot to mention another ancestor, Joe Louis Sr.—The Champ—a man who like Woods had a rainbow of heritages in the river of his bloodstream, but who overcame the forces of racism nonetheless.

The Next Generation

When exploring the legacy of Joe Louis, we should look no further than his son, Joe Louis Barrow Jr.

Joe Jr. explains that his father's full name was Joe Louis Barrow, but signing in for an early bout, his father noticed that "Barrow" wouldn't fit on the line. So "Joe Louis" became his father's professional name.

Joe Jr. knew early on that his father was famous. "With my sister, he would take us to lunch and dinner. We were constantly interrupted by people seeking autographs. Dinners were not a fulfilling time together. The golf course was meaningful time."

Joe Louis Barrow Jr., son of The Champ, is the only man on the planet who played a round of golf simultaneously with the greatest tennis player of all time and the greatest boxer of all time. The tennis player was Althea Gibson, who won

11 major championships in tennis, becoming the first Black, Native American woman to win a major, who twice was given the Venus Rosewater Dish at Wimbledon by the Queen of England. This is the same Althea Gibson who, at the height of her tennis career, became the first Black female professional golfer and worked to integrate the LPGA.

Joe Jr. is alive and well, still golfing in Jacksonville, Florida. He recounted that day, in 1958 or 1959, when he golfed with Gibson, on a layout called the Pipe O' Peace in the southside of Chicago, one of the golf courses Blacks were allowed to play. (Pipe O' Peace Golf Course was renamed Joe Louis The Champ Golf Course in 1989.)

"Althea was a bit upset that day. My father and Ted Rhodes and Charlie Sifford were in the foursome in front of us." Instead, she was playing with the 12-year-old son of The Champ. "She wanted to be with the big fellows in front of us," Joe Jr. recalls, referring to Ted Rhodes, Charlie Sifford, and his father Joe Louis. That's quite the group—and as pros, they were Althea's equals.

"I understood that they were special, yes. By the way people treated us. But I didn't understand how important they were at the time. People around the course would treat them differently than other golfers. He was heavyweight champ, and she was the tennis champ." They were both transitioning from their championship sports to the great game of golf.

"One of the lasting impressions from that day is how far she could hit the ball," Joe Jr. says, smiling. He would go on to play on the golf team at the University of Chicago High School and could shoot in the 70s.

Recalling his lessons from his father, Joe notes one of the ironies of The Champ's game: "He had enormous hands, so you wouldn't think he would be a good putter, but putting was his strength."

About besting his father, Joe Jr. laughs. "Once in Las Vegas, he four-putted the 1st green and I thought, *this is the day I am going to beat him*. I was in college then, at the University of Denver. On the 16th green, we were tied. He asked me,

'How are you going to go back to Denver and tell your friends that your old man beat you?' I said, 'You haven't beat me yet.' Well, he birded 17 and 18."

Joe Jr. mentions again his father's soft hands and his putting touch, and admits that "After college, I beat him once. Yes. I remember him talking about his service, yes. He entertained the troops. Did 96 boxing exhibitions. He hosted more than 3 million troops during those. He had a desire to help people see they were important, that he would support the war. People forget that even through World War II, the armed services were segregated. My father was unhappy when he saw segregation in the army. But he had a friend from Chicago, Truman Gibson. Gibson worked for the Secretary of the Army. He was close to my father. My father didn't like the fact that the Black soldiers were put in the back of the exhibitions. He would call Truman to fix it, and they did."

These first-hand testimonies to history can heal as much as clarify. Joe Louis Jr. notes the southside was home to the Champ in later years, and his home included Pipe O' Peace Golf Course and the Archway Lounge, which at that time was owned by The Champ's former trainer, "Killer" Johnson. He held court there, and Joe Jr. tells me of those later years when The Champ would pay for Charlie Sifford and other's tournament fees.

Joe Jr. remembers, "My father had an overwhelming desire to help people."

He recalled the time when the Max Schmeling sought out Joe Louis to heal old wounds, to close the loop on the politics of their fight, which had pitted Black versus White, Freeman versus the Nazis.

"After that second fight, Max had accused my father of a low blow, but when they met, Max apologized. My father had been hitting him so fast and so hard that [Max] had turned away. He was trying to escape. It wasn't a low blow." That 124 seconds of fury and the punch in question landed on Schmeling's back, a blow that crushed a vertebra: Schmeling was just trying to survive.

"They became friends," Joe Jr. reveals. His father had travelled to Germany with Howard Cosell at one point, to report on a fight, and he had met up with Schmeling in Hamburg. In a return to the states, Schmeling had come to Milwaukee to referee a fight. "When he was in Milwaukee, he asked about my father," he shared. "When he learned he was only 90 miles from Chicago, he drove down and found my father at The Archway. Max apologized that he made an uproar about the punch at the time."

There at the Archway Lounge, a wrong was made right. The two combatants would appear together in 1961 on a popular television program, "This is Your Life," which reunited The Champ with a host of people from his past, including his sister whom he helped through Howard University, and Schmeling, who sincerely calls Louis "a great man."

"When my father died [in 1981], President Reagan intervened so that my father could be laid to rest at Arlington." Reagan made an exception to the requirements, allowing Louis to be interred with a full military honors funeral. After all, he had helped to integrate the services, as well as professional golf. "Though he couldn't be there, Joe Jr. recalls, "Max helped pay for some of my father's funeral," he continues.

On the long trail that was blazed by Jim Thorpe, Dewey Brown, and countless of unnamed others, the Brown Bomber appeared—the man who Muhammad Ali called "The Greatest"—the Black Cherokee with hands big enough to change the direction of history.

The Louis Barrow Legacy and The First Tee

"I know what golf did for me," Joe Jr. says. "And when I took over the First Tee Program, we realized we could develop a curriculum based on the values of the game. These kids might not grow up to be professional golfers like my father. They may be lawyers and doctors and teachers, but the values ... Golf is hard. Perseverance is needed. The nine-core values curriculum. I caused that to be." He is referring to the Life Skills and Leadership Academy put in place by the

PGA in their youth programs. For all that, he was awarded a lifetime achievement award in November 2022.

The First Tee began in 1997 as a partnership among the LPGA, the Masters Tournament, the PGA of America, the PGA Tour, and the USGA to make golf affordable and accessible for all kids. Joe Louis Barrow Jr. introduced a life skills curriculum that supported the development of nine values found within the game of golf, including honesty, integrity, perseverance, and respect.

Joe Jr. became the second executive director of the PGA's First Tee Program and ran it for 18 years. He explains, "The First Tee says to everyone, that golf is open. We married the game and the values in our core curriculum. The par-birdie-eagle-ace curriculum. That made all the difference. Most of the young of colors didn't think about golf. They don't think about golf as a way to grow. I incorporated the life skills and nine core values: golf skills and life skills at each level. Many of the young people ended up finishing college and going on to a career."

Joe Jr. credits George H.W. Bush with helping to establish the First Tee program, though he sees more work needs to be done. "First Tee can't do it alone," Joe Jr. says, and notes that programs such as N7 and the NB3FIT Junior Golf program are also committed to shaping the lives of young people, in this case Native American children, by teaching them the fundamentals of golf. The program focuses on leadership and nutrition education along with elements of integrity, respect, and perseverance.

"One of my disappointments in the golf industry, as an industry: it's not as open as it could have been or should be ... there are people taking it on forthright, but in my years in golf, you could still count the number of African Americans and Native Americans on two hands on the high end ... that saddens me. For many years I was the ranking individual of color. I was the only one. It's very tough. I figured out a way to stay out there, but there are barriers still there." Thank God he—and all the others before him—did.

Joe Jr. says, "Perseverance is the big one. Golf is hard. You have to have that value to begin to understand the game." And not only the values of golf, he sees that fight to make the game integrated, to look more like America, that fight still goes on.

Joe Louis Barrow Jr. tees it up in front of Ted Rhodes, (l.), and his father (r.). (Courtesy of Joe Louis Barrow Jr.)

Chapter 8

THE OSAGE AGE

> "If you let your White man tongues say what is in your Indian heart you will do great things for your people."
> —Fred Lookout, Osage Tribal Chief, 1926-1949; Great Grandfather to Walter Acey Junior Hopper

In Martin Scorsese's film, *Killers of the Flower Moon*, there is a brief clip of Osage tribesmen in ceremonial blankets out on a track flailing away at golf balls. The film implies that with the rush of oil money, the Osage discover golf. Wealth = golf, the rich man's game. But the history of Osage golf goes back well before the oil rush. For the Osage, golf has long been a way to connect to the land, and their people, and that history can be seen in the transformational golf instructor by the name of Walter Acey Junior Hopper.

Money is—as we know—the dirtiest thing in the world. Cash picks up the scents and soils and biomes of the germed—murderers, grifters, and thieves among them. The Osage Nation's experience with sudden wealth in the 1920s proves this to a tragic fault: the oil wealth brought in every manner of murderous crook and criminal and conniver, and the names associated with the crimes are still being sorted.

And it's true that during the Reign of Terror, Chief Bacon Rind and the Osage likely hired Perry Maxwell in 1919 to build a nine-hole course in Pawhuska.

The ghost of this nine-hole layout sits on the hill in Pawhuska, a large area that is senior housing now. At the time, you could see the oil derricks from the course. Now, there's a K-8 language immersion school where the Osage language survives. People remember a time when the tribe wanted to purchase the course back.

"It's still there. I mean, the greens are, but it hasn't been used for golf in a long time," explains Anthony Shackelford, who runs Prevention and Primary Treatment at Osage Nation. Shackelford's programs offer a series of community and school events on life skills and to promote suicide awareness and prevention. Anthony is also first cousin to Walter Hopper, whose life in golf helps to overcome incorrect representations of the tribe's history with the game.

"My dad's grandfather went to school at Carlisle in 1872. My dad used to talk about his grandfather. The Old Man was always very proud that he learned how to play golf. He was ten when they moved down here. Walked a path down here from Kansas. Literally walked. Of all the things he did in his life, he talked with pride that he learned how to play golf."

Shackelford's pride in this history runs deep. His father, who studied with the painter Charles Banks Wilson, created the Osage Nation Seal. Anthony runs the Osage Nation Prevention Department, which operates in most of the Nation's schools. He oversees life skills and protective practices. Suicide prevention and the core of the program is known as ATOD (Alcohol, Tobacco, and Other Drugs). He recalls the day Notah Begay III visited.

"Notah Begay came in, a friend of ours who went to Stanford. Notah is well known in the golfing industry ... he'll go into communities that are underserved that affect Native American youth across the country. And it was the largest participatory soccer clinic in the history of Osage Nation. University of Oklahoma women's soccer was here, and we had 180 kids. Roaring success. I got to play nine with Notah."

Golf and basketball are the two favorite sports of the tribe. Soccer is growing as well, and sports have been a way to keep the young ones out of trouble. No one knew this more than Walter Hopper, whose life in golf helps to overcome incorrect representations.

"Junior is my first cousin," Anthony recalls, noting their blood lines go back to the Tribal Chair Fred Lookout and to Lookout's father, and beyond that, to the hundreds of years of our First Nation's history. Walter's great grandfather on his mom's side was Chief Fred Lookout, and on his dad's side his great grandfather was Chief John Oberly.

Mr. Shackelford and his family have lived out the legacy of Osage Nation over many generations, and that continues to this day. When I ask him about the clip in Scorsese's film, of the Osage in blankets playing golf, he laughs and says, "Akin to Scottish kilt, the blankets. Even during heat of the summer months. Same as putting on a scarf and hat. Just part of what they wore." At least the fashion was accurate.

Shackelford continues, reflecting on the 1920s:

> "Work was slow, then all of a sudden, money rolling in like crazy. Yeah, and when the money was coming in the country, as there was in the Great Depression, there was no middle class. It was haves and have nots. Tens of millions in today's market. But it was a double-edged sword. Less than popular choices were drinking and drugs. And then they put a target on our backs. Now it's been glamourized on the big screen. Osages were victims, victims of the government entrusted to look out for our wellbeing. Even the government wanted to get their hands on our money. 'Guardians,' and all that. It was like winning the lottery. If you didn't have an attorney, a lot of money flipped sides. But some were studious and saved and planned and helped facilitate a good lifestyle. They worked and left things to their kids. There was the other side of it, too. People focus on the bad side. There was a good side too. But overall, the government fumbled the ball in taking care of our people."

Shackelford sees the loss of the Pawhuska golf course as a shame: "I mean, it was a nice course like that in a town of 3,000. Very unique. A wonderful setting. Crying shame of course. The new owner tried to open up a disc golf course.

That fell to the wayside. Granite markers that are still there. You drive by and don't even want to look over there. It's all gone to seed." An eye sore from the Reign of Terror, the neglected course obscures the fact that golf was in the DNA of the tribe long before the oil rush of the 1920s.

To Mr. Shackelford, Indians are by nature athletic people. Not only Jim Thorpe and John Levis and Billy Mills: "A lot of them went unknown. Look at the Hominy Indians, they had a professional football team. the year The New York Giants were champions. 1929. Hominy Indians beat them. There's footage of that game. And an account of it in newspaper print. That team had a bunch of our relatives on it."

This love of the land and excellence in sport is embodied by the spirit of Walter Acey Junior Hopper. Ask any golfer in the region and most will immediately reflect warmly on an encounter with Hopper.

"I saw him just 24 months ago," Jason Dochney (Cherokee) said recently. Mr. Dochney is now a PGA member and runs a teaching school, APA Golf. He lauds Walter Hopper as someone who brought golf to life for him. "Walter was very prominent in our PGA section, a figurehead for junior golf in our section, and we all learned from him. It was super cool to connect with him again."

Since Walter passed in 2022, his wife Marilyn upholds this legacy. Her voice is soft and warm as she tells their story and their history together which started one of the biggest PGA junior programs in the nation.

"He worked with Tahlequah Wilma Mankiller, Chief of the Cherokee," his wife Marilyn says. "He involved Indian students through several different avenues. He thought that the kids who played golf, it introduced them to being good human beings. It was the kids who played golf stayed out of trouble. It gave them an opportunity to advance and be good people in life." Of the thousands of kids that came through the PGA Junior, many advanced to great heights: doctors, lawyers, and so on; and many became great golfers and are on the PGA and LPGA Tours, including Bob Tway, Matt Gogel,

Bryce Molder, Tag Ridings, Brad Elder, and Stacy Prammanasuh.

"Walter's great grandfather was Fred Lookout," Marilyn recounts, Chief of the Osage from the Reign of Terror until 1949. "Walter and his sisters are the only ones who could claim to being great grandchildren to both Chiefs of the Osage tribe." Lookout is a generational figure in that history. In 1926, following the downfall of Chief Bacon Rind, Lookout was elected and served until his death in office in 1949. During the Osage Indian murders, Lookout's family claimed he survived a shooting attempt and then hired Chicago Mafia members as bodyguards.

Walter's life was not as dicey, but just as transformational.

"I learned how to play when Walter and I were at OSU," Marilyn continues. "That was our pastime, going to the golf course and playing. They had two courses at OSU, and we just wanted to play and be together."

Just after he enlisted, Marilyn and Junior made their love sacrosanct, before he left for Vietnam. Like many of our First People, he enlisted, selecting the U.S. Air Force and serving in Vietnam. He reached the rank of sergeant and received the Airman of the Month award for the 58th Airlift Command in July 1969. When he returned, he took up work in education.

"He was working in education," Marilyn recalls. "He was Director of Indian Education for Oklahoma public schools. But he just loved to play golf every day. He determined that is probably what he should be doing. Golf and working with the youth were Walter's biggest passion."

Marilyn and the family knew him as Junior, but everyone else called him Walter. When he started in golf after quitting Indian Education, he started at Mohawk from 1979 to 1982. Then became head pro at Pryor Creek Golf course in 1983. He was at Pryor as head pro and developed the PGA Junior program while at Pryor and developed it into one of the biggest and best Junior programs in the nation.

"We worked together as I ran the pro shop," Marilyn recalls. "And he coordinated running the course and running the PGA Jr program. Then in 1996 he was hired on at the South Central PGA office in Broken Arrow, Oklahoma, where his title was director of Junior Golf. They moved the Junior program into his office, and he then later became the tournament director for the club pros as well as the juniors, until he retired in 2011."

Marilyn's memories span time and this history is marked by raising a family as well. After she and Walter started at Pryor Creek, Walter landed a position at Mohawk Park in Tulsa. Marilyn recalls, "We raised our boys there, and they did all the junior golf. They all went to college on golf scholarships. They were very involved. The oldest, Acey went to University of Central Oklahoma ... Travis went to University of Nebraska and Adrian went to Paris ... Texas. Adrian is still with it."

As a professional, Walter actually got the PGA's First Tee program started in Tulsa. Some others took it over and will take credit, but Marilyn and everyone else know Junior started it.

Walter achieved many awards and recognitions: 1989-special award from the South-Central PGA for excellent work and dedication to Junior Golf; 1980s and 1990s—served on the PGA National Junior Golf Committee; 1993-1994 PGA Service Award for dedicated service as a member of the PGA Junior Golf. On Nov. 17, 1995—the Governor's Award for all his work providing quality fitness and sports activities which have helped Oklahomans of all ages live happier and healthier lives. In November of 1995—PGA Junior Golf Foundation Award for Excellence; June 2004—Jim Thorpe Award and induction into the Oklahoma Sports Hall of Fame for all his work in promoting junior golf.

And just as golf was part of the Osage culture before the Reign of Terror, it will continue to be part of Osage history going forward.

Brian Davis followed Hopper on the South-Central Section Junior Tour, which has grown to a 40-45 person event behemoth capped by the season-ending Tournament of

Champions, later renamed the Walter Hopper Championship in his honor.

"It's not very often that you meet someone who is truly generational in their work, but that's exactly what Walter was," Davis said. "Every junior event I attend, I run into a parent who would ask about Walter and then proceed to smile and tell me about how he was running the junior tour when they were kids and now their kids are playing on the same junior tour."

Walter was also known for saying, "I never met a stranger." All were welcome. He didn't play in a blanket, and golf wasn't an elitist game that arrived with the filth of the oil wealth and the murderous grifters and thieving crooks who came with it.

For the Osage, golf has long been a way to connect to the land, their people, and the lasting traditions of a resilient, sovereign nation.

Portrait of Walter Hopper by David Bunn Martine

Chapter 9

INDIAN OF THE YEAR

> "When the world was covered in eternal darkness, the animals and beings brought together a council to discuss how to divide the time between day and night. The sun was tasked with bringing daylight, while the moon or stars would be responsible for the night. The council agreed on a harmonious division of time, ensuring that both day and night created a balanced world."
> —Choctaw parable

> "Balance, rhythm and timing. If you have that you can golf."
> —Junior Moody, Choctaw golf instructor

Orville Moody was known as "Sarge," in part because of his long history in the U.S. Army, and for his everyman persona. When he won the 69th U.S. Open in 1969 at Cypress Creek, little attention was paid to Moody's triumph as a Native son. Nevertheless, Choctaw Nation whooped it up.

"They had a parade in Anadarko," Junior Moody recalls. Junior would have been 10 when his uncle was named Indian of the Year in 1969. He couldn't be there for one reason or another, so his mother and some of us went. She rode in the car. I was a young kid." Junior remembers that convertible go by that said: Orville Moody, Indian of the Year.

The parade is now called the American Indian Expo and has been running for 89 years. In '69, the star of the show was a man they called Sarge on the PGA Tour—Orville Moody, Choctaw, an Everyman. He had captured the U.S. Open with a 14-inch putt that held off three players lingering one stroke behind.

While her son was unable to ride in the parade, Orville's mother Sarah soaked up the glory, riding past the Hall of Fame of Famous Indians, which would have included, fittingly enough, a monument for most decorated Indian soldier in United States history: Pascal Poolaw, Kiowa Warrior, who received 42 awards and medals, including five Bronze Stars, four Silver Stars, three Purple Hearts, and one Air Medal. He was the ancestor who bush-whacked the path: Orville would learn his golf chops in the army, in Korea.

"I can still see her face like it was yesterday," Junior Moody recalls. At ten years old, he would have felt like a kid at the candy shop window watching his grandmother sitting in a car that had the family named in golf. All the Indians had their gear on, for a golfer. His uncle! Indian of the Year!

"Golf was the family's game going back four generations," Junior recounts, so far back the names don't come as easy. "My great granddad ... I never met him. Then there's Dale, Cleve, Leon, Spanky, Michelle ... Orville. Every one of us is in the golf business still." At 65 years old, Junior Moody speaks in that musical Oklahoma twang, what he calls "South language." He works at Twin Oaks Country Club, in Duncan, Oklahoma. His father Leon—who was Orville's brother—worked at Lawton Municipal Course and now, 88 years young, he drives a cart at the Comanche Casino. Junior's sons work at a golf course in Duncan.

Junior Moody has to turn off his lawnmower to talk. Currently superintendent at Twin Oaks in Duncan, he taught for 26 years at the Duncan Country Club, and he's won a tournament or two himself.

"One of them pro-ams," Junior says. "Maybe 1993 or '94. I beat em all. Including my uncle. And all them local pros. I think it was the Graham Texas Pro-Am." Junior agreed that a history of Native Americans in golf was a good idea.

"All of us have our cards," Junior said. The Moody clan are all registered Choctaw tribal members. Their lives are anchored in the heart of Indian Country, where the Trail of Tears was a reality. Orville's father, Cleeve, was the greenskeeper at Chickasha Country Club, where young Orville got his start. The family later moved to El Reno and then Oklahoma City, where Orville started at Capitol Hill High School as a junior.

"He became a good golfer at that time," Junior Moody said. "He won the state championship there at Capitol Hill."

After high school, the story gets a little complicated. Orville won a scholarship to Oklahoma University, but—like a lot of Indigenous folks—school didn't capture his fancy. And a scholarship at that time was more like work study.

"He was in charge of the tennis courts. He never did understand that," Junior recalled with a laugh.

And when his girlfriend back home broke up with him, Orville joined the army where he served for 14 years. Eventually his duties became organizing and maintaining golf operations within the army. And he won the Korean Open three times while still in fatigues and quartertones.

Junior's favorite Orville Moody story is the time Lee Trevino was on a tour in Korea to entertain the troops. Trevino bursts into the shop and says, 'Who's your best golfer? I want to play him.' Well," Junior laughs that soft Oklahoma lilt, "Orville steps up and says, 'I'll play you.' He went out and beat the stuffing out of Trevino. They became friends for life." They also became playing partners. In the 1969 World Cup in Singapore—what could be considered an all-Indigenous team—Moody and Trevino represented the U.S. The duo won by eight strokes over the Japanese team of Takaaki Kono and Haruo Yasuda.

Junior recalls one tournament, during a rain delay at a pro-am, where their foursome all huddled in a shed out of the rain, "We were playing at Falcon Head, and there was a guy named Danny Williams who had a TV show out of the city. He was an Indian, too. When the rain started, we took some cover, and Williams asked Orville to tell a story. Well, he started telling stories about the tour and the army. I laughed so hard I thought I was going to bust a gut."

Orville liked to eat, hunt, fish, golf, and tell stories. Just like the rest of us.

And we could say some Choctaw balance was returned to the world when Orville won the U.S. Open in 1969. With that win, a Native had claimed the top—the elite of the elite—in the least violent and most difficult game in human history. An everyman, a staff sergeant, someone just like us had won the big one.

Reflecting on his life after emerging from the U.S. Army and winning the U.S. Open, Orville is reported to have said, "I always had a place to sleep, a place to eat, and I always got paid. The money is too good to go back now, but I was happier then." He was comfortable as an Everyman, as Sarge. Bob Hope had a joke about that Everyman persona: Moody was on the tour for two years before he stopped saluting his caddie.

There's got to be a word for this phenomena, this rooting for someone like us: the psychologist or sociologist or economist must surely have studied the phenomena in which we root for someone because they are seemingly as normal and seemingly average as we are. *Twin flame* implies some sort of intimacy. *Doppelganger* also doesn't quite fit the bill—too much of a sort of cosmic twinship. And we all can't have the same doppelganger. *Anti-hero* implies they've done something wrong, intrinsically conflicted between the forces of good and bad. Whether there is a word for that phenomena or not, Orville Moody was like all of us in another way as well: putting was his Achilles heel.

"He was the best ball-striker out there," Junior recalls. "If he could putt, during his heyday, he would have been up there with Nicklaus and Palmer. Trevino used to say that all the time. He could hit it good, but then would get the yips." Many a reader knows this story well: from tee to green is the easy part; from green to cup is a gauntlet of outsized challenge.

For Orville, that all changed on the senior tour for two reasons: he took his teenage daughter Michelle on as a caddie, and he started using a long putter.

"Charley Owens. That was his name," Junior brings the memories back. "Owens had a knee that was locked up. He was putting with the long putter. That's the first time Orville ever used one. He tried it once and then didn't put it down. Went from being the worst to leading the Senior Tour. If he had that long putter [earlier], he'd be known with Nicklaus and Trevino. Such a good ball-striker."

Junior would know. He taught golf for 26 years at Duncan Country Club. He laughs when I tell him Frank Dufina's line: "The first hundred years are the hardest."

"Today, I listen to those young guys, and they're all so technical. No one knows what they're talking about. Golf is about rhythm and timing. Balance, rhythm, and timing. If you have that, you can golf."

If you can putt. Ben Hogan famously said golf was two games in one: there's ball striking and then there's putting, a whole other challenge.

"Talk to Michelle. Michelle balanced that all out," Junior says laughing. Michelle won't take all the credit for her father's resurgence as a senior.

"Credit where credit is due," she says. "There was a golfer named Charlie Owens. He deserves credit because he was a great guy. He was a paratrooper in the military, and he could not bend over. One of his knees was fused. Might have been his left one. He used a long putter, and dad said, let me try that. After that, he fashioned his own long putter. I've still got it at my house."

Where people might think it was a "fluke" U.S. Open win, they forget that Orville Moody went on a tear afterward. He was the leading golfer on the Senior Tour, winning the Senior Open, and all because of his daughter Michelle. Long before Nick Faldo met his caddie Fanny Sunesson, Melissa Orville Blackmon was the woman caddie on tour lugging around a giant bag. Michelle remembers that her father, like many an army vet, had some choice vocabulary. And an attitude. She remembers a tournament—maybe it was in '87—when Orville ripped the head off his putter with three holes left to play.

"Those were going to be a long three holes," Michelle says with a laugh. She was a teenager in the late '80s. She might have been grooving to Rich Astley's "Never Gonna Give You Up" or Def Leppard's "Pour Some Sugar On Me." Any teenager might have felt like she was wasting her time listening to an old man with a paunch curse his fate.

"I told him he had a rotten attitude, and he should change it." With Michelle on his bag and a long putter in his hand, Sarge started winning. He won twice in 1987, added three more Senior Tour victories in '88. He book-ended his U.S. Open victory from '69 with a Senior U.S. Open win in '89.

"That's when he made all his money," Junior recalls. People forget that. Once he learned how to putt, he was unbeatable. "After he started putting, one of the companies signed a deal with him. ... They made a long putter that had the name 'Moody' on it. I used to laugh. I told him the putter made him look like he was handicapped. But then one winter, I was golfing and started putting with him and his putter. That's all I use now. I wouldn't go back now if you paid me."

If any of this sounds like the U.S. Open was not the highlight of the Moody Family's golfing life, you'd have his daughter in agreement. And Junior as well. For the family, golf is a part of the landscape, the family is part of the land. The 69th U.S. Open in 1969. The U.S. Senior Open in 1989. Indian of the Year. These USGA national titles are just part of the story.

Michelle remembers all these days with great fondness: "We had a rapport," she says. Rapport sounds like a nice word for good-cop, bad-cop. After blowing a four-foot putt on the last hole of the Lexington tournament, Orville cussed and told Michelle, "Ray Charles could have read the greens better than you did today."

Michelle could take it. Besides, she knew what lurked behind the tough-guy exterior. He had cried like a baby when he won the Havermeyer Trophy. The family wouldn't let him forget. And in the years when Orville had conquered his putting fears, Michelle was on his bag.

Her favorite story comes from a pro-am in Florida: "They were notoriously slow, the pro-ams, and we were stuck on a par three. Well, there is a noisy seabird perched in a tree. My dad said, 'Michelle, give me a 7-iron.' I asked him what he needed a 7-iron for. He said, I'm going to get that bird out of the tree. I told him I wouldn't give it to him because he would kill that bird. That's when he said, I'll hit in between its feet. Sure enough, he hit that ball right between his feet, and the bird flew off. That's how good he was."

Michelle was born in 1969: the same year Moody won the big one, the U.S. Open, the year the Choctaw Nation named him Indian of the Year. On the living-room wall, the family long kept the eagle headdress he was given, that came with a big leather band with a proclamation: "Indian of the Year." Rod Curl is often called the First of the First People to win on the tour, but Orville Moody knew where he came from.

"About Sarah," Michelle recalls, "he used to talk about how she walked the Trail of Tears. She was a young girl who walked with her parents. That's how they got to Chickasha. Grandma Moody. When I was in 5th grade, she was 89. She was considerably older when she had him. He was the youngest of ten."

And the stories endure. One heard many times notes that, in the final round in '69, taking what would no doubt have been a nerve-wracking stroll from the 17th green to the 18th tee, a marshal mistook Moody—the leader of the tournament—for a spectator, and instructed him to get behind the ropes. Another marshal intervened, saying, "He's a player. Let him through. He's the man." Sarge was The Man, and once he was let through the ropes to finish, he made a 14-inch putt to hold off a playoff with a threesome tied for 2nd place, which included Al Geiberger. (Geiberger would be the first tour pro to get home in that magical number—59—in 1977.)

And during that same U.S. Open in Houston, when one of

our First People captured the country's top spot in golf, a fan followed Moody and cheered every shot. Asked why, the fan told the *New York Times*, "Because I'm short and fat and want to root for someone just like me."

If only he could putt.

Orville Moody lines up a putt in the U.S. Senior Open, holding his long putter, with daughter Michelle.

Chapter 10

THE ANCESTORS OF ROD CURL

> "My native name is Yoso, which means Jonny comes from behind. But I was given the name 'Yoso' by my mother, which is also the name of a flower."
> —Rod Curl

On a stormy day in early June, I steered a rental car through a Florida rainstorm that had me thinking I had been, well, snake bit. But by the time I made it to the Clearwater Country Club, the intense sun was breaking out and had the shadows scared. Rod Curl and I met at the appointed time in the appointed place. At age 80, he could pass for 55: built like a brick, with a warm and knowing smile. Little did I know, this erstwhile anthropologist would be getting a half-day-long golf lesson with no water breaks.

The first ancestor Rod Curl mentions is his father-in-law. "Bonnie's dad, yeah, he played. I was 17, and there was one girl in the world. I had to marry her. I couldn't let her go out of high school. Her father didn't really like me that much. Anyway, that's what I could feel, you know. I was a no-good, construction-working Indian. That's what I felt. Well, he played golf, and to win her I had to win him. Lake Redding is still there. And it's one of my favorites. I started there when I was 19. That's when we married. When I was 23, I played in the 1966 U.S. Open. You see? I had the touch and feel. God gave us that. We had that feel. I got long in '72. And then I won, okay? Now, hit this ball between those two trees."

We headed to a shaded area beneath massive willows where we would spend a half a day discussing—not all the mechanics of a golf swing, but—*the* golf swing. The perfect swing. My hopes were to have a lemonade and talk about the bridge we were building between Native American history and our times. Mr. Curl had other ideas.

"I only teach people who want to learn," he said with purpose. We had found the shade of two giant willows, and I again tried to lead him back to his ancestors, as in: who taught him? After all, it was my 64th birthday, and on my birthday, I'd been visited by a black snake. A black snake is a symbol of the ancestors, and I felt emboldened. The spirits had gathered again. I was filled with questions.

I began, "You had 46 top-10 finishes in the age spanning Hogan and Casper to Johnny Miller? Arnold Palmer taught you the grip? When you walked the landscapes, did you see the land as yours, mine, or ours?"

"People ask me, haven't you played here? What did you think of that? With who? I've already played with the best in the world. If I have to answer stupid questions, I would just as soon go play poker and eat ice cream. I teach golf. Only people that want to learn. You have to listen every word I say. That's who I am. I'll give you my life." He paused here only for a breath.

"Now hit that ball between the gap in those trees," Rod instructed, pointing at the turf between us.

"What ball?"

"That ball," he pointed again.

"An imaginary ball?"

"There's only one swing," he said with a smile as warm as the Florida sun. "There's one golf swing, and you don't need a ball to learn it."

"I don't need a ball?"

Mr. Curl swooped down and plugged a tee into the earth.

"Does that help?" he asked.

I didn't know. I'd grown up a poor, White kid in northern New Jersey. Golf balls were like a fool's gold. Learning golf was about having a bucket of castaways and whacking 'em as hard as I could. I had spent years reading the hundreds of logical fallacies about the golf swing, but now in the presence of one of golf's greats, a man who knew a little something about touch and feel, all of that became instantly moot. Is he talking about Hogan's mythical motions?

"Now hit that ball between the gap in those trees." He pointed at two spear-shaped cypress trees about 100 yards off.

When I did swing at the invisible ball, Mr. Curl laughed.

"You only have 32 flaws."

"Only 32?"

Rod Curl smiled his warm, big grin. "About that, yes," he said. "Now. Let's start with your grip."

When I humbly suggest that my 12 handicap is secure, that I had traveled to hear about his history, he ignores me and begins to arrange my hands and shoulders and hips.

"Now hit that ball."

"What ball?"

"It's there on the tee."

Rod Curl made contact with the White world's game to win the hand of the one girl in the world and the respect of her father. If his tribe had once owned California, Rod Curl would regain America in a different way. When the *New York Times* reported on Rod Curl's one-stroke victory over Jack Nicklaus at The Colonial, in 1974, the lead was: Curl was "the first Indian to win a battle on television." The sly remark was a nod at the John Wayne inspired views of Native Americans as warring, grunting, feather-wearing wild men on horses, who couldn't shoot as well as the White guys.

"Everyone dreamed of beating Nicklaus by one stroke," he tells me. "Indians, White guys, Black guys, you name it. But people forget that field had Raymond Floyd, David Graham, Hubert Green ... here."

Mr. Curl stands behind me and demonstrates Nicklaus' upstroke.

"Note the 'L.' Look at the 'L.' No. Look. Really look." Mr.

Curl roughly pushes my arms back and up until my right arm forms an L at the top of my backstroke. "That's the Nicklaus 'L,'" he says with a grin. "So powerful."

In a previous lesson, my teacher had told me not to try to swing like Nicklaus, to instead leave my left heel fixed on the earth. I would learn soon what Tom Lovell, the Native American activist, had told me about Rod Curl: "Some teachers will work with what you got. Rod is the kind that will remake your whole game in a three-hour lesson. Rod will teach you the idea about the perfect swing and all that. Then you'll be all bent out of shape for a month."

Mr. Curl's son, Rod Curl Jr.—a PGA teaching pro—had told me the same. "When I take my girls over there, they just want to hit it and have fun. But my dad, like ... you got to do it the right way. He's pretty intense."

How intense? We were standing in the willow shade of the practice area at Clearwater Country Club in Florida. And while I pestered him with questions about his history and our shared heroes, he was very intent on showing me how I had learned the golf swing wrong.

"There is only one swing. Now hit that ball."

An invisible ball. Again.

Like light is both a particle and a wave, for Rod Curl, the golf swing is both a perfect, Platonic form, and yet every one is different. I seemingly couldn't distract Rod Curl from teaching me the up-and-then-under, and the perfect grip, I still wanted to get the story.

"I don't know my mother's last name," he says impatiently. "My father owned a nightclub in Redding [California]. I watched him play poker until I was 21, then I started playing. I was a construction worker." Pool, or bowling, or golf were ways to beat the man. Bonnie's father, Rod Curl's first father-in-law, taught him golf. An excellent baseball and pool player, in three short years, Rod Curl would be playing the '66 U.S. Open as an amateur at the Olympic Club in San Francisco. There Rod befriended Arnold Palmer, who taught Rod the grip: the same grip he was teaching me.

After meeting Palmer, he became what is known as a rabbit. A *rabbit* is the now-archaic term for someone who had not finished in the top-60 money winners the year previous and had to qualify for each tournament. Rod, Bonnie, Susanna, and Rod would drive the high-ways and bi-ways so that, on Mondays, Rod could qualify for the upcoming matches. A '66 Mercury was their chariot, carrying Bonnie, and later on their first two children, Suzanna and Rod Jr., as well. Golf became the purveyor of an American dream that gets realized with the win at The Colonial in '74.

"Palmer?" I query. "You played with Palmer?"

"You don't want to swing like him," Rod says, briskly taking my club and showing how Palmer hit like he was hitting to the first baseman.

"You do that, try to hit this ball to first base."

What ball? What base?

He plugs a tee into the earth. "Does that help?"

There's still no ball. And no first base. In Rod Curl's world, the swing exists separate from the ball, and there's only one swing—a perfect arc—and there's only one grip: the one Palmer showed him in '66. I was beginning to understand, but don't I just need to stand there and whack balls into the turf? And what about our heroes?

I ask, "You were on a driving range with Ben Hogan?"

"Hogan? I read his book. When I saw him on the range, I didn't stop, but then I came on Palmer. He's my god," Mr. Curl says. "Such a special person. I became friends with him. You know when he's your friend. I watched Hogan hit a couple of shots at Olympic. But this is one of the highlights of my life. Palmer was playing with Dave Marr. I went and asked him, 'Can I play with you?' A little ole Native boy. I was a 10 handicapper. He put his arm around me and said, 'sure.' Then we suddenly had 5,000 or 10,000 people following us. On the 11th hole, he turned to me and said, 'I have a fetish with grip. When I look at someone's grip, I know whether I can beat you. You need to get your grip straight.' Up to that point, I was a hooker. Palmer was very adamant about teaching me how to hold the club. Both my sons have benefitted. Both my sons have close to a perfect grip."

He is referring to his sons Rod Jr. and Jeff: both pros with a number of wins and with current teaching practices. They had both told me the same thing.

"He's not wrong. He knows what he's talking about," Rod Jr. told me. "The swing and the grip. Same thing. He'd put my hands on perfect and tell me to hold the club for 15 and 20 minutes. He'd take pictures and then make me walk away and come back and do it again until it was natural."

So, I relent.

"Ok," I sigh. "Show me Palmer's grip. I'll take pictures."

"No," Mr. Curl says. "I'll take the pictures. Give me your phone." Rod Curl put me in place, shoulders just so. He had me reveal three knuckles on my left hand (strong grip). He had me put my left thumb in the lifeline of my right palm, with my right thumb touching the forefinger of my right hand (between weak and strong.) He put the club in the fingers of my right hand (don't palm it!). Then he circled me, carrying my phone, taking pictures of my grip and stance once he had me where he wanted me.

"Now hit this ball. The one on the tee there. Hit it between the gap in those two trees."

I had begun to understand you didn't need a ball to learn the swing, but when I took a swing, Curl smiled his big smile and took a pause. "You have some hand-eye coordination, but you need to go to Japan and Korea. 90 percent of the ladies there know what I'm talking about."

"Both my sons have near-perfect grips," Rod Curl continued, a passing remark as he evaluated my poor-boy-from-New-Jersey grip. He has taken my phone, insisting he would take the pictures. He aligns my shoulders (left up, right down) before coming to my hands. He pries open my right hand.

"You're palming it," he says with a comic alarm in his voice. "You'll get no distance that way." He resets the club into the fingers of my right hand and then presses both hands together.

"You?" He laughed, "You need to show four knuckles on your left."

For all he has been through, Rod Curl Sr. is a bright teacher with a sense of humor. He's also had to endure more than a few racial inanities. Because he is only 5'5", he was quickly nicknamed Little Beaver, after the sidekick in the Western comic-strip character Red Ryder. One sportswriter wrote, "Big Chief Little Name shoot many birdies. Kill White man's golf course."

He has taken headline this with good humor, although without inviting pidgin Indian exchanges in the way that Mexican American Lee Trevino has cultivated his Super-Mex image. "I never say, 'I'll do a rain dance,'" Curl says. "I'm an Indian boy who grew up in the White man's ways."

We might also want to file this under one of the mysteries of golf that will never be solved: The same tournament where Palmer taught Rod Curl Sr. how to hold a golf club to correct his hooks—the 66th U.S. Open in 1966—is the same tournament that Palmer—due to a series of snap-hooked tee shots on the back nine led to an incoming 39 and a blown seven-shot lead. Billy Casper made up seven strokes on the back nine to force an 18-hole playoff. Eventually, Casper lifted the U.S. Open trophy for the second time.

Mr. Curl is clearly joyful just thinking about Palmer's place in his game. In addition to Curl's many accolades for breaking the racial barriers in golf, he might also say he is one of the few folks in living memory whose grip can be traced directly to Arnold Palmer, whose own grip is traced to his father, (Jerome) Deacon Palmer, who worked as a greenskeeper at the Latrobe Country Club in Pennsylvania. Overcoming that challenge, not laying claim to intergenerational trauma, one might say this allowed intergenerational knowledge to make its way through time: a simple grip, handed down from father to son, legend to legend. Palmer often spoke about how, during the Depression years—and after his sister was born and his mother needed time—Arnold began to go with his father to the course at the ripe old age of two.

Anyone who has been around golf long enough knows the rumor is true: the Vardon Trophy, given to the lowest scoring pro on the tour, is modeled from a cast of Palmer's club grip. According to *Golf Digest*, Arnold never denied or confirmed the rumor, but what is true is that Arnold was taught the grip at age three by his father, along with the directive, "Don't ever change it, boy."

The strong father-son bond is at work in so many levels in the game of golf, and Rod Curl's teaching mannerisms—tough and uncompromising—felt fatherly to me as he tried to teach the Palmer grip on that hot June day in 2023. Over and over he said: "Show as many knuckles as you can on your left hand." "The 'V' in your right hand should point at the right eye—not the shoulder. This creates a kind of natural torque in the hands as they go back and then swing down through the ball."

When I relate this to Curl's son, Rod Jr., he laughs and claims to knows this lesson well. "Oh yeah, I know that story well. And he would make me hold that grip and walk around the house for 20 minutes just holding it, as if that were a normal thing." Rod Jr. laughs. He remembers being in the rabbit's car, his father's dream-chasing chariot, racing around the country in the early years as his father played the qualifiers.

When I tell him his father told me that both of his sons have near-perfect grips, Rod Jr. laughs. "I'm not sure about that."

In this world—as it is—perhaps it's hard to suggest anything is perfect, but both Rod Curl Jr. and Jeff Curl have a trophy case to make the argument that the intergenerational knowledge passed by the Deacon to the King, then to the Little Beaver and to his sons—well, there might be something to this idea of perfection: what cannot be improved on. Jeff Curl won the Connecticut Open twice, while he and his father worked for the Mashantucket Pequots in Foxwoods. Rod Jr. is the teaching pro with a 68.67 scoring average and boasts seven top-10 finishes in competitive golf.

That day in Clearwater, Florida, two hours passed like

this before Mr. Curl and I walked the short distance to the matts, where there are actual golf balls—real balls, or range balls as the case may be. He poured out the bucket and began to separate the balls based on their quality and age.

"Save these for the driver," he said, putting aside the newer balls. We both smiled and laughed at this. I could see that, like me, he was no millionaire's son. I was in the company of someone who learned the value of frugality. My Jersey-Boy heart had found his kind. There is good and bad in range balls, as well as this world, and you need to be able to tell the difference. And then Rod had me begin to practice what he's taught. The Nicklaus 'L,' the Palmer grip, Trevino's arched wrists, the Hogan lag. And with each shot, Rod would give me an instant analysis.

"That's the second best 8-iron you've ever hit."

"That's a 190-yard 3-wood. That's all you need."

We didn't even make it through a small bucket. Apparently, I was either hopeless or a good student. He indicated we would go to the putting green where he would teach me 7-Up, the game he invented with pro golfer George Archer. On the way, I tried to regain a tone in my voice, a register above the despair and dejection of realizing that I have 32 flaws in my swing. Rod had unschooled me of all my swing thoughts.

When I returned to my questions and asked about the Great American Indian Shootouts, Rod didn't miss a beat.

"Everyone says I only have one win. I have two. I won the first World Indian Open. I liked being with my people. Tom Lovell and Johnny Miller. Bob Hope and Steve Young were there. Gerald Ford. The Indian guys would follow me. They were shy in the sense of that I was a star for them. Tom Lovell started the first World Indian Open, which I won. We had good friends who supported that. Bob Hope. Steve Young. They encouraged the young boys, but there's only been one of me for the last 50 years. Until Notah Begay."

I begged off the putting green, after—it must be said—taking a beating in the game of 7-Up. Rod found me in the clubhouse shade, sipping a water and still wanting to talk about saving the world, of merging our histories, and bringing a new methodology to golf courses. I still wanted to connect our living days with the eternal clock of history. Rod Curl did not want to bear the burden of carrying the hopes of all Indigenous people. He wanted to teach me how to play golf better than a 12 handicap. And the intensity of his instruction was belied by his kindness.

Still the elephant in the corner—the core of my interest—was the fact that he was one of the first of our First People to win an event on the PGA Tour. And The Colonial at that! Once the shame of the Caucasians-only clause was brought into the light, Pete Davies, Charlie Sifford, Ted Rhodes, Althea Gibson, Orville Moody, and Trevino were all able to notch victories. Trevino had taught me that differences and quirks, a sense of humor, these are what make us beautiful and special. Trevino had inspired me because he was an outlaw, a brown-skinned, dominant force in a White man's game. I had loved his antics, the big wins, and the jokes. I liked the chip on his shoulder. Both he and Rod Curl had been outsiders and winners in the 1970s.

"Trevino and I were good friends," Rod said quickly. "And no, I never felt disrespected." He then did what I had hoped for in our four hours together: He reminisced.

"I think it was '68. We were in the Hawaiian Open. Downwind I was outdriving Trevino by ten yards, but into the wind, Trevino could hit a quail-high. You know what that is? You ever do any hunting? He could hit a low ball like no one else. A quail-high is a line drive. Into the wind he could get me by ten yards. We went back and forth like that all day. And he had 32 stories to tell per hour."

Rod Curl allowed me to feel close to the ancestors: Hogan, Hope. Nicklaus, Palmer, Dave Marr, Trevino. George Archer. The names had fallen off Mr. Curl's tongue, honey to my ears. Solving the world's problems would have to wait. I had also been relieved of the myths of the golf swing and grip: there is only one—the perfect one—and you had to learn them both if you want to be any good.

There's an old saw that Native Americans are certain that Columbus brought anthropologists on his ships when he came to the New World. How else could he have made so many wrong deductions about where he was? Wearing my anthropologist's hat to Florida, I found America had delivered other surprises as well. In Rod Curl, the Indian Wars had been won by a "little ole Indian boy," playing golf, and in subtler ways than through retribution and warrior tropes. From that first U.S. Open in '66, to his win at The Colonial in '74 and his 46 top-10 finishes, Curl had attained one version of the American dream through the game we all love, and along the way had made a lot of friends. Despite his intense teaching style, he hadn't discouraged me from bringing home a story. As if to make his point about giving his life, he walked me to my rental car, parked in the shade.

"You know, I lost my mother to all that," he said.

I thought we were done, but he had more to say. The ghosts of history still recall that 40 percent of Native American children had been forcibly removed from their families and taken to boarding schools. His family bore the scars of the days of transition, what Native historians would call the Termination Era (1953-1970) through the rise of Self-Determination (1975-present). Rod Curl's storied career on the tour fell in between those changes.

"I don't know my mother's last name. She was a wonderful woman, the best woman in the world. She worked for the tribe. We didn't see her much. My dad started a nightclub ... I was five years old, and I watched my Dad play poker in 1949 in Cali and Vegas. 1948, '49. My mother worked for the tribe, fought the government, for the land. In the end, what did we get? $29 million for the whole state of California. What was that? Like, $600 for each member of the tribe. It should have been $29 billion."

He told me this not in bitterness, but as a friend. Just as he had told me, that for those who wanted to learn, he would give up his life. And that much was true. We stood together in the shade of a tree, loading my sticks back into my rental car.

"I have a number for you," Rod said as I prepared to take off. "Call Tom Lovell," he said, texting me his friend's digits. "And come back in February when it's cooler. We'll play some golf."

Tom Lovell had founded the World Indian Open and the Great American Indian Shootout, to raise money for Native Americans wanting to go to college. Rod had won and played in all of those, alongside Gerald Ford and Miller, Young and Hope and Begay. If my golf game was less than perfect, perhaps I could help in other ways, and I had my next clue. That's how oral history works.

I would call Tom Lovell on my way back to the airport.

Chapter 11

LOVELL'S LOST TRIBE

Tom Lovell calls me from the cab of a truck loaded with firewood on its way to Navajo Elders in Monument Valley area. We're decades gone from the spaghetti westerns and Hollywood films shot in this grand valley, when Monument Valley was looking to depict the Indian Wars. But Lovell's trips are not the stuff of Hollywood tropes. It's winter, and the elders here need his help. He's been doing it for years, and he tells me to open my checkbook.

"Come on, Mark" he practically shouts into the phone. "Get out your checkbook." It's a moral imperative, to bring comfort to the elders. He sends me a picture of a female elder whose face signals a thousand hardships. Even if she can no longer hear or speak, the photo seems to say, her memories are sacred. The elders need to be alive.

Over the last two years, after taking a lesson with Rod Curl, Tom Lovell—Curl's friend and one-time sponsor—has become another Native spirit directing, cajoling, and showering me with stories of a life in golf and a life lived for others: for the elders, for his family, for his people. He's raised tens of millions of dollars for scholarships, had rounds with the game's greatest, and ex-presidents, and our nation's most notable comedian: Bob Hope.

When the perils of winter weren't threatening his tribe, he laughed and recounted the many jokes Bob Hope brought with him to the Great American Indian Shootouts. Bob Hope might be said to have founded the throne of the crown prince of golf. Lovell told of a time Bob Hope pulled up to the Monticello Golf Course for one of their fundraisers in a Brink's truck. He spills out smiling, and, before a round of golf with President Ford and Johnny Miller and Steve Young, among others, Hope spent half the day on the phone raising money for educational scholarships. The greater part of the day involved telling jokes at the after-party, playing with the Native American kids while 140 folks looked on, having steaks and ice cream.

And then there was the time Hope greeted Tom Lovell—who organized and ran the Great American Indian Shootout for many years—took his hand, looked in his eyes, and said, "My putting's bad, but my long-game stinks."

When Tom breaks out his scrapbook, a collection of pictures and stories and anecdotes of the eight years of The Great American Indian Shootout, a golf tournament that raised more than $50 million, Hope took a look and said, "this is historical."

"Historical," Tom replied ... "as in?"

"Well, you remember Gerry Ford?"

"The president?"

"No, the pro at the White House. He'll be here soon."

"And I won't be giving the President strokes? You see, I wear Arnold Palmer shoes, Arnold Palmer pants, and Arnold Palmer shirts, but I play golf like Betsy Palmer. You'll see what that means when I hit into a tree and the tree becomes a Secret Service man and walks away."

Tom flipped the page and landed on a photo of a bunch of school-aged Indigenous kids singing happy birthday to Bob Hope on his 80th birthday.

"I remember this. This was taken before golf was even invented. I'm that old."

Yes, Bob Hope, the same man who said "When you're from Cleveland, anything's historic," admired Tom Lovell's scrapbook, and three times answered the call to raise money for scholarships for Native Americans to get an education. "After all," Hope told Lovell, "I killed enough of them in the movie *Paleface*."

With roots in hundreds of generations and thousands of years, Tom Lovell calls his folks Lovell's Lost Tribe: Bob Hope, his wife Delores, Gerald Ford, Melvin Pervais, Steve Young, Johnny Miller, the boxer Gene Fullmer, Rod Curl, Frankie Avalon—they all worked together for eight years and brought in a whole lot of donations for scholarships, plus or minus $53 million. Not exactly chump change.

Lovell's scrapbook is a multiverse, in which past and present and future have equal value; in which the past's broken policies forced present action, with an eye toward the futures of the young. And as an elder's memory travels, fails, and then remembers, it's important to capture the stories before they are gone.

Native children sing Happy Birthday to Bob Hope. (courtesy of Tom Lovell).

Is the Great American Indian Shootout Tom Lovell's legacy? His work has—directly or indirectly—led to 47,822 scholarships. Still, Tom would rather tell stories than evaluate his life, and he's quick to note he has played Augusta National and shot a round of 66 at St. George's in Utah, which is the highlight of his golfing life.

Tom shares another great memory: "I happened to get the chance to play with Johnny Miller at a golf tournament. We immediately hit it off as friends. Johnny, being a strong LDS church member, believes the words of Prophet Spencer W. Kimball. To help and improve the lives of the Laminates is our purpose on earth. He believes the Book of Mormon to be the word of God. He and Linda Miller dedicated their lives to family and the LDS churches. My meeting Johnny couldn't have been better timing. It was the year we started the Shootout. 1981 or '82."

Lovell himself is a full-blooded Diné (Navajo) and full-blooded golf-lover. "My dad gave me the time off work to work on my golf game. I started golfing at the old age of 27," Lovell recalls from his ranch in Idaho. "I'm self-taught with a lot of practice. When we started the fundraisers, Rod Curl and Johnny Miller gave me playing lessons. Grant Leavitt in Monticello helped me on chipping and putting. Jimmy Thompson and Bill Korns worked with me also. I played with Gardner Dickinson and Mike Donald. And Peter Thompson and Larry Zeigler in one week. Hit balls with Miller Barber in Montana. Took me two years to break 100. But after that, low 80s and 70s. I was invited to play Augusta National by Vernon Loucks Jr. in fall 2001 and spring 2002."

Tom Lovell's picture book includes a shot of him on Hogan's Bridge. He is a legend in Native American golfing history, not for any feats as an amateur golfer, but the man who started events that have awarded so many scholarships and raised so many millions for education programs run by the American Indian Services, an organization that currently runs out of BYU. He's also someone who keeps certain things in perspective and considers Rod Curl's most impressive feat setting the course record at the first World Indian Open.

"That first World Indian Open at Rose Park, Curl set the course record after bogeying the first," Tom remembered. "I was 2-Up on him going into the 4th, then Rod blitzed the course, shot a 63, and I was 10 shots back at 73."

Lovell doesn't use the word *Navajo* to describe his heritage, and he is not alone in this preference. Navajo is seen as a word imposed on the tribes by the colonists, the kidnappers of history. *Diné* translates to "The People" or "Children of the Holy People." It's a term of respect and refers to a culture and language and connection to the land and tradition that existed long before European contact, and it will be there when his multiverse creates a world of equality and equal opportunity.

"I am full blooded Diné," Lovell said, as he recounted his history in both golf and his tribe. "I didn't have too many prospects and didn't like school much. I opened a used car and truck lot outside Provo, Utah."

As a businessman servicing equipment to ranchers in Utah and Idaho, Lovell first attended the Indian Shootout in Monticello, Utah. Monticello was located close to the Navajo Reservation. The local tribes were not well-received, despite the fact that $10,000 was donated by the State of Utah to help the city with a first go at a golf event.

"I didn't like how we were treated, so we started the World Indian Open in Salt Lake City with the blessings of Mayor Ted Wilson and Utah Governor Scott Matheson. The only celebrity I knew was boxer Gene Fullmer," Lovell recalled. "I gave him golf lessons. He was known as the Cyclone of the West, a great boxer." About that first outing, Gerald Bagley asked Lovell why we didn't have our Native American tournament. He offered Jeremy Ranch for free. The World Indian Open was born.

Why did this band of politicians and comedians and golfers see education as a way for the tribe to advance?

"We didn't have much opportunity," Lovell said. As is well-documented, even today only 65 percent of Native students graduate high school—the lowest graduation rate among American demographic group. The college success rate is even more disparaging, with only 9.3 percent of all Native Americans earning a college degree.

Tom explained his goals further: "I wanted to help American Indian Services at BYU. Paul Ream and I were board members. I suggested we do a fundraiser for scholarships for Native children to attend college. I told Paul I could get Johnny Miller to attend. He said he could get the Utah food industry to buy teams. I knew Dr. Gerald Bagley who owned Jeremy Ranch. We sold out every year at $2,000 a player, or $8,000 a team. My first celebrity was Gene Fullmer. And then I got PGA pros involved." Johnny Miller was followed by Steve Young, Frankie Avalon, Bob Hope, and President Ford, and legions of folks doing it for the children."

With such big names, it's a lot to soak in. Tom continued, "Rod Curl came into town and won the first one. I became Johnny Miller's good friend. After five years, we moved to Thanksgiving Point in Lehi, Utah, and now the Riverside Country Club in Provo, Utah. American Indian Services benefit from these tournaments. Now I think there's something like six satellite tournaments held throughout the west."

Lovell joined the board of the American Indian Services so he could shape the polices around the funds. He said, "Nationally, our tribal youth face many challenges, including poverty and higher than average rates of chemical dependency and teen suicide. Education can break that cycle and uplift our youth to become tomorrow's leaders." Part of his quest was to ensure that as many Native Americans as possible received the access to education that he didn't have.

With the federal government's recognition of tribes beginning in 1961, another era began: an uneven one, one in which tribes began to gain sovereignty, economic resources, and land. Many in the tribal cultures had rejected ideas of Western education. The untold history of schoolchildren running away from schools—both western and Indian—are legend. But one of Lovell's Lost Tribe—one of his supporters in promoting education—was a man of the Ojibwe: Mel

Pervais. Once they had established a measure of success, with Hollywood stars and ex-presidents, Pervais came knocking.

Lovell recalled a dinner with Pervais. "His grandfather was a tribal chief, he said his father pushed him into the non-Native American world at an early age. It was the most traumatic thing he ever did. But it was the best thing he ever did."

Lovell recalled their first outing. Pervais took Rod Curl and Decon Chabon, among others, up to the Chief Joseph Ranch and "paid for everything." An advocate for self-sufficiency in the Native American community, later in life Pervais spoke before students and other groups arguing that Native Americans must stop relying on federal aid and must begin supporting themselves in the free-enterprise system. In 1982, Pervais was invited by President Ronald Reagan to serve on a private-sector task force that encouraged support of community projects, including homes for the elderly and day-care centers. He responded by building Sunbrook, a golf and retirement community in St. George, Utah.

For Tom Lovell, Mel Pervais is a Secretary of the Future, with Native tribes gaining social ability and skill building necessary for individual and tribal success. "He is the person who could bring about a future where we all have equal opportunity, the opportunities none of us had," Tom added.

In another way, that future is now, and the future can be seen on the face of Chauma Jansen. Jansen is not only one of the recipients of a scholarship from the money raised by the golf and galas of the American Indian Services. An Assiniboine Sioux and Navajo, she has gone from being a scholarship recipient to the executive director of American Indian Services. She's in Pervais's department and sees education as a vital part of society, enabling access to upward mobility and economic freedom. "Native Americans have been historically left out of having a positive experience in this institution and gaining the economic advantages that their non-Native counterparts have had." For Jansen, if more Native Americans were educated, you would see more of them "seated at the table. ... If we want to see Native American communities contribute to the mainstream economy, then supporting them in higher education is the key."

Jansen noted that next to their annual gala, golf outings are the biggest fundraisers, and they now sponsor two: at St. George and Riverside. "We're dedicated to helping Native Americans access a quality education, while still preserving their culture and honoring their heritage. Our mission is to provide preparatory programs for children and financial assistance for those in pursuit of a college degree." Toward this end—all of it funded by golf—Jansen listed three programs where donated funds go: college and trade-school scholarships and STEM Prep.

If this current era is called the Age of Sovereignty, then this cross-pollination of golf, Hollywood, education, and money honors the past, present, and future for Lovell's Lost Tribe—those elders already passing from the world.

I can still hear his raspy voice as he shouts over the phone, "Come on, Mark. Get out your checkbook." The elders were struggling through the winter's cold and needed firewood. We can all help, one way or another. Like light to rainbow, Lovell is not going to stop. Life is golf, family, tribe, and care for the elders. Even if they can no longer hear or speak, their memories are sacred.

Tom Lovell, Mel Pervais, Chebon Dacon, Rod Curl, Bryan Pervais, at Jeremy Ranch.

Part 3

A Snow Bird Swing

Late on a Long Island winter's day, Connor Flanagan mentioned the book—a pamphlet really, more like a collection of pages held together by old glue and a spirit of not giving in to time. At that time, Connor was Director of the Southampton History Museum, where Mike Smith, Dave Bunn Martine, and I had gone to see a glass-encased display of carvings and leather jewelry that Oscar Smith Bunn had gifted to the Parrish family around 1908. We were standing in what had once been the Parrish family house: a gorgeous carpenter's gothic which sits proudly on a prominent corner of Main Street, Southampton. As we marveled at the collection of Oscar's carvings and an early mashie carved by Willie Dunn himself, Connor brought the fragile pamphlet out, perched on a pillow, as if to acknowledge our common fight against time and dust.

In 1923, attempting to capture the history before broken memories intervened, Samuel Parrish had written an account of the forming of Shinnecock Hills, in the form of a letter addressed to then President Colonel de Lancey Kountze. To our surprise and delight, along about pages 13 and 14, Samuel Parrish recounts the first golf match in this country played between members of opposing clubs: Shinnecock versus Ye Ole Apple Tree Gang in Yonkers.

And as proof that museums and libraries are the very soul of civilization—the repositories of long and collective memory, in support of golf and all the great things of human evolution—what came with a great surprise was that Samuel's account of the first golf match played in this country had a connection to the history of our First People and the struggle to grow back their territories.

The title of Mr. Parrish's book is indicative of Victorian titles of the late 19th century, and one has to love the thoroughness: *Some Facts Reflections and Personal Reminiscences Connected with the introduction of The Game of Golf into the United States more especially as associated with the formation of the Shinnecock Hills Golf Club (Incorporated September 22, 1891.)*

Toward the end of these facts, reflections, and reminiscences, a reader comes on Parrish's note about the first golf match played in America. Here is part of his account:

> In the month then of October, 1891, I was called upon in my 44 Broadway Office by John C. Ten Eyck, who said he had heard that we played golf down on Long Island, at Southampton. I replied, "why, yes, does anyone else play golf in this country?" He then informed me, to my great surprise and pleasure, that a little group of them had been playing up in Yonkers for two or three years past, and he would be very glad if I would come up and play with him. ... On the following Saturday ... I proceeded on my way to Yonkers, where I was met by Mr. Ten Eyck and taken by him to the now celebrated, but at that time practically unknown links situated on the outskirts of Yonkers, which has the now famous Apple Tree for headquarters.
>
> I have only two distinct recollections connected with this event, first that the players kept their clubs at the hospitable vestibule of the neighboring house of the late John Reid, and, second, I was beaten by Mr. Ten Eyck, his recollection that I was only one down at the finish, while my impression, though the impression, rather hazy in my mind, was to the effect that the match was much more to his favor. This, then, would appear to be the first game of golf ever played in this country between members of different clubs. The Yonkers links consisted of six holes around which we played three times, thus making our eighteen holes. If my memory serves me

> the 'putting greens' were of dirt, fairly well levelled off, with the hole scooped out in the middle of each 'green.' Altogether the day was a very delightful one, even if the links were of a primitive character.

The man who beat Mr. Parrish that day in the first golf match on this continent—John C. Van Eyck—was the son of a New Jersey senator. During the course of his political career, Van Eyck had become an abolitionist and—before and during his congressional tenure—had a role in dealing with Indian treaties. In the mid-1800s, there were numerous Indian treaties being re-negotiated and ratified, particularly as westward expansion in the United States created land-grabs and disputes between settlers and tribes. Senator Van Eyck had worked with Thomas Hartley Crawford on a commission investigating the fraudulent sale of Creek Indian Lands in Alabama. An early legal finding in support of Native claims to their land, the 1831 findings upheld the Creek tribe allegations of improper land transactions and inadequate compensation.

Ned Blackhawk had written about the inextricable relationship of American history and history of our First People, in his book, *The Rediscovery of America* (2023). "You cannot tell one without the other," Blackhawk writes. In the DNA of golf history, we find a deeper layer of our First People's history as well. Through memory and oral history, one clue led to the next. This person gave me the name of that person. A phone call led to receiving someone else's digits. One story led to a truer story, from the living who had remembered the living who had remembered the dead who were there at the start.

But I needed to turn to those in the game in the Right-Now-Time. While I would be returning to Shinnecock, in the near term I made arrangements —like many a snow-bird and golfer—to go on a southern swing out of the wintry north. And I wasn't going to play a golf course in a retirement community or sign on to The Villages. I was heading for Indian Country, to meet some living legends—golfers in the Right-Now-Time—to take lessons with some of the first of our First

People to win their PGA Tour cards and to watch a wave of Native Youth who had that beautiful "nothingness" in their swings. I went in search of the untold stories of legends and to get a glimpse of a new generation where golf was the fastest growing sport. I went to witness how the golf industry has taken a place on The Red Road and to walk with the dew sweepers in the desert.

Next up: The Black Mesa, no-go zones, and the Native American Open with my tour guide, Ou Yea Wa.

Chapter 12

THE NATIVE AMERICAN OPEN

Day 1: Chaco to Cochiti

We had come to Cochiti after touring the Black Mesa and Valles Caldera, rolling through the high desert down to the headwaters of the Rio Grande. I had taken a guide, named Ou Yea Wa, because I'd heard that a rookie traveler can get lost in the desert. I wanted to see the beauty of the place up close, and I needed help capturing that beauty, so I took a guide for what golfers call "local knowledge." For the caldera here is a vast geologic region shaped by volcanic eruptions long ago, and the earth has embraced and limited the lifeforms as a way to define a stark beauty.

Near the edges of this red desert, I asked about the markers and signs that noted that stealing Indigenous remains and artifacts is illegal. Apparantly, treasure hunters go out into the desert looking for untouched settlements.

"There's still a lot of untouched lands," Ou Yea Wa told me. "No-go zones. Not even the sheriffs will go there. ... It's where the missing people are. Young women in particular." In this era of having all kinds of information in the palm of our hands, I looked up more information and told my guide that the National Center for Missing and Exploited Children report that Native American children comprised 415 of the 27,733 children reported in 2021. Ou Yea Wa laughed at these numbers.

"The local tribes will tell you the number is much higher than that." He pointed out past a tabletop mesa. "Not even the cops will go out there."

We rode in silence for a bit, then came on another warning sign about removing artifacts.

"When the tribes win back items in museums and other institutions," Ou Yea Wa said, "they put them back in the grounds. The Navajo even have a word for this: *gozhoo*." While a lot of the archeologist types don't understand this practice, Ou Yea Wa told me it makes sense for the tribes. Returning things to the way they were is an important part of correcting the past. This goes for artifacts as well as swaths of land.

After some jokes about how this land calls for a 2-iron, and after taking some photographs to try to capture the daunting beauty of the desert, we rolled out of the areas where the streets have no names and into the Cochiti Pueblo, located southwest of Santa Fe: where some tribes had taken over existing courses (like Ak-Chin), and where some tribes had built courses with the resources from gaming. The Cochiti Pueblo—without the aid of a casino—had built a desert golf course in 1981: a Robert Trent Jones II design that was once the toast of New Mexico.

"I want to show you something," Ou Yea Wa said. "Follow me." I rolled out of our car, and my guide led me off the high point of Cochiti, past where the clubhouse held court over fairways running out in three directions. We strolled past the 10th tee, a platform overlooking a gorgeous sloping fairway that rolls down to a large, green pond. Rising above the mirror of the pond—calling the eye to the distance—were the desert god's sand sculptures, rising out of the golf course. A seemingly inhospitable landscape populated by road runners and turkeys and the wind. Ou Yea Wa was fearless and leaped up onto a flat that the wind had carved into a cliff, a shawl made of sand. Ten feet up, carved in the volcanic ash known as *tuff*—a kind of whitish-gray Play-Doh-like material that made this earth habitable—he pointed to a cave that the golfers and visitors to this place have turned into a makeshift memorial.

"You don't need metal tools to carve into the tuff," Ou Yea Wa noted, grabbing a small handful and putting it into my palm. You could feel the water in the tuff, and all jokes about Play-Doh aside, this was the material that had sustained eons of civilizations in the harshest of climates. Not only the wind lives here. Shielded from the wind and the rain by tuff, humans did, too, since before recorded time, well before land deeds and titles.

The Hopi, the Utes, the Anasazi, Apache, Navajo—all the descendants of the Pueblo Indians might have carved this cave. The floor of the cave was lined with turkey and buzzard feathers and a flower arrangement of desert flowers—what I would later learn are Desert Primrose, Desert Lily, Desert Sunflower—stood in memorial. There was a name and date carved into the wall. A scratched-out heart shape. We couldn't make out the writing. Not even Ou Yea Wa knew the Keres, but the feel of this memorial reiterated a theme that recurred again and again on my trip to the Native American Open: We come bearing our ancestors and when we look back, we see the branches of our families and tribes are not separate lines, but a web, and the strands of that web lead us back to the primordial Eve.

We share the same mother, and we call her Earth. Ou Yea Wa smiled and attempted to translate: "Where they once were, we are now. And where we are now, you will be."

The drive from Chaco to Cochiti took about four hours, including some side jaunts and stops that made the day's time bend. After a few of these, I felt like I had woken up in the future on another planet. At first, the eye is drawn to just see the black streaks of the basalt against the white sand and pale limestone. The black streaks run down the sides of the mesas like black tears or warpaint. And in the way car travel dominates the vision, there's the black asphalt of the highway, a dark ribbon of tarmac laid into the reddish brown of the Valles Caldera: the geologic term for the area around Santa Fe, where volcanoes once splashed an ash fall over what once was ocean floor. The phrase "totally uninhabitable" comes to mind, and it became easy to relate to the quotation seen at the O'Keefe Museum on a previous night: "I've been absolutely terrified every moment of my life, and I've never let it keep me from a single thing that I wanted to do." A desolate landscape, a terrifying beauty that at the same time urges action, and yet also forms in the soul a desire to become some part of it.

"When the lake at the top of the world overflowed," Ou Yea Wa said, "all this was ocean. Human life arrived much later."

Just weeks before I arrived, archeologists had found footprints in White Sands that were formed 21,000-23,000 years ago: dates that shatter the current understanding of human habitation in this corner of the world. Ou Yea Wa sounded proud of this: "This is where people first came and were able to survive." And this is surprising given the current harshness of the landscape. But then we don't know what was here then. There's a quality of hardiness in the creases on the faces of the people here; it speaks to the unknown, a history that no longer speaks itself.

From a distance, it looks stark and uninhabited, but up close? Just below the mesa top, Ou Yea Wa gave me a lesson about tuff. Cut into the sides of the cliffs—in this hardened volcanic ash—are a vast network of caves and apartments, beautifully defensible in their remote location, unseen from a distance. They could clamber up the sides on sage wood ladders. They could plant the mesa tops with maize (corn), the crop that originated in this harshness, the unisex, all-complete beauty of a plant that—along with wild turkeys—could sustain a civilization in the limited moisture of the desert.

The volcanic eruptions had marked different eras in geological time, largely driven by the San Francisco peaks, in what is known today as Arizona. The largest of these, Sunset Crater, is now a national monument. Terms such as Pueblo 1, Pueblo 2, and Pueblo 3 are used to demarcate the Hopi migrations that rose and fell between the eruptions, which brought the distribution of the ash—*tuff*—which they could carve in and make dwellings.

After my brief lesson in the architecture of the black mesa, we turned south again, and just then the green and yellow ribbon of the cottonwoods along the Rio Grande and its tributaries begin to come into view: vegetation surrounding and protecting the water source. And then there's Cochiti, the first pueblo (settlement) to put up a golf course, five miles in from the highway and astride Cochiti Lake: an oasis that defies the unrelenting sun and the wind and anything else that tries to steal the water.

Ou Yea Wa is a photographer by trade, not a golfer. He would have more than likely agreed with John Updike's assessment that "life is too short for golf." And at first he was only interested in the fact that I had an appointment to speak with Robert Trent Jones Jr. (RTJ2 for short), because it meant that he would have some free time to take some pictures and feel the earth under his feet. But we would find some surprising common ground in RTJ2's ideas about the golfer's eye.

Sight—in golf and photography—is the critical sense. It's easy to understand the allure of being a photographer in the Southwest. As the eyes acclimate, the purples and blues and yellows seem to flower out of the sand. In addition to the colors, the landscape comes to life in shadows, in a lone figure in a poncho walking the highway, the abandoned shell of a car pushed up against the side of a ravine, the stand at the road selling fireworks and pottery. The sun rules the desert. Only shadows and wind survive at midday, sculpting dramatic shapes and shades in the sweet noon time. (For a White man with fair skin and no hair, it's best to keep passing through.)

Anyway, it's easy to see how Land, with a capital "L," is something you don't own. As the Pueblo historian Monica Murrell told me when I was preparing my visit: "We don't think of the land as ours. We feel that we belong to the land." That sentiment would speak to the Tamaya's ability to not only survive eons in this stark place, but to build a culture of historians and athletes and veterans.

And it seems almost second nature that the Cochiti Pueblo would hire RTJ2 to build one of the first Native-owned courses in the country—one carved into the desert along the headwaters of the Rio Grande—before even gaming would aid and add to the cultures and landscapes of our First People.

RTJ2

I got through to him on the phone at his retreat on Lanai, at midday. He had just played a round of golf with Pierce Brosnan, who that very day had called Jones "the architect of all my joys and sorrows."

"Lanai is the Florence of our times," Jones said. I'd heard that a conversation with RTJ2 can be expansive and cover a lot of ground. I tried to bring the focus on Native American golf courses, Cochiti in particular.

"When we were preparing to build Cochiti," he began, "the tribe held a ritual, asking the great spirit if my spirit was right to design and build a golf course there. That was my interview."

And in that way, RTJ2's company's motto "Of the Earth—For the Spirit" seems prescient. 'Heaven with a zip code' is the motto of Cochiti, and he recalls that with a smile in his voice, a voice that riffs through history and memory in daunting speed.

"One tradition at the Yale [University] graduation ceremony is that graduating seniors smoke a peace pipe. That's true," he says, with both humor and gravity. [They now don't smoke tobacco from them, but blow bubbles.]

"Being an American Studies major at Yale, I follow my own flute. The work wasn't pro bono, but it was modest. And literally they had a ceremony, and the elders surrounded me and had some aspen-covered drums, and some flutes, and played some Indian chants and asked the spirits if their spirits and my spirit would be invited to work with the land. That felt natural to me."

If the ritual and the peace pipe made a difference, the spirits shined brightly enough such that he carved Cochiti into the desert as if it was meant to be there. *Es muss sein*, the Germans say of something inevitable. Like any great work of art, Cochiti makes us feel that golf and water and the desert are all interconnected. This is not a comfort, but an intensity: an unrelenting encounter with the elements. You have to feel the fear Georgia O'Keefe spoke of, but still must be willing to take your shot.

RTJ2 has worked with three tribal nations on golf course designs. By my math, RTJ2 and his brother Rees have designed about 10% of today's Native-owned courses.

Native American council leaders say they are attracted to golf courses because they bring added revenue and jobs without devastating the land. And in the pitched battle for water in the West, these courses also help tribes preserve their water rights. Cochiti is privileged by having a reservoir, which is not without controversy. The state made a contract to deliver some of the water to its neighbor (Texas), but instead the Cochiti Pueblo dammed it up and—by most accounts—just said no.

"It's their water," Jones laughed. "They can do what they want with it. And half of it is invisible [underground]. The Natives know the invisible. They did not apply pesticides and

Cochiti, in New Mexico—one of Robert Trent Jones II's designs.

almost no fertilizers."

Water is its own story in these parts. And in the religion of rituals of the First People, prayer and sacrifices are made to the great living source of life: Water comes first, worshipped as the rain, giver of the corn and the thunder, brother to the sun. All is alive and interconnected because of water, which finds the common denomination of depth and flow.

We can be glad RTJ2 passed that interview with the tribal council, assuming the spirits shined brightly on him, because the result is Cochiti Golf Club, once considered one of New Mexico's finest designs. In a turn of history, golf has brought Native Americans back to their own land. It's not corn and buffalo, but the sustenance comes from a game, which might be said to be a fair alternative.

"Golf course design is an artform," RTJ2 says. "There are so little rules. I mean, there are the five elements of defense. Length-width, vertical-horizontal. Fine tuning around short game. Compositional mode. All those are in a structural sense. My drawings have arrows, and I am showing the shape of how I want them to drain. But I don't use a formulaic approach. Donald Ross, Seth Raynor: they are civil engineers, formulaic. ... Their bunker faces are like a highway cut ... For me, real, real people who are the great designers see a sequence of holes: 18 little rhythms, 18 compositions that hear the tempo of the land. And real golf is continuous—not a return to the clubhouse. You're in it. You're playing like you're playing an instrument. You're interacting with the routing."

Jones feels that the Golden Age greats—his father among them—were great at routing, and Tillinghast was the best of all on how to use land in a sequence. "He makes you look forward to the next hole. Great golf courses are collaborative: the land, the golfer's eye, the designer. A composition and collaboration, like an orchestra that is playing the land."

The bunker faces at Cochiti transition into desert sand and brush with little fanfare, what might be called waste bunkers if the bunkers weren't connected with the entire desert. In the same way, the present-day design blends with a distant past here—the course becoming a form of economy, empowerment, and resistance.

Keith Herrera is the current manager at Cochiti, and he and Ou Yea Wa tell the same story, at almost the same time. All the Pueblos originated in Chaco Canyon, to the north and west, where four states now meet. Some event—no one is really sure what—broke up the ancient Chaco Pueblos, and the region's First People migrated to other areas, including Cochiti and Santa Ana and all throughout the southern Rocky Mountains.

Later, life with the Spanish became taxing to the Cochiti people, because of the endless mandatory taxation and tributes, and the banning of traditional religious practices, and slavery, and false imprisonment. So the Cochiti participated in the Pueblo revolts of 1680. They fled to more defensible positions near their present-day village, the headwaters of the Rio Grande. And that is, centuries later, where RTJ2 was brought in to survey 50,000 aces, where the Kereseyn-speaking natives live today, on land they never left, and which was reclaimed in a series of lawsuits against the U.S. Government.

"It's a revolutionary spirit returning the land to original usage," Jones says. "I mean, having an economy separate from the White settlers, golf was a way to capture the traffic between Albuquerque and Santa Fe. They didn't need a casino in the early days."

As has been noted by many, an interview with RTJ2 can range from golf design, to poetry and grass types, to Mckenna in the Asia-Pacific decolonizing Indonesia and Malaysia. And then back to Yale, his American Studies classes, where he played in the #1 slot on the golf team (1957-1961).

"A golfer who has played competitively is looking for ways to use the layout—18 little puzzles—to his advantage and the opponent's disadvantage. They will play away from challenges off the tee. On the greens. I like lower-profile greens, unlike my father. I like shot values and appeals to the golfer's eye."

Jones considers Cochiti one of his poems, and what he calls the "invisible hazard"—wind—flows over his routing like a song. The course has aged some, and Jones feels they now use too much water on the fairways. Where once the fairways bled into the desert, there's more grass now, but that does not interfere with the flow of life, or RTJ2's thought: "Mother Earth calls us back," he says. "We smoke the peace pipe into autumn's sunset ... to learn what the natives knew ... because it was on their wilderness we fed." He is quoting the composer Nolan Gasser and also Abraham Lincoln, about the declaration for Thanksgiving, something Native Americans might have something to say about.

Jones' knowledge of American history will extend to comments on the Great Law of Peace of the Iroquois Federation, which declared a basic right for all people and influenced some of the authors of the U.S. Constitution: Franklin and Jefferson among them.

"I do not bring a cretin's eye to these projects," RTJ2 says distinctly. "The land speaks to me. The land is everything, in a routing. I walk the land, feel it through the soles of my feet. The land itself is teaching me as I walk it. I feel it through a golfer's prism. Using all the senses, six senses ... I'm a three-dimensional architect. With a different style in the West. Add elements of wind. Change of elevation. Shadows in the far West. Bunker patterns and shapes of sculpture that light up and give direction when the sun is at different angles."

When I get off the phone and back into the car, I explain my interview with RTJ2 to Ou Yea Wa on our way to the next Pueblo—Santa Ana—and he nodded, as if in agreement. I asked him if he agreed to the following revelation: "Does the land itself teach us, as we walk on it?" He didn't disagree, but pointed to his eye. For him, a photographer—and for a golfer as well—the land teaches us to see. Beauty comes in at the eye. And my tour across the Valles Caldera closed on this note: While the historian searches for facts, the golfer's eye and the photographer's eye share the same search for beauty made by sand and sun, shadows and wind. Beauty is why we play.

Day Two—Santa Ana Golf Club

As the crow flies, Santa Ana Pueblo is 22 miles across the desert from Cochiti, and both Pueblos acknowledge their Chaco forebears, though neither offer a clear reason as to why the original settlement was abandoned. The Mayan civilizations in Mexico and Guatemala also have similar mysteries to former homelands and why the people left them.

"Perhaps we all will before long," Ou Yea Wa commented, and it's hard not to agree. The desert land, punctuated by Oasis-like golf courses—surrounded by the green tops of black cottonwoods—reminds one of geologic time, time before zones and hours and days. The shade and shadows call the traveler further on, and our temporary home after Cochiti is Santa Ana, with the adjacent and stunning Twin Warriors Golf Course.

I learned that Santa Ana is a center-point in the world of *Native Links*, with numerous golf events advocating for the protection of tribal families, on two magnificent desert courses, adjacent to the adobe office of the Notay Begah III's NB3 Foundation. They nurture Native Americans through their fitness and activity initiatives, and golfers through their NB3 Elite golf program. Santa Ana is also home to Jason Montoya, who works as a teaching pro and player development at Santa Ana Golf Club—where I would prolong my life long efforts to lose the over-the-top move I'd learned in baseball. And while there are a lot of claims to be various "firsts" among the First People in the game we all love, Jason's claim is for real. In fact, he is the first Native from a Pueblo to be a PGA member.

As a young boy on the Santa Ana Pueblo, Jason loved sports, and—like many of us—he was coached by his father and uncles, who were skilled, Montoya says with a grin, "at yelling and screaming." At the age of eight, Jason began to find refuge on the driving range at Santa Ana Golf Club.

"Listen," he says, pointing to the area where he honed his skills. "It's quiet. I would spend hours there to get away from the yelling."

We are standing in the shade at the far end of the range at Santa Ana, on the weekend of the Third Annual Native American Open. Of course, he had a noted role model in working out the techniques of the notoriously difficult golf swing: Notah Begay III.

"Growing up, there was Tiger—yeah—but Notah for me was the standout and the role model. He was a Native American and showed me how to take my game to the next levels. I had an internship with him at Turning Stone in New York."

Jason Montoya remembers a moment in 2002, when he was the age of some of the junior champions he has coached—Zachary BlueEyes and Maddison and Olivia Long. He was in the practice sand bunker at Twin Warriors, hitting shot after shot, as he puts it, "some better than others." Notah Begay III came over to watch him. Twin Warrios was Begay's practice course during those years when he was a four-time winner on the PGA Tour. He took time to engage with the 16-year-old Montoya, demonstrating bunker technique.

"Notah came over and told me to listen to the club hitting the sand," Jason recalls. "He said there was a sound I should hear. I'd never thought of it that way, in terms of sound, but he told me I should hear the clunk of the club on the sand in a certain way." We might venture that the golfer's eye looks to the fairways and greens, but when in sand: It's the golfer's ear that matters. Whether sound is the secret to playing out of sand, Montoya sees it as a moment of transformation in his life. A four-time PGA tour winner came over and took an interest in the young Montoya.

Jason's manner is one of appreciation, and it brings up a key teaching of the game: A lot of golfers are familiar with the phrase, "it's a humbling game." But why is humility a good thing, if it is? Most of us will have a clear and stinging memory of having high expectations—for a love, or a game, or a movie. The dashing of these expectations teach us: It's a common theme in Native cultures. One of the wisest characteristics one can bring into the world is a natural humility of spirit. This allows us to avoid the disappointment following high expectations and to live an appreciative spirit. When we're humbled by golf, it is part of the process of learning these difficult lessons.

For Montoya, the results of humility and appreciation speak for themselves. His school is thriving. And while Jason is also the first Pueblo Native to become a certified PGA teacher, he is not the last. The folks who have followed Jason Montoya into the mix include Aiden Thomas (Laguna Pueblo) and Justin Montoya (PGA Associate at Sandia Pueblo).

"One of my good buddies from Cochiti, Travis Pecos, will be a member soon. Patrick Herrera at Twin Warriors, he's an associate now. I am encouraging them and pushing them."

Jason Montoya with pupil Maddison Long.

From those silent sessions on the range as a boy, through high school recreation programs, Jason began to be attracted to golf management programs, and—following a childhood memory about liking Las Vegas and a trip to Circus Circus with his brother—he completed his studies in golf management at UNLV in 2010. Montoya served a number of high-end internships—notably with Notah Begay III at Turning Stone in New York, and also hooking up with N7: the Nike program run by Native Sam McCracken that sponsors Native athletes.

He did a turn with Vision 54, the coaching program that claims Annika Sorenstam as a founder and client, all leading him back home to Santa Ana, where he a teaching pro to young junior champions and serves as a tribal ambassador, and not only to all things golf. His school takes a holistic approach, one that rings from the mouths of many of the elders—diet, education, sport, care for each other.

It works. By midday, Santa Ana is bustling with golfers. The Notah Begay III (NB3) Foundation's truck, with its motto "Water First," held sway in a parking lot filling up with license plates from all over the country. I left Ou Yea Wa in the good hands of Jason Montoya and drove farther out into the desert, where Twin Warriors—designed by Gary Panks—is laid out on a moon-like landscape, and where the grounds-crew follow the advice not to overwater. The resulting routing is sublime. A golfer's eye scans the desert's reds and browns and purples—looking for a little green on which to nest a little, white sphere.

After a lesson with Jason, who had focused on the pressure of my hands on the club, Chairman Jay Garcia and the Tamaya's treasurer, Larry Pasqual, and I grab carts and head to the 1st tee at Twin Warriors. Jay and Larry have built Santa Ana into a hive of activity and excellence for Indigenous golfers. As I do my usual bidding about history, Jay sounds a similar theme: "The feds were going to take our water if we didn't use it. At the time, we didn't know anything about golf. Or Larry did. He'd learned golf in the Marines."

Larry Pasqual is a big man, who had spent 10 years in the

Marine Corps, doing a tour during Operation Desert Storm. He tells me the ideas of Santa Ana's golf program were simply notes on a napkin until they attracted the assistance of an investment firm. In 1991, they paired up with Via Grande, who put up the capital, and the team built 45 artistic holes designed by Gary Panks. During these same years, the Pueblo constructed the Prairie Star Casino. Gaming and golf here grew hand-in-hand.

"Now we're hooked." Both Chairman Jay Garcia and Larry Pasqual laugh. They are talking about golf, not gambling. At Larry's urging, Chairman Garcia tells me a story that stirs my own ancient memories. At about the age of 10, I found my grandmother's hickory sticks in the tool shed. Fascinated by their smooth handles and this strange game that had a lot of rules, my first swings were made with clubs two times too big and weighted for a world before time zones. While this might explain my enduring slice, it's a story many of us shared. We all started swinging with stuff passed down.

"When I first started playing," Jay begins, "I had a set of Wilson clubs. I'm not sure where I got them. I played with them a few years until one day, at a tournament somewhere, someone tells me they were women's clubs."

Larry and Jay share an extended chuckle at this. It's not a story of "it's gotta be the shoes," but good equipment does make a difference. And we pressed into Gary Panks' gorgeous landscape at Twin Warriors. Desert golf and links golf have this in common: no trees, though the shot-making is more about targets than rolls. Larry and Jay have mastered it well and boast about being in the money at any number of area tournaments, including one of Tom Lovell and Johnny Miller's fundraisers at We-Ko-Pa, held for the American Indian Services in Utah. Whatever handicaps that came with the wrong set of clubs have now been made up.

The stories and the years roll off Jay and Larry's tongues as we play the sublimely beautiful Twin Warriors, which will be the site of the final round of the Native American Open: an event that has grown exponentially three years running. Jay

Garcia has the details:

> Along about 2017, the idea of a competitive open strictly for Native American Golfers began to entertain their thoughts. They had two successful golf courses and were the site of the Notah Begay III Foundation. They had a golf school and were developing recreational programs. Jason Montoya had involved N7. What would complete the picture? The Native American Open was born: Santa Ana Pueblo, 2021. By 2023, The Open featured 160 golfers from 71 bands, nations, or tribes, with 17 states and Canada represented. For the second straight year, the club had to turn golfers away. What's more impressive is the growth of Juniors: In 2023, 62 Native juniors from as far away as South Dakota and Minnesota were teeing it up.

This is not a surprise. The NA Open is a well-run competition, with prize money and bragging rights—and the publicity that might bring sponsorships—all in play. The courses had on their finest trim, their edges sharp. When I'd spoke to the Chairman about the future, he told me he would like to eventually grow the Native Open into a 54-hole event.

"But if we start and develop a championship-only event apart from the Native Open, then I would make that a 54- or 72-hole tournament depending on what amount of prize money we can offer. Then I may keep the other event at 36 holes, being cognizant that many people are working and need to return home. We have great support from our vendors, business partners, and so not sure if I want to hit them up twice for supporting us."

The idea of Native Americans making their own tournaments and leagues is a not a new strategy but—at Santa Ana at least—the growth in the game is bearing amazing results. Does he see the NA Open here being a national, penultimate event?

"I am not sure if I would call it the penultimate event, as I support the other Native golf tournaments, but I will say I aspire ours to be the 'premier' Native event. I am also interested in the team concept along the likes of what the LIV Tour is doing or now the PGA Tour. I think that would be awesome for tribes to represent and play for their respective tribes, while still playing individual stroke play. Just ideas for now. But stay tuned."

I asked about Cochiti and Sandia, did they feel the heat of competition?

"We are the standard," Chairman Garcia said, as we nursed a cool drink in the shade, out of the desert sun. And there was proof enough of that. "Golf is the fastest growing sport among our First People," Jay said. "The changes seen are attributed to accessibility. With more tribal golf courses available, our younger generation has more opportunities to play and practice than my generation and those before. Television and internet coverage have helped."

As they set me up with a cart to photograph the proceedings and to follow the players, Jay and Larry had other duties. I was about to follow the action of the third Native American Open.

Twin Warriors has a peek-a-boo effect. The course draws the eye to the immediate, but some part of the infinite also calls you to admire the distance: the painted desert mountains. The golfer's eye surrenders to all time and space, and at the same time there's privacy as you deal with the up-close, which is necessary, as the local plants can be prickly and some of the local resident creatures inhospitable. The out-of-bounds might be deadly. Following your nose means paying attention.

So it was, I stayed on the cart paths, and on the 10th tee, As I began to follow the women's flight, I couldn't shake the image of no-go zones and all the missing young women in the desert. The foursome I followed included Skyesong Alexis (Alexis Nakoda Sioux), Sadie Kelley (Oneida), and one of the Long girls (Coeur d'Alene and Navajo). All of them were escorted by men I took to be their fathers or their coaches. It was a cool comfort that competitive golf would allow for this type of support and protection.

I asked one of them, “Do you mind if I take pictures?,” not sure if he was either a father or a coach. He smiled as if I’d mistaken him for a player. “She’s the one playing,” he said and pointed out onto the fairway where a slight 16-year-old with a big club was lining up a shot. I learned later I was watching the Chickasaw junior champion—Peyton “Beans” Factor—who was playing in the NA Open for the first time.

Like the many names I’d learned in my travels, Beans Factor is a name synonymous with Native golf. You hear it mentioned with both awe and expectation. She was coming off a hole-in-one at an American Junior Golf Association (AJGA) event at Twins Hills Golf and Country Club in Joplin, Missouri. With no junior flight at the NA Open, Beans was playing in the championship flight along the older women.

Sadie’s father Lance would later tell me about a tournament in Phoenix. “Last week, my daughter played in her first college tournament of the spring season. There were three Native girls playing in the tournament. Just another example of the interest in golf and how it’s improving for women, especially for Native women.” Sadie plays for Colorado Mesa University in Grand Junction. The other two Native players were from Bemidji State and Western Texas.

Kristi Daniels-Long is the mother of Maddison Long, who has committed to the University of Maryland to play Division-I golf. Maddison and her sister Olivia both went through the N7 and NB3 programs. Both had taken lessons with Jason Montoya, and Maddison played in the 2023 Begay Championship and was part of the PGA Pathways to Progression program. A proud mother, Kristi had been around the junior golf scene to offer a long perspective.

“The girls will smudge their bags and clubs before they leave the house for a tournament. They know that we come from some proud blood lines on my Coeur d’Alene side, and also on their Dad’s Navajo side. I have taught them that some people have no idea where they even come from, but we do, and to always walk with pride."

Looking out on the women's flight, she added, "A Beans Factor would not have been possible even ten years ago." These women golfers were supported by the NB3 and N7 Foundations, and now had role models like Gabby Lemieux to look up to.

I was reminded of something Rod Curl had said, many moons ago: "Go watch the ladies ... 90% of them get it." He was referring to the idea that there was a correct way—a perfect way—to swing a golf club. And further back, my mind searches for an image of Althea Gibson, the club lifted high after impact. And I remember what the fictional character Shivas Irons said in Michael Murphy's *Golf in the Kingdom:* "Let the nothingness into yer shots." Beans Factor had a preternatural smoothness, a relaxed manner that had no unnecessary glitches. Her swing finished with a pronounced lift of her body at impact, hips sliding upward and forward. No magic or secret to it: just one graceful motion with all of nothing inside.

And I'll long remember Factor's face returning to her cart. She had a look of both determination and acceptance. Her face seemed to say what any real golfer knows: good or bad, I have to play the next shot. They go where we hit them. No one else can play our shot for us.

Meeting Wisdom

Back in the clubhouse at the end of Day 1, and hungry from two days' travel through the Valles Caldera, I made a plate of bison burgers and coleslaw and found myself a spot at a round table with an 80-year old Chickasaw golfer named Beaman Wisdom. As we spoke, he lamented that there was not a Super Senior flight. He had to compete with 70-year-olds, and that was just not fair! His eyes were warm, and the creased skin of his face carried some of the colors of the earth in a way that said, this skin would not be shed. And as the room noise and activity ebbed and flowed around us, he asked me why I was there. I told him that I was working on a book, and that I confessed to being a member of the White tribe from New Jersey, which made him laugh, but then Wisdom—added with authority—remarks I could tell he had spoken before: "The worst things White people brought to these shores is Christianity and alcohol."

This comment—to be sure—had the effect of keeping me away from the bar, but his point about Christianity is one I had heard in my travels. Our First People's ancestors had paved the way, and the figure of Jesus was a late-comer to the Earth Ecstatic spirituality of our Natives. At the same time, even here at Santa Ana, Christianity had melded with some of the original traditions, in ways that were too big to address over lunch, and too heavy to go into here. In short, the Pueblos had blended Spanish Catholicism into many of their rituals, but I didn't argue the point with Wisdom.

I didn't argue it because as the late lunch wore on, and as Wisdom told his story in stride, with a reflective smile, I realized I was in the presence of an elder who had found in golf many of the finer ways of living. At 80 years old, he had an easy smile, and we developed an immediate and warm rapport. We each did our elevator speech, and his included the fact that he joined the army because it was one of the only options open to an Oklahoman Native on the res. "After high school, I joined and got housed with Elvis Presley at Fort Hood."

When I told him that my wife—when I met her—believed that Elvis was still alive, and confessed that our wedding song had been "You'll Never Walk Alone," Mr. Wisdom paused and smiled. "Elvis got a lot of privileges."

Mr. Wisdom is the first and only person I would meet in this life who had rubbed shoulders—and marched alongside—the 20th century's eternal hip-thrusting heartthrob.

"Oklahoma is rich in golfers," Wisdom went on. Golf gave meaning to their history, to the suffering. The tribes had indeed walked and not alone. Not only Jim Thorpe and Orville Moody, but Sarah—Orville's grandmother who had walked The Trail of Tears—but also Michelle and Spanky and Junior Moody, Junior Hopper, Steve McDonald, and others in the Midwest tribes—J.C. Wright and Michael Powell among them—a new generation that accessed golf through education and had made good livings in the industry.

"Education first," Beaman said, as the young ones lined up to greet him. Our chat gave way to people coming over to greet Mr. Wisdom. The line grew as he introduced me to both old friends and new, among them some of the country's finest young, Native golfers: folks like Robert Komahcheet III (Shawnee and a grandnephew of Jim Thorpe), Aiden Thomas (Diné), Peyton "Beans" Factor (Chickasaw), Glynnis Price (Diné), Sadie Kelly (Onieda/Ojibwe), and Jimmy Squire (Absentee Shawnee).

Some of the young men, after saying their names, announced how long they were sober, all to Wisdom's delight.

The parents came too, pushing their young ones up to greet this living elder. And as these young golfers—with skin colors as varied and as beautiful as desert sands—came over to greet Mr. Wisdom, I thought of the phrase Ou Yea Wa had taught me in the desert: *they will stand where we once were.* I also couldn't help but wish they would live out Elvis's wish for us all: "you'll never walk alone." May the golf gods hold and protect them. If Wisdom has a say, they do and they will.

And as an elder, he was not imparting knowledge or stories. That would come at another time, perhaps from other folks. He was simply being greeted, sharing smiles, making sure they acknowledged me and shook my hand.

When this parade of acolytes faded, Wisdom and I sat at the table, and I told him my favorite story of my life in sport: I was coaching youth soccer. My son Myles was on the Under-12 team, and we had a schedule for rotating captain. Each game, a new boy would take out the colors for the coin flip. One year, a young boy named Wilson was on our team, a savvy kid who would grow into a boxer and himself a soldier. We were playing a city team—the city to our north—and while we were an all-White team, while Worcester had

Black and Brown players. Wilson went out for the coin flip and met up with a handsome young Black man sent out to captain for his team. Without prompting, Wilson said, "I'm sorry for what my people did to your people."

The parents and referees smiled at this, a little uncomfortable at Wilson's precocious apology. It remains my favoite story in my life in sport. And I told this story to Beaman Wisdom out of respect, but also because we had a rapport that would let in the humor and truth of it—even at 10 and 11 years old, we can know what is just and unjust.

As the late lunch party broke up, Wisdom clasped my hand warmly. He handed me a flier about a new golf club and plans to start a Chickasaw tournament in Oklahoma. He would land it at WinStar, the massive casino and golf course there, in a part of the country where the five nations had made a home after their removal from their ancestral lands. It was Jim Thorpe country, and it had given rise to many great Native golfers. There was no quit in Wisdom.

"It will be bigger than this," he said with a knowing grin.

As the events of the first day broke up, I gathered my notes on the back of that flier, where I had written down the names of the people I needed to meet, a living history on my swing through the south: Steve McDonald, J.C. Wright, and Gabby Lemieux among them. The elder himself had given me a map in my own handwriting, a map made up of names of some of the living pioneers in the least violent, most difficult game in human history.

But first came the finish and meeting the champions of the Native American Open.

Chapter 13

CHAMPIONS DECLARED

In the desert, if you're lucky, you're playing early in the morning. Out here, dew sweepers rule, and the golf starts early. Before the final round of the third Native American Open, as another desert blue emerged from the gold of the early morning sky, Emmett "Shkeme" Garcia of the Tamaya Pueblo gave a blessing. He led the crowd in a Keres prayer, then his brother Jay offered this translation: "On behalf of his current tribal chief, and the humble people of the homeland of Tamaya, we pray you watch your words, be mindful of the homeland, remember you came carrying your ancestors and family and friends. Be safe, be strong, and be blessed on this special day in this special place. Have a great day and go hard."

Chairman Garcia then acknowledged the Twin Warriors—Mae'Eqi and Uyuye'ewi—who long ago showed the Tamaya the path to the upper light and the upper world along the banks of the Rio Grande. He added, "They have led us to our modern existence."

I learned that blessing the players before a tournament was common practice at the LPGA events that have been held at Circling Raven and Thornberry. At Santa Ana, the blessing was accepted by all and the daylight was as clear as yesterday's was, and tomorrow's will be: a brilliant blue sheltering a skein of golfers as they took to last-minute hugs and well wishes before they headed to the tees. Game on.

I made my way to the 1st tee at Santa Ana, which is shaded by a giant black cottonwood tree. The NB3 Foundation's adobe is not even 100 yards off from this point, where the starter Derek Gutierrez—general manager of Santa Ana Golf Club and board director at PGA of America—announced the names of the golfers one by one.

As four young Native golfers each hit their first drives in a quest for a trophy, one of the young men hit a slice that, at first, appeared to be heading out of bounds and toward a small pond. (Water may be precious, but not for a golfer.) Suddenly, the ball nicked a tree or a mound and took a "member's bounce." The drive had come back into play. The player turned to the gathered crowd and said, "Notah told me to hit it there."

All of us gathered shared a good laugh. Among Native American golfers, Notah Begay III (aka NB3) is ubiquitous: as an inspiration, a north star, and, in this case, as the purveyor of good luck.

A four-time winner on the PGA Tour—all four coming in a remarkable one-year span—Begay's heritage includes Navajo, San Felipe, and Isleta people. He was born and raised in Albuquerque and found his way to Stanford University, where he roomed with a fellow by the name of Tiger Woods and claimed an NCAA Division I team title in 1994.

As is well-known, Begay's success on the PGA Tour was relatively short-lived. A debilitating back injury took away his golf swing for nearly four years. That was far from the best thing that could've happened for him, but it may have been for some Native American children on Indian reservations. Begay became a philanthropist when he started his foundation in 2005. The organization helps to improve health and wellness of Native American children on Indian reservations nationwide. It also nurtures young golfing talent.

"If it wasn't for the back injury, this thing never would've gotten off the ground." He was referring to his foundation during a recent interview. Between the years of '02 and '06, with free time allowed by a back injury, he surveyed the landscape. "I spent the time in Native communities," he told a gathering. "That's where I saw many of these kids after school just sitting around on the couch or on the bench outside. They were doing nothing. Doing absolutely nothing. I took it upon myself to figure out a way that they could be doing something productive. Sports had always been instrumental in my life."

Ask any parent or person about the success story in Native American golf, the names Sam McCracken (of Nike's N7 Fund) and Begay are universal, and that includes the two winners of the 2023 Native American Open: Skyesong Alexis and Eric Frazier.

The Champions Declared

As noted, I had fallen into a cadre of parents and coaches following the play of the young women—Peyton "Beans" Factor, Sadie Kelly, Olivia Long, and Maddison Long. The tournament bore proof of a growing culture among young women in golf, and one particular golfer stood out and took top honors: Skyesong Alexis.

Skyesong is from the Alexis Nakoda Sioux Nation, located in Alberta, Canada. She began playing golf at eight years old. "I am self-taught," she says, "I just watched Tiger Woods videos and Notah Begay on TV when I was a little girl. I would watch their swings, then go outside and swing the club. Tiger and Notah, with all their accomplishments, showed me anything is possible if you believe in yourself."

That Skyesong did not name a female golfer is of note, and it raises the question if this self-belief can be even harder for Native female golfers.

"I faced a lot of challenges being Native," Skyesong tells me. "I heard a lot of bullying comments along the way. But that didn't stop me and just made me more motivated to keep showing up, because I belonged playing at that level in golf."

In 2022, Skyesong secured the backing of a sponsor—Backwoods Energy Services—and played on the Epson

Professional Tour. She lived for a time in Florida, played alongside Gabby Lemieux and other top women. While she continues to seek sponsors for her professional career, this was a step toward her dream of playing on the LPGA.

Her biggest win?

"The Sun Life Open in 2019 as an amateur," she says with little hesitation.

Skyesong has two kids: her son Cory Saddleback is 7, and her daughter Kaya Alexis is 12.

"Not being rich," she says, "we always have to grind through, and it's a good feeling to accomplish what I have so far being the first Indigenous in Canada to do what I have done. And I'm proud that I have pushed through it all, to be playing at the level I'm playing at now, knowing I'm where I belong."

She loved this year's Native American Open for being able to play alongside such a strong field that are Native just like her. "It's good to see more young ones coming up," she says.

What would such an accomplished and talented Native golfer tell the young ones? "To always chase your dreams. Goals in life can be big or small. No matter what happens, know you are good enough. You belong, and there's nothing in this world you can't do, there's always a way, if you just believe and push through and keep showing up. 'Cause hard work pays off."

The goal of being the first female Native golfer with a win on the LPGA is still there, and that October weekend at Santa Ana Pueblo, Skyesong not only showed up, but she showed us all that golf was women's work as well. She took top honors at the NA Open by 15 strokes ... winning going away, and setting an example of the young junior females playing in the championship flight. A win on the tour can and will be done.

In the men's championship flight, Eric Frazier won by 1 one stroke, needing an eagle in both rounds to gain the victory. When reached on his cell phone, Eric was already on to the next tournament—the San Diego Open—the very tournament where Joe Louis had broken the color barrier 70 years ago. He says, "I've played professional golf the last three years of my life. I don't want to walk away from it altogether. I enjoy every aspect of it."

Like Notah, Eric Frazier grew up in Albuquerque playing at Paradise Hills, on the city's west side. He started at the age of six, taught by his father and grandfather, who came to Albuquerque from Windrock, Arizona. Eric is a third-generation golfer, though he is quick to note the differences in their lives in golf.

"My dad and grandfather, they would go hit balls in the middle of the desert. They grew up in a time of golf when courses weren't accessible. It's a different time now."

In addition to family, he counts Notah and Tiger as primary inspirations. "Those are the pinnacles of what I wanted to be."

At the same time, as every athlete knows, the element of time comes into play, and Eric admits his thoughts have turned to "staying in the industry and enrolling in a PGA Associate program." When the road fatigue of professional play gets too much, he can stay in the golf world, which has given him so much.

"I'm getting a little older," the 27-year-old Frazier says. "As a professional athlete, I wake up early, go to the gym, practice, and play. It's every single minute of the day."

He is not shy in stating how hard this life is. He adds, "There's no money in it unless you win. It's an investment every week as far as expenses. If you don't make the cut, you are losing money all day long."

I recalled Rod Curl and his rabbit days, chasing the dream. For both Curl and Frazier, golf has given much. "I'm talking about friends and people I've met. It's more or less like a commonality thing. Now some of my friends, getting older, are starting to take up the game, and I'm playing with old friends."

What's changed from Eric's father to his own life is accessibility: "Golf is more accessible to our people now. There's a lot more drive from the community and tribes. All the tribes that have a golf course are getting initiative." He notes that the tournaments his father played were word-of-mouth, raising money for scholarships and causes. The Native American Open is different. Santa Ana boasts the first Pueblo PGA Professional in Jason Montoya. It is also the home of the Notah Begay III Foundation, and, in its third year, the NA Open at Santa Ana continues to have to turn entrees away. As well-run as it is, this is not a surprise.

"I really liked that it was more than the New Mexico community. I met people from everywhere. A lot of the tournaments are basically word of mouth. The Open did a great job of marketing. There are several different communities from all over."

What would he say to the youth movement that was so apparent at this year's tournament?

"Never take it for granted. Always find that passion for the game and stick with it. One way or another you'll come back to it. ... I would also want to add: Never forget where you come from. Always appreciate what golf has done for our community. Whether that's for themselves or their family or the community as a whole."

That same spirit of appreciation and humility of spirit came through community—of tribe and family, school and peers. Win or lose. Even in victory, Skyesong and Eric carried forward the wishes of the ancestors and the living. Like Jason Montoya and Jay Garcia, like Derek Gutierrez.

And it would appear other organizations have begun to follow these teachings as well. The PGA Tour—which has dipped its toes into the water with the Pathways to Progression program—had its inaugural year in 2023. Two of the juniors at the NA Open—two who had paid their respect to Mr. Wisdom and had a certain nothingness in their swing—would represent their tribes and families and teachers on a national scale.

Chapter 14

PGA PATHWAYS TO PROGRESSION

Watching the beautiful nothingness in the swings of the Native golfers—the young ones in particular—I was reminded of what John Updike wrote: "The correct golf swing is a web of small articles of faith, all of which strain common sense." Given this strain on common sense, given the colossus of literature on trying to fix it, one of the glaring ironies in our shared history is the lack of systematic instruction. Sure, some golfers refer to muscle memory or swing thoughts. Ben Hogan called it all a secret. Rod Curl claimed there is a perfect swing, and you have to learn it if you want to play well. Some refer to golf as implicit learning: knowledge that is not gained by top-down teacher-to-student relations, but by self-observation and perseverance. The last and best word goes to the man who taught the game for the longest stretch of time on earth: On learning the golf swing, Frank Dufina had said, "the first hundred years are the hardest."

This last point might be said for golf organizations as well as the teaching of golf. A codified way to learn "the small articles of faith" of the swing, has evolved quite slowly. For example, in 2023, The USGA announced the U.S. National Development Program, which the organization celebrated as "the country's first unified pathway to nurture the potential of America's top players, starting in competitive junior golf and progressing to the pinnacles of the sport."

In the late 1960s and into the '70s, the PGA Tour began to express interest in growing the game by forming the Q School, but this largely focused on how to make it to the professional playing circuit. In the 1980s, The PGA began to offer a certification program that required passing the Player Ability Test, completing qualifying courses, and passing a test on various subjects, including golf instruction. The program takes three-to-four years to complete and includes fees and travel for examinations. As witnessed by Jason Montoya and others, the PGA has also since partnered with some colleges and universities in order to grow the game, offering programs in turf management and golf operations for those who love the game but don't want to go through the grueling task of making the tour.

Nevertheless, in the era when televised golf made the game look like it was played by all-White players who were freakishly good, and as golf faced the existential crises of shrinking playing population and course closures, more focus has been put on growing the game and involving communities that have been notoriously left out—those communities include Native Americans.

Speaking again with Kristi Daniels-Long (Coeur D'Alene), the mother of the young competitors, Olivia and Maddison Long who both had come through NB3 and N7, it's clear that Kristi is a champion of these programs for Native youth. She sees more Notahs or Gabby Lemieuxs coming along soon. For example, the Santa Fe Indian School (SFIS) started a golf team in 2022, for the very first time in its history (dating back to 1890). Jason Montoya assisted SFIS in developing the foundation for the team. Haskell Indian Nations University also started a golf team in the past few years.

"We had several participants this year who play on the Haskell team," Daniels-Long says. "For tribal golfers with potential, it takes a community to raise them and propel them forward. It also takes a lot of financial support, and many tribes are now in a position to offer that financial support. A huge shift from my generation and those before."

To add to this support, in 2023, the PGA Tour announced the Pathways to Progression program as a way to grow the game among communities that have traditionally been underrepresented.

Kenyatta Ramsey, the PGA's vice president of player development who oversees the Pathways to Progression program, said the 24 athletes chosen for the program were recruited from a number of junior programs, all focused on junior golfers from under-represented groups. NB3 and N7 were involved in identifying Maddison Long and Zachary BlueEyes (Navajo). The two were among 24 junior athletes in the inaugural year of the PGA's new Pathways to Progression program, which works to develop junior and collegiate golfers from traditionally under-represented communities. BlueEyes and Long are the two Native Americans participating in the program's inaugeral year.

BlueEyes' parents, Donny and Lisa Hale-BlueEyes, said the program helps even out the playing field. "As a Native American in the game of golf, the challenges that are faced are financial shortfalls," they told me. "Many of the students and fellow golfers that Zach has played with in tournaments have private coaches, have expensive golf gear and equipment, live on a golf course/country club and can travel the country to many golf tournaments."

Long's mother agrees. "I really feel that sometimes Native youth golfers are looked over and not sought out," she said. "My family is just fortunate to have such people in our corner."

BlueEyes and Long both developed their abilities at the hub of Native golf—Santa Ana—and were identified for the Pathways to Progression program through NB3Fit Golf Team: a collective of 15 elite Native golfers ages 13 to 17 from across New Mexico who train and play at Santa Ana and Twin Warriors.

The other 22 participants were scouted through the PGA's programming with historically Black colleges and universities, as well junior programs that include the Jim Thorpe

Invitational, the Mack Champ Invitational, Steph Curry's the Underrated Tour, and the PGA's First Tee program.

In the Pathways to Progression program's first year, Ramsey said his role involves securing investments and recruiting organizations that will help to eliminate or reduce the barriers young minority players face when it comes to advancement in the game of golf.

For Ramsey, these barriers relate to resources at an earlier age. "Tiger Woods didn't lead to more Black and Brown golfers," Ramsey said. "It takes a lot more than talent. We aim to have the right people developing that talent. Why? We want golf to look more like America."

For the 24 young golfers participating, the program began six months ago in Florida, where they spent four days in college prep and healthy lifestyles programs. They also got to play the TPC Sawgrass course and received developmental grants from the PGA to cover costs for instruction by certified PGA coaches and to secure top-shelf equipment.

The players also signed on for college prep once a month and regular programs on playing fitness.

Ramsey endearingly calls the 24 athletes "The Squad." He said, "Our goal is to put them in a better position to succeed at every level. And it's not just about talent and gear. Coaches and parents are the two most important pieces to this puzzle."

A History Lesson

As previously noted, Tiger Woods and NB3 roomed together at Stanford University and both were named All-Americans multiple years before moving on to the PGA Tour. They are often cited as inspirations for Black and Native golfers, but there are historical differences between Native and Black athletes in the game.

From 1916 to 1961, the PGA had a Caucasians-only rule, excluding Black, Native, and other players of color who had participated in tournaments in earlier decades, including the first Native professional golfer. As we explored in

Chapter 6, African American players formed the United Golf Association (UGA) in the mid-1920s, which was led—in the following decades—by inspirational leaders such as tennis great Althea Gibson and champion boxer Joe Louis. The UGA held national tournaments and had its own leagues and courses. Many excellent golfers emerged from these efforts, including Dewey Brown, Charlie Sifford, and Lee Elder. Some of the players—including Bill Spiller, along with Louis and Gibson—were also strong voices that agitated against the PGA's Caucasian-only rule until it was repealed in 1961.

Native Americans did not organize in a similar way. There were fledging efforts, like the First Nation's Tour. And The Great American Indian Shootout focused on fundraising for education, as did many other Native-only events. But we could say competitive golf in Native communities did not begin to arise until the 1990s, after gaming licenses allowed tribes to expand their economic bases to include museums, schools, and—yes—golf courses. Cochiti was an early go, but Santa Ana Pueblo was also an early adoptee, building Santa Ana Golf Club in 1993, and adding the exquisite Twin Warriors facility in 2001.

Today, more than 55 tribes operate golf facilities, many built by the finest architects. One of those is Paul Albanese, who designed courses for the Santee Sioux and Potawatomi. He sees golf as a way to celebrate the culture of our First People: When he built the courses, he wrote, "all members of the community came. Because we made it clear from the beginning that these landscapes were *not* just for golfers, but for all members of the tribe. And non-native golfers that play my designs will walk away with *more* than just a score, but an understanding and appreciation of the culture of the tribe."

The results of these efforts are becoming obvious. From high-end facilities and landscapes that incorporate the stories and legends of our tribes have come teaching professionals, competitive tournaments, and—as witnessed by BlueEyes and Long—a youth movement that indicates Native golf is on the rise. None of this happens without programs designed for access.

BlueEyes, one of the more decorated of Native junior golfers, began with the First Tee of Four Corners and participated in Junior PGA League, U.S. Kids Golf and Sun Country Golf, all before the NB3 Foundation began its program.

"I know that people don't know what Native people go through on the reservation," Zachary said, "but I know that being the only Native person at a tournament, I can show other Natives that they can be in sports, and they can show off their Native side of things."

Coaches also contribute to the development of young Native golfers. When BlueEyes and Long returned from their weeklong training in Florida with the Pathways to Progression program, there was no question who their coach would be: Jason Montoya.

"You learn how they learn—that's the biggest thing," Montoya said. "When I get a player who's been coached by dad or grandpa for many years, I have to assess how they learned and then ... how do they get over that to improve their game? We learn together."

Montoya has known both players since they were very young. "With Zach," Montoya said, "when he was a little guy, I was in Arizona teaching at Talking Stick. He came to one of my Nike N7 camps in Arizona. Then he found out I was at Santa Ana. Even though he lives a two-and-a-half-hour drive, he'd come down for lessons."

Zachary cites Jason Montoya but also Gerome Espinoza. "These two have helped me with my swing, swing thoughts, and mental game. Jason works with my swing and how to play different shots around the golf course. Gerome helps me with the mental game and how to control my shots and control my spin on the golf course."

BlueEyes' parents cite Begay and Montoya as positive influences on their son's personal and athletic development.

"They have worked with him by providing golf lessons on the course as well as player development both on and off the course," they said. "This player development includes patience, attitude, and strategy."

Kristi Long said the program inspired her daughter to work harder. "NB3 is what really lit the fire for Maddison," she said. "I loved how they instilled in the kids the rules and course etiquette. They also really taught the kids about their short game. We were thrilled when Clint Begay, Notah's brother, started working with Maddison, and the girls when they started on the NB3 Elite golf team."

For Ramsey, the Pathways to Progression program and other outreach efforts are not only an extension of efforts to grow the game but also a means to involve more Black, Brown, and Native junior golfers.

"This will be my last job," Ramsey said. "This is not a one-year thing. ... Our leadership wants this program ingrained into the fabric of the PGA. It's hard to be what you can't see. Bringing these kids forward will grow the game."

Ramsey notes that Zachary, as a junior, will be supported in his senior year, and the PGA Pathways to Progression Program will work with the NB3 Foundation again to include Native golfers in the years going forward.

Begay likes to tell the story of how he started in the game. He fell in love with the game at the age of six, but couldn't afford to play. When he was nine, he told a local golf club, "You don't have to pay me. I'll sweep and clean up. Just give me a plan to practice." His negotiating skills were inferior to his golf ones, but the point is made, as he has said in public remarks: "It all starts with the younger generation. We're hoping to do it piece by piece and program by program, exposing these kids to sound ideals and principles. It's not because we went out and got research from Stanford and Harvard. It's because we go in and work with these communities."

Joined by the resources of the PGA and visionaries like Kenyatta Ramsey, and by facilities such as Santa Ana and Twin Warriors, the future of Native golf is bright, and the pathways for women are being carved out by the legacies of legends like Althea Gibson and by younger gamers like Gabby Lemieux. Their stories help to right the wrongs of the past and write a brighter future.

Chapter 15

DREAM CATCHERS

It's not only caddies that have stories in their bag, golfer Gabby Lemieux likes to spin a happy yarn as well.

At Texas Tech, under the tutelage of Coach JoJo Robinson, Lemieux was having a great season (2015-16). Turns out Notah Begay was friendly with Coach Robinson. Both were from Albuquerque and grew up playing golf together. Coach Robinson and Begay began to exchange notes about this young champion who happened to be Native American.

"He was talking to her," Lemieux begins, "and coach says, 'yeah, she's really good. Up there on the leaderboard in D1 college golf.'"

Begay began to scroll through the rankings, but couldn't find Gabby's name. "He was checking to see where I was ranked," Lemieux says with a laugh. "He kept scrolling down. He couldn't find me, and then he decided to scroll up. Yeah, he found me."

Lemieux was ranked #1 in the country. And that's not all. While at Texas Tech University, she had four collegiate wins, was Big 12 Player of the Year, and held the lowest scoring average for all four years.

Out of this networking between NB3 and Coach Robinson, as Lemieux transitioned to professional golf, a friendship—and mentorship—was born.

"Crazy how the universe is," Gabby says, "so many things

are supposed to be there. He knew my coach and now he's my mentor. I'm so fortunate that he can show me the ropes. I want to help the next girl after me."

While telling these stories, Lemieux was in Phoenix, on a rare break. She had a week off and would begin the grind of the tour again in short order. When asked if there was a key moment when she knew golf was her game, she replied, "When I was a part of a team, when I was hanging with others who loved golf as much as I do."

The transition from the team sport of collegiate golf to the lonely, fishbowl life of professional golf was not easy. "I didn't know anything," Lemieux continued, "how to book flights, how to get sponsors. Professional golf is a job. Notah was trying to teach me how to do a job, the business side of it. That is where he has guided me. He has benefitted me as a person and a golfer."

The importants of this relationship between mentor and mentee, of a Native who can model success and show the ropes, should not be underestimated.

There is a well-known story about Althea Gibson (African American, Lumbee), the professional tennis player and golfer. In 1995—the same year a 14-year-old Serena Williams made her professional debut—the 68-year-old Althea Gibson called her former doubles partner, Angela Buxton, to say goodbye. She couldn't make rent or pay her medical bills. She was in bad health and had been living a reclusive, depressive life. In short, Gibson saw no reason to live. In response to Gibson's call, her former partner Buxton placed a letter in *Tennis Week* magazine, asking the tennis community for help. For the rest of her life, until she passed in 2003, Gibson received envelopes with cash, in multiple denominations and currencies, from those whom she had inspired.

As we explored in Chapters 6 and 7, Gibson was a pioneer in golf as well as tennis. In 1958, at the height of her own barrier-breaking tennis career, Althea Gibson left tennis and went to knock down a few barriers in the world of professional golf. In an era when golf clubs would make her change clothes and shoes in her car—not allowed to use the clubhouse because her skin was dark—Gibson heard what she called "the siren song of golf." She returned to the sport she had learned to love at Florida A&M, and she played 13 years on the LPGA Tour. She did this without organizational support or a mentor. One can only imagine how tough Althea Gibson needed to be.

Likewise, Gabby Lemieux's journey to be the first female of a tribal community to achieve that elusive first win on the LPGA Tour is not a wish on a rabbit's foot. At the Native American Open, her name is on the lips of many of the young women. Her name has become synonymous with something eternal in the game. To face that difficult moment, to balance on a high wire, to be her best self in the fishbowl of professional golf, these are dreams many hope she catches, in part because she plays for the right reasons.

"I have a lot on my shoulders," Lemieux said. "There's this perception that I do it for Indian country. But it's almost the opposite. Indian Country wants to see me succeed. They hope it's in golf. It's becoming a big sport in Indian Country. And I love that I am able to share my story and be a part of history being a Native woman playing golf. But they want me to succeed as a person as well. I'm the person leading the way. I might have a couple of bumps in the road. But if I can give back to youth, I want them to face down the challenges, 'cause there are lot of Native golfers that are going to succeed after me."

Lemieux is a member of the Shoshone-Paiute Tribes and grew up alongside the Duck Valley Indian Reservation in the high plains of the American West, near what is now the Idaho-Nevada state line. And where she grew up in Caldwell—a suburb of Boise—a few hours from the border of the reservation property, her father introduced her to golf on the fairways of Fairview, Timberstone, and Purple Sage golf courses. Like many of the champions and players that this book has documented, golf and family and Native heritage are the supporting legs of the chair for Lemieux.

There are pictures of a very young Gabby happily swinging a club, with her father in the background. "My dad picked it up as a hobby. Then it turned into getting me and my sister [Tyler] out. And then it became a daily thing. We were fortunate that we had a driving range nearby. We didn't have the best equipment. I think our first sets were from a second-hand store. But it soon turned into a family thing. My mom wasn't a golfer, but ran the junior league that I was a part of . ... She became president of the Caldwell Junior Golf Association."

At the same time, Lemieux is an example of what many a golfer of any heritage has maintained: to make it to the elite levels of golf is a long and arduous journey. Most of us would have stopped after achieving half of what Gabby has done: qualifying for the U.S. Girls' Junior Championship three straight years (2012-14), two Idaho Golf Association Junior Championships, earning Big 12 Player of the Year at Texas Tech University, where she also helped lead her team to two NCAA Championship appearances. On the Epson Tour, she registered a pair of top-10 finishes in 2021, including a share of third in the Circling Raven Championship. In 2022, she qualified for the U.S. Women's Open at Pine Needles.

While we are not far removed from the years when Althea Gibson lost hope, what has changed is the network of support and organizations growing the game we all love. What has become clear is that elite Native golfers like Lemieux, her mentor, and golfers like Skyesong Alexis and Eric Frazier and the youth movement that is represented in the Pathways to Progression program, these are part of a living culture that is growing and changing Native golf. It's a newer golf culture that includes organizations and facilities, teachers, industry employees, a culture that represents what Kristi Daniels-Long called "a generational shift in our First People's lives." As Gibson said herself, "No matter what accomplishments you make, somebody helps you."

Each January, a number of Native organizations release the year's calendar of dozens of Native-only golf events, many at Native-owned facilities. Each month lists numerous events. They might be fundraisers for education, celebrations of sobriety, events praising the name of someone gone on to the spirit world, or more heady competitions for elite golfers such as the Native American Open at Santa Ana in October.

As one example among many, here is Curtis Osceola, Chief Council of the Miccosukee, one of the first recognized tribal nations (1963), on what golf has brought to their culture:

> "We have long had alligator fashion dances and arts and crafts, the green corn celebration, but then gaming gave us a source of revenue. Gaming transformed the culture of the tribe. So much so that the tribe is now one of the most successful in terms of its governing administration in the country. The golf course came after secondary education and health care. We now have wealthy and educated Natives in the eastern style. And we support the traditional style too. We have a language arts program. ... And in 2005, we purchased Kendall Lakes, a course designed in the shape of a horseshoe. It's become part of the dance we have to do with western society, to engage in an enjoyable activity, so we can bond and communicate and build relationships with other people."

We might venture that this affiliation of golf operations and organizations holding tournaments is akin to the UGA, which nurtured both great male and female golfers of color. From 1934 through November 1961, golf associations for African Americans included the African American Golf Association (AAGA), United States Black Golf Association, United Black Golfers Association (UBGA), Western States Golf Association, Black Jewels Ladies Golf Association, and the African American Golf Foundation. During this time period, African Americans also established Black-owned golf courses, such as Mapledale in Massachusetts, or Clearview in Ohio. As noted earlier in the book, Joe Louis the Champ Golf Course in Chicago was at one time called Pipe o' Peace, and primarily a course played by Black players, much like the William J. Devine golf course in Boston's Franklin Park.

And in the same way that the UGA gave rise to Charlie Sifford, Renee Powell, and Althea Gibson, the culture of golf in Native American communities—including access to facilities and first-rate coaching—is giving rise to elite golfers among both juniors and professionals. For Lemieux, this is not just about golf.

"I love taking pictures," she says. "And when it's on Native land it's so cool. When I play on the tour sometimes, we have tournaments that are Native-run, on Native-owned courses. Our cultures are being shared with people from all over the world. Like, before the pro-am starts, the tribes are blessing the courses. Our rituals are including people from the outside world in our traditions. I can go to Michigan, to Idaho, to Nevada. Golf has become a way to experience Native culture through a different lens that is native owned and supported. It's super beautiful."

For the game is not about birdies and technique. Like many of us, she sees the game in a philosophical light: "Golf isn't just hitting a ball around a course and trying to shoot the lowest score. It's so much more than that. It teaches you patience, controlling what you can control." As she approached Qualifying School in 2022, she said, "Just to be the first Native American women's professional golfer on the LPGA, I think, speaks thousands of words. I just hope that maybe one girl, one Native American girl who's playing golf right now would see that and they'd want to do that, too."

Maddison Long has played with Lemieux when she has visited New Mexico, and Maddison cites Gabby as her north star and motivator. Following the Native American Open, she told me, "Gabby Lemieux has been a big role model to me as a Native American woman and a golfer. I met her at a junior golf clinic and after got to play nine holes with her. Since then, I have followed her journey through the Epson Tour and her debut in the 2022 U.S. Women's Open. She inspired me to pursue my passion in golf and show that with enough dedication I can succeed in it."

Gabby Lemieux has been through this process and knows

the risks and rewards. She recently had a moment of reflection before deciding to chase the dream again in 2024: "After some conversations with those close to me, and figuring out what my next step is, I plan to take on a new journey. That journey is finding ways to make the most fun out of what I got left ... in golf. ... I am still going to compete professionally in golf in 2024!!!"

Chasing the dream of a win on the LPGA Tour is not over. To be a first, to walk that high wire, about this journey, she said, "I am not a golfer first. I am Gabby Lemieux, a woman who [likes] to play golf, compete, and most importantly, do it because I love it."

In a society in love with instant access—with too much information, with all-seeing, all-knowing media—this speed of access can add to the challenge of what we know is the most difficult game in human history. It can add to the challenge to do what we love. And there are many examples of how the fishbowl of professional golf—the media and public scrutiny—can add unnecessary pressures. Calvin Peete won 12 times on the tour, including the Players Championship in 1985. He later said, "I would not want to be Tiger Woods." Peete was 23 when he took up the game. By the time Woods turned 23, he had seven tour victories, including the 1997 Masters. It was the fishbowl life—of being constantly in the spotlight—that Peete did not envy about Tiger's success.

That Gabby Lemieux can be in that spotlight, chasing her dream, and can continue to be an excellent role model for the young—like Peyton "Beans" Factor and the Long sisters—perhaps it's part of the process, or perhaps it's the mettle of a true champion. There is also the element of having a caucus of other champions on her side.

"I was super lucky to find N7," Gabby says about the Nike program designed to support Native youth in athletics, as well as lifestyles for health and wellness. "I didn't know about it until all the talk about turning professional. I was like, holy cow, I didn't know it existed. Now that's a big part of who I am."

This network of mentors and organizational support involved coaches and friends, but also came to her through Jason Montoya. "I got lucky," Lemieux says. "Jason knew my sister Tyler. They met in Arizona at Talking Stick. My sister became assistant there and helped Jason with an N7 clinic. Jason knew Sam McCracken." And another partnership was born. Lemieux signed on as an N7 ambassador, a group that includes Montoya, and notable Native athletes such as Jacoby Ellsbury and Sam Bradford. As an N7 ambassador, she also meets her goal of helping younger peole who one day will be where she is now.

For even at 28 years young, we might mistake Gabby for an elder when she says, "Golf is about being yourself and letting the game come to you."

From talented individuals to organizational support, from Santa Ana and the Native American Open, to N7 and a growing golf industry in Native communities, we are witnessing an evolving ecosystem of economy and family, individual excellence embedded in a wider *#landback* narrative. Taken together, along with the voices and profiles of people associated with the game, the development of Native American tribal culture and landscapes designed around golf, these map out the continuance of Native peoples in a recovery that we can celebrate as we also reconstruct—and rediscover—the history of the game.

And in addition to the genealogy of family, there is a deeper genealogy that connects present to past. Like Althea Gibson and Joe Louis, like Orville Moody and Rod Curl, and reaching back to Frank Dufina and Oscar Bunn, the place of our First People in golf is a story not only about the game, but the best part of American history: the story of barrier breakers, of those who flew first. A history of human resilience and determination.

In the 2015 documentary on Althea Gibson, Serena Williams identified Althea Gibson as "the most important pioneer."

There is also an eloquent clip of Renee Powell, whose father was the first African American to design, build, own, and operate a golf course. Powell's father had built Clear-view, the famed course of the UGA circuit, a course that had the motto—"Golf for Everybody." These are the words Renee Powell has lived in her own pioneering career. In the documentary about Gibson, Renee recalled a UGA Tournament in Boston in the 1960s when she was paired with her idol. She saw up close how Althea Gibson was "a force of nature" and a woman "completely unafraid."

What were the costs of that courage? Some of these powerful, pioneering individuals paid a high price. In his autobiography, Joe Louis lamented his addictions and how he would recover from fights with booze and drugs. The story of Gibson reaching a point of considering suicide is another example of those costs. Such that, if we can avoid even one scene of a 68-year-old champion losing the will to live, all of this history will have been worth the effort.

Our dream catchers must have the tools. For Gabby Lemieux and the many histories recorded here, that has become about support and belonging.

"I want them to feel like they belong in the game," Gabby says. "I want them to see me and be like, I can be like her. I'd be super proud to be that for them." Along with father and mother and sister, along with tribe, many others are now on board.

On this subject of the high cost of chasing dreams and the pressure of being first, the same is true of another challenge: playing without one of his limbs.

Chapter 16

JIMMY SQUIRE: THUNDER CLAN

> "Jimmy Squire has been working to help disabled athletes for more than 20 years, and the world is finally beginning to catch up."
> —Dianna Hunt (Cherokee Affiliation)

> "Golf taught me how to walk."
> —Jimmy Squire

Hummingbird (aka Micah Jones), who is the heart and soul of the golf operation at Santa Ana, had told me, "look for him." And it was soon obvious how I would recognize Jimmy Squire, Absentee Shawnee of Oklahoma.

Jimmy's left leg is solid, while his right is a prosthetic device on which he has learned to golf, and golf well. I met up with him on the putting green at the opening ceremony of the Native American Open. As the Sandia Mountains turned to their evening watermelon-pink, Jimmy showed me what he can do with a golf club.

Watching Jimmy swing, I was reminded of the story of Ernest Jones, a British golf pro who came to America and became Babe Zaharias' coach. Jones had lost his right leg during the war and played off his left leg. Developing faith in a simple pendulum swing, he famously scored a 38 on a front nine just four months after his amputation. Jones had said to Zaharias, "I watched you. The day you can stop experimenting is the day you will be a great golfer, maybe the greatest of all."

Jimmy Squire had implicitly taken some of Jones' teachings to heart. The golf swing is a simple pendulum. "Just hit standing on your left leg," Jimmy tells me in characteristic good humor. "That's the best way to learn it."

When Squire was first adopted into the Sac and Fox Thunder Clan in 2008, he had been representing disabled veterans and Native Americas for nearly ten years when Jack Thorpe, the son of Olympian Jim Thorpe, approached him and offered to adopt him into the family. Squire cites the adoption ceremony as a key source of his determination to make the world of tournament athletics more welcoming to disabled Native American athletes.

"His son [Jack Thorpe] told me, 'work on his legacy, work on your legacy.' We want to be like him. The reason is because of my grandpa, Jim Thorpe. He is the one who gave us that motivation. If I open doors for other tribes, other athletes and the disabled, as well as our veterans, to get them more motivated in playing a sport—or being an athlete—it begins with grandpa."

He also has run into another golfer of note along the way: Tom Watson.

"I was 23," Jimmy tells me in his musical and soft Oklahoma twang. He was still learning to swing with one leg, and he loved golf enough to volunteer for the 2001 PGA Senior Championship at Southern Hills in Tulsa. As luck or fate or the golf gods would have it, Jimmy was told to ferry a fellow by the name of Tom Watson from the practice area to the starting tee.

"Yes. Tom Watson. He told me. Just like Jack Thorpe had told me. He said, 'there's only one of you. You can be that inspiration for so many in your situation.'"

After giving that blessing, Watson won that tournament by one stroke over ... the other Jim Thorpe. And since representing the Absentee Shawnee of Oklahoma at this year's Native American Open at Santa Ana, Squire's legacy has only grown. I had heard he had recently won a golf tournament for adaptive golfers.

"Actually, I won three of them," he confessed. Two of those wins were back-to-back tournaments in November, run by the Veterans Golf Association. Squire's schedule is as relentless as is his good nature, and it wouldn't be possible without his team: Sherry Smith (Comanche), is his "partner, rider, and caddie." He has, in his words, an "Indian brother": Robert Komahcheet III, whose mother is a Thorpe. Financial sponsors of Jimmy's golfing and outreach efforts include Absentee Shawnee Tribal Veterans, and Hill Country Prosthetics, Texas Adaptive Sports, and The Southwest Amputee Golf Association (SWAGA).

Roy McCoy has run SWAGA since 1980, and he counts Jimmy Squire as an ambassador to Native Americans. The organization offers three annual tournaments and clinics for veterans and amputees, most recently at WinStar: a Chickasaw Nation resort in Oklahoma.

"Jimmy is a great ambassador and a great help," Roy Smith shares. "For many years now. Especially for our outreach to the tribes."

With a high rate of diabetes, with remote communities removed from adequate health care, and with veterans of war all part of the story, limb amputation affects Native Americans at much higher rates than the general population. McCoy's organization has developed clinics to help men and women who have lost limbs get active. He sees Squire's efforts in these communities as invaluable. McCoy said, "Jimmy's a great spirit. A good guy." And not only an ambassador: Squire won this year's SWAGA Championship Flight at WinStar.

Squire's Native name is Ko Ti Ke Pe Ya Se Ki, which translates as "changing the feathers of a baby eagle." He lost his foot at age three in a lawnmowing accident, an event indicative of a difficult childhood. Born and raised in Shawnee, mostly by his grandparents, his father's father was William Squire (Absentee Shawnee) and grandmother Darby was Shawnee and Creek. Married for 63 years, they were involved in the Absentee Shawnee stomp dances.

"I would sing and drum at the pow-wow and she would dance," Jimmy recounted. "She took me to the drum circles. I stayed with them on the weekends. If there was a pow-wow going on, we would watch cowboy rodeos and a cultural education. They never forgot where they came from."

Squire remembers early on hearing the name of Jim Thorpe from his grandparents. He and they would pack up and go to pow-wows. He played the heartbeat drum.

"That is what makes the pow-wow," Jimmy tells me. "The center drum. We would go to Jim Thorpe Memorial Sac and Fox Pow-Wow. I went to his birthplace. On the way to Stroud, there is a road marker that I saw. I wanted to be a role model and athlete like him. If he could be a tribal member and inspiration, I would like to be like him and play all the sports my body would allow."

Jimmy described his life evolving out of a difficult childhood: "There was a lot of bullying and being picked on. Fighting all the time. With my parents, we went from one housing project to another. I was different. They had never seen anybody like me. They knew I was different. It drove me to become suicidal. I was always fighting, always being picked on and being called names, and my mother didn't know how to handle that. From 4th grade to 'til about ... I would say at least 7th grade, I would have to take my leg off to defend myself. I was at my lowest."

Athletics opened the door. When Jimmy was picked for soccer in 5th grade, he felt a door opened. "I was making a name for myself as far as being an athlete. Sports pulled me out of that desperation. I can go back in time and remember and process. I wrestled from 7th through 11th [grades], and that's when they revised me to above knee. At the Endeavor Games in Oklahoma City, in 2007 I got gold in the long jump as an above-knee amputee."

After this event, he met Paul Clark III. "I was sitting on the bleachers and he asked, 'what are you doing with all the medals?' After a time he asked me, 'If you had one wish in this world, what would it be?' I said, 'I would go to pay my respects to Jim Thorpe.'"

And that's how it happened. In 2008, Paul Clark III picked

Jimmy up at his grandmother's house, and took him to the town of Jim Thorpe, Pennsylvania. They hung out with the councilmen. They went to the grave site and sent up a prayer. They got to hold the Olympic medals, and Jimmy was made the chair of the Jim Thorpe parade. Not too many people have a chance to go from their lowest to these accomplishments, and that was because of love.

Jimmy Squire believes—no, he knows—that the love of Paul Clark lll and Doyle Black, his adoptive father, helped to make his positive life possible.

"We're not taught how to raise a disabled child. My mother didn't know. So, I had asked my leg guy if he would be willing to raise me. Out of the blue one day, I asked him to raise me. He thought about it, and one day he told me, '"I want to raise you.'"

Doyle Black, a prosthetic technician, took Jimmy in at the age of 15. "He took me in and loved me and gave me the inspiration of learning what an amputee life was going to be for me." Jimmy has endured two operations, first removing his leg below the knee and then a second operation removing his leg above the knee. To these challenges, Squire has responded with empathy, enthusiasm, and good humor.

"If I throw my leg, rather than a club," he jokes, "then you know I'm in trouble."

The likelihood of such a meltdown is slim. Squire loves the game and loves to give back to those who need it, particularly veterans.

"I couldn't serve," Jimmy said, "But I have buddies who came back from war without limbs. I don't want to see them whine and cry. I encourage them to move with the world. To be with the Veteran Golfers Association (VGA) and the family flight and to represent my family, that's the best honor to ever ask for."

Randy Norris is the president of the Oklahoma Branch of the VGA. He notes that out of approximately 290,000 Oklahoma veterans, there are over 100,000 with some level of disability. "Jimmy's work is invaluable for the adaptive athletes in the state's veteran community. It's work to get these folks to stay active, and Jimmy is a great advocate for that. Especially among our Native American veterans."

"I'm not one to sit at home," Squire brags. "I put my leg on in the morning and take it off at midnight when I go to bed. And if I can open some doors, so others don't sit at home and stare at the wall, I've met my goal."

While he has worked at numerous golf clubs since he was 20, working on the range and in the cart barn and the starter's shed, Squire currently works for the Shawnee Tribe in their recycling center, while continuing to thrive in a game he has loved since he was 15.

"You just need one leg to stand on," Squire says with a ring in his voice. "In golf, you're on your own. It's between you and nature. The game gave me a better sense of looking forward to that next shot. Walking was the best gift the game could give, to make me the best walker I could be. There was no time clock. No coach screaming in your ear. Golf taught me how to walk."

At the 2023 Native American Open, Squire was one of two disabled golfers. When he heard the organizers of the Native American Open are planning an amputee flight in the future—in part because of his participation—he bristles with excitement.

"We need 10 disabled golfers for them to make a flight." He is hopeful that next year's Native American Open at Santa Ana will include a handicap category. We need to branch out and get disabled Natives and veterans to be more involved."

As a disabled golfer, Squire is ranked 11th in state, 88th in the region, and 343 in the nation.

The World is Catching Up

While Jimmy Squire has been playing in tournaments and advocating for disabled athletes for more than 20 years, the world is beginning to catch up.

While Blind Golf has been formalized since 1990, in 2021, the USGA and U.S. Adaptive Golf Association established categories for golfers with a variety of impairments. The classifications go from G1 to G15, and cover legs, arms, eyes, intellectual diversity, and body size. In addition to these classifications, the USGA and U.S. Adaptive Golfers Golf Association have established a national Adaptive Open, which began in 2022 and took place at Pinehurst in July 2023. The championship follows through on a 2017 pledge by the USGA to establish this championship for the adaptive golf community, and despite the pandemic, the organization fulfilled that promise.

The Adaptive Open is the USGA's 15th national championship, joining such iconic events as the U.S. Open, U.S. Women's Open, U.S. Amateur, and U.S. Women's Amateur. Champions of this new event will see their names recorded in the annals of golf history alongside many of the game's storied figures. Eligibility is open to both male and female professional and amateur golfers with an official handicap index of 36.4 or less, and an eligible impairment confirmed by a WR4GD pass. (There is no self-reporting of disabilities.) The 96 players in this year's Open competed in one of eight impairment categories, as well as for the overall titles. When the dust settled, Kipp Popert of England and Ryanne Jackson of Seminole, Florida came away as the overall men's and women's champions, respectively.

John Bodenhamer, the USGA's senior managing director of championships, said, "Since 1895, our championships have provided the world's best players with an opportunity to showcase their skills on a global stage, compete for a national championship and achieve their dreams. After years of planning and delays caused by the global pandemic, we are proud to bring that same opportunity to the adaptive golf community through this championship, and to do so at Pinehurst, our second home. We believe this effort will spur participation for golfers with disabilities and hope it inspires others in the industry to make the game and its competitions more welcoming to all."

Ken Green is also a G1 adaptive golfer. Once a PGA professional who lost a leg in a traffic accident and who competed in the Adaptive Open, he shared this sentiment in an email: “To me, it’s as positive as any other tournament I’ve ever played. It’s about life and golf, and then the mixture of both and what golf can do for a person who has been given the worst of the worst blows. They use golf to help them fight through all the negativity that happens sometimes when you lose limbs or eyesight or paralyzation or any of those other impairments.”

The Path Lit by the Same Lightning

Jim Thorpe may be the greatest athelete of the 20th century, but he also had his struggles. As we’ve seen Joe Louis and Althea Gibson even had struggles of their own. They did not have a UGA or a USGA, or a N7 or NB3, to take them in, support them, provide them mentors or opportunities or funding. By 1929, Native Americans would have had only five years of legal citizenship.

Thorpe’s gifts and his role in this history are indisputable. According to his grandnephew Robert Komahcheet lll, the first time his great uncle played golf he shot a 76. Nevertheless, by 1929, “the greatest athlete in the world” was rebuilding his life.

Whatever hardship Thorpe faced—on a golf course or elsewhere, as witnessed by his family—his stamina lives beyond his time and is carried along by Jimmy Squire and others. Squire’s unwavering enthusiasm for Native American veterans and amputees is an extension of that legacy and motivation.

“If it means opening doors for Native American amputees,” Squire says in his soft Oklahoma accent, “I’ll play.”

On the last day of the Native American Open, I found Jimmy and his partner Sherry coming home on the 18th green. When I got to their cart, Jimmy was on the green, and Sherry gave me a look and a shrug. The least violent and most difficult game in human history can humble even a member of the Thunder Clan.

“The first hundred years are the hardest,” I whispered to

Sherry. Maybe we're quiet around the golf course for concentration, maybe the quiet is for the recently humbled, so they don't come down to tears.

Whatever the answer, what was clear in her smile was that Sherry would be there at the finish—good round or bad. And what was clear from Jimmy's expression was: he'd had a bad day, but he wasn't going to give up. That resilience and support, which Jimmy Squire has exhibited for more than 20 years, is critical in ways we are beginning to see in Native American golf.

I'd witness it again on my swing through the Southwest, down the John Wayne Highway, deeper into both Golf Country and Indian Country.

Jimmy Squire teeing off at the Native American Open.

Chapter 17

TRIBE. FAMILY. MENTOR. MENTEE.

The last stop on my Southwest Swing took me to Scottsdale and Phoenix, the same weekend when the PGA Tour's Waste Management Open was raising the hackles. While listening to radio accounts of rowdy, beer-drenched fans and PGA players fed up with the over-served masses, I slid a rental in the cradle between mountains ranges, driving the John Wayne Highway, deep into desert again. My destination: Poston Butte, to meet a man named J.C. Wright.

As with every stop on this journey, one thing led to another. To get this history right, one person knew someone else I needed to know. From Mike Smith and David Bunn Martine, to Jay Garcia to Mr. Wisdom, memories became the names of legends, living and dead. I'd get another set of digits, another story in the history of the First People in the game we all love, and all these roads led to Poston Butte. And as with other stories involving J.C. Wright, this one began with a good omen.

Sitting on the patio overlooking the practice area at Poston Butte Golf Club in Florence, Arizona, J.C. and I are interrupted before our conversation begins.

"Excuse me, Boss," the course superintendent politely interrupts a meeting that had yet to start. "Mrs. Sykes? She got a hole-in-one on 7. Wanted you to know."

If that hole in one is any indication, J.C. Wright, a Lakota, might be said to be a magnet for good luck. And not only luck. J.C. is also a pioneer. According to the PGA of America,

Wright is the first Native American to achieve his membership (in 2009).

"I was told I was one of five members at that time," he says. If you ask Wright, or anyone else for that matter, the story of our First People in the golf industry is complex. There are many reasons for this. As one example, when Orville Moody won the U.S. Open in 1969, there was little mention in the press about his Choctaw heritage, nor that his grandmother walked on the Trail of Tears. In two years of research on the connections between our First People and the game of golf, the best way to "tell the truth" about the past is to listen. J.C. Wright's story includes a family and tribe born with talent and for good fortune. He is fourth generation on from Tribal Chief Hollow Horn Bear, who fought alongside Sitting Bull and Crazy Horse, and who passed away on his way back from Herbert Hoover's inaugural. From this auspicious genealogy, J.C. Wright's story connects the past to our modern life and Native golf.

Many years ago, Wright was dealing blackjack at the Rosebud Casino, on the Rosebud Reservation in South Dakota. It was a job, it and came after his success at Black Hills College, where he starred as a walk-on the football team. With a natural charisma, Wright attracted regulars at his table, one of them was a rancher by the name of Charley Doby. Charley brought along his friends. Long into the night, Charley and his rancher friends would work J.C.'s table, then dawn would call them back to the needs of their cattle and land. Charley was also a golf enthusiast and mentored J.C. in taking up the game.

"He's passed now," J.C. recalls. "Just a few years ago. He introduced me to the game as a career. He also introduced me to Joe Prue and others. Playing with those guys, I got good quick."

Joe Prue and Charley Doby knew about golf, yes, they also knew about the vocational scholarships. J.C. did his homework, researched the vocational schools and ended up qualifying for a tribal education program. That program would afford J.C.—and other members of the tribe—the financial ability to attend the golf school.

"Joe Prue was a family friend," J.C. goes on. "Our mothers were best friends. Joe was always out playing golf and that is how we met, and the relationship grew to hunting, fishing, and traveling, playing golf prior to his passing."

J.C. knew champions when he saw them. All ears and eyes, he learned from Prue and Doby about the game, as well as school programs for vocational pursuits. As a talented athlete, those same programs had money for matters other than industrial pursuits. J.C. took what he learned from Charley and Joe Prue and found himself at the Golf Academy of Arizona in Chandler, a two-year program that would be a life-changer.

And just as one story leads to another, and as one phone call turns up two more, J.C. Wright's journey led back to Prue, a Sioux golfing legend, with a legacy that carries on through J.C. Wright and Joe's youngest daughter, Cassie Prue, now director of golf operations at El Dorado Country Club in McKinney, Texas.

Cassie said of her father, "He would talk about golf as a humbling game, and how the golf gods would humble you, and you have to walk humbly on the earth, but then he would go out and whoop up on you." This is the kind of legendary figure one hears of when digging into the history of our First People in golf. In another world, Joe Prue would be the Charlie Sifford of Native golf. In his heyday, according to both J.C. and Cassie, other players would drop out when they learned he had entered the tournament.

Cassie saw it all up close: "He was not a humble man at all. He knew he could beat you, and he knew when you were done, and he would let you know."

Some readers will have played in a tournament that offered $10,000 for a hole-in-one. Win a car or win $10,000? These are usually on a long par three, an uphill shot into the wind and to Redan or turtle-backed green. Impossible, right? Well, Joe Prue (Lakota) hit one for ten grand while his young daughter Cassie looked on.

In addition to the hole-in-one worth $10,000, he has made 16 other aces, as well as a 59 in competition at 27 Flags Golf Course in Sioux City, Iowa. He counted Rod Curl as a friend and mentored not only J.C. Wright and Cassie, but a generation of Native golfers. One day he birdied the 18th hole at a tournament then drove his son and son's girlfriend to a hospital where she delivered a baby daughter. His tribal name given at birth was Cangleska Luta Hoksila ("Red Circle Boy"), the name for a sundancer: the ones who dance as a sacrifice for family and tribe. And while golf was his passion, the game was a vehicle for a broader philosophy of life.

He had told his daughter, "As soon as you are created, an ending date is already there. Some die at birth, others in the womb. How we get to that time and place is up to you." Mr. Prue passed onto to those who knew him the great challenge of life: He who is not busy being born is busy dying, and this wisdom lives on in mentees like J.C. Wright and his daughter.

Cassie's tribal name is Wiwang Waci Win ("Sundance Woman"), a name that her maternal grandmother gave her. "My grandmother has worked hard in order that the language never dies," Cassie says. And she keeps one of her grandmother's favorite phrases close to her heart: "Ni Lakota! Tuweni he ektuja s'ni yo." ("You are Lakota! Never forget that!") That pride and association would explain how Joe Prue influenced not only his daughter, but his daughter's mentor, J.C. And he's played a protective role in her life.

"We are all from the same reservation," Cassie told me. "If you played golf, you knew my dad. As J.C. got older, he would play with us."

J.C. was a pallbearer at Joe Prue's funeral in 2022, and he now serves as an uncle figure to Joe's youngest daughter Cassie. When J.C. received his membership card, there was fewer than five Native American PGA instructors in the game, Steve McDonald being the first. Now, according to the PGA, there are 73. As witnessed by the parents of the junior champions, the challenges facing J.C. and his mentee Cassie Prue are not only golf-related, but come with the challenges of access, resources, and support. That's where Charley Doby's influence comes back in.

"Charley got me playing," Wright explained, "with the help of his rancher friends. I ended up managing a little nine-hole 'pasture golf course' called Prairie Hills. I ran that little club for a year, and even with all the challenges, I got to be a pretty good golfer."

About these challenges, Wright tells a story that harkens back to Jay Garcia and how many of us tried to learn golf with a set of inherited clubs.

"I mean," J.C. says with a laugh, "My first clubs didn't really fit me—they were way too small—and it was all pretty new. But Joe Prue was good to learn from and somehow in the back of my mind I kept thinking about this golf school that a rancher had told me about in Arizona and that kind of ended up being my salvation."

In South Dakota, J.C. recalls, "while growing up, myself and my peers were faced with the challenges of drugs and alcohol combined with life on the reservation. It was never easy, finding golf and the golf school was my salvation."

"It knows no color," he says of that world of pain. All of us know someone turning on that wheel. J.C. wanted no part of that. He shares, "But believe it or not, all that alcoholism and drug abuse and other problems associated with the reservation, they motivated me into a positive light. ... I think it's important that I have succeeded as a kind of trendsetter among my people, because I'm not sure what could have happened had I failed. I mean, Notah Begay has done a lot nationally, and Sam McCracken from Nike has really supported Native Americans, too. That's really the kind of impact that I'd eventually like to have."

J.C.'s grandfather had warned him, with his stones. The stones had spelled out danger and possibility both. J.C. understood it, and his coaches had told him the same. You're one of the best we've seen. When J.C. would laugh, his coaches and mentors would say it again: I am completely serious. You have a pure spirit. You can do good things. Rocks tell stories.

J.C. was a rock. The year was 2000, and J.C., who had been looking for a way off the res, found one. He boxed up a few clothes, his second-hand clubs, and a hunting rifle, and he headed for Phoenix: a golf mecca in the heart of Indian Country. After arriving, he joined Troon Golf at Whirlwind Golf Club at Wild Horse Pass, applied for the grants he had heard about from Charley and Joe, and enrolled in the Golf Academy in Chandler.

"I never dreamed I could get that far, but all of a sudden I'm 25, in the golf business, and actually closer than I'd ever been to my goal of being a Class-A PGA professional. ... In 2002, I made it reality when I got my first real job as an assistant golf professional at Ak-Chin Southern Dunes Golf Club."

Ak-Chin is a storied course—a work of art—and a unique story in the world of Native American golf. It began as a private men's club, with a course designed by Brian Curley, with help from Fred Couples and Lee Schmidt. Its opening day was attended by notables such as John Daly, and the idea was to be modelled on the Bohemian Club—all men. Not even women employees. It never caught on, and ownership

Ak-Chin Southern Dunes in Arizona.

changed hands before landing with the Ak-Chin Indian Community in 2010.

Wright worked with the club and the tribe and the federal government to secure a Fee-to-Trust arrangement, the same Fee-to-Trust agreements that were established in the 1934 Indian Reorganization Act and that continue to be a central part in helping to rebuild tribal land bases. In the case of Ak-Chin Southern Dunes, with the help of J.C. Wright, the land again became the tribe's, and the course has continued to develop high-end events and tournaments, including the famed Copper Cup between the University of Arizona and Arizona State University.

Wright left Ak-Chin in 2013 to take his first director of golf job at Lookout Mountain at Tapatio Cliffs a Hilton Resort. Later in 2022, Wright accepted the GM job at Poston Butte. He oversees a staff of 86 for Troon Golf, a staff that accommodates 52,000 rounds of golf each year. His teaching stints at We-Ko-Pa, Boulders, and Whirlwind are in the rear view, and he's now a world and lifetime away from the green velvet of the blackjack tables at Rosebud.

This is Indian Country. Poston Butte sits in an enormous bowl made by the Superstition Mountains in the distance, skirted by a rust red fog. The roads out of Phoenix take you through commercial zones that could be in Kansas City, Cleveland, or Boston. Then, a little farther out, this commercial ring succumbs to the desert. Phallic cacti spring up. The hardiest of all earth's plants, they can survive on a spit. It's sunny and 75, today and forever. Any water is being pulled up by the developments, and the few cottonwoods direct you to whatever rivers have endured, from time immemorial into the 21st century.

More than a two-decade run from the Black Hills and Rosebud Casino, J.C. is now GM of a well-appointed and well-run golf course 54 miles from Phoenix, and this makes the point again: With the national approval of gaming licenses, officially sanctioned in 1984, recognized tribal cultures have begun to create revenues that have in turn allowed for them to more readily rebuild their culture. In 2023, the market size of golf courses and country clubs in the United States amounted to around $27.24 billion. And where many in the industry are plateauing and in a "hold" pattern, even after the surge in outdoor activity during the Covid-19 pandemic, according to *Golfweek*, "there is one group of builders as bullish as ever on course construction: Native Americans. This group is quickly earning a reputation for clubhouses and golfing." And as long as land, water, and cash continue to bless their reservations, Native Americans have built a culture of resort golf, and PGA pros and players have followed.

This success has enabled J.C. Wright to grow the game in a personally meaningful way. "In that regard, I went back to my people," J.C. said, "to see if I could get a few other [Native Americans] involved in the golf business." Cassie Prue, the daughter of Joe, is one of those people.

"My dad got all of us into it," Cassie explained. "He was a big person at home trying to keep courses open and promoting golf. I went everywhere with him."

Cassie is the youngest of Joe's daughters, who travelled with her father to and from a lot of Native golf events in her youth. Her father strictly played in Native events only, and one she remembers fondly is a hole-in-one worth $10,000. She was by his side. North Dakota. Sioux City, and then eventually a wider turn to Nevada, Vegas, Santa Ana, and all over South Dakota.

"Strictly Native events," Cassie repeated. This point comes with a certain wistfulness. Before casinos and the new generation of golfers, before the N7 Fund and NB3 Foundation, how many legends escaped onto the sanctuary of golf courses? For Joe Prue, the journey included the Army. He served from 1974-79 as a police officer and as an x-ray technician. And he believed in the values one gets from golf and service are a lived experience, and he passed this pride and skill to J.C. Wright and his daughter, Cassie, to name just two.

That pride in both tribe and golf came to the forefront when Cassie spoke about this at the annual PGA event in

Scottsdale. The year was 2020, the same year she received her associate's certificate.

"Community is so strong in our culture," she recalled saying to the PGA gathering. "You're connected to everything in one way or another. In the Sioux tradition, you belong to the earth. You are related to everything and everyone. Golf is such a big part of that. My father learned from his father, so the game is finding my people. Native or not. I feel it in the golfing community. And not being at home [in South Dakota], we look for community. At that PGA conference, I told them how I never thought I would be where I am now, and that's because of community."

A lion's share of that journey has been with her son. Landon has been with her the whole way. "I was going to take care of him, and he was going to take care of me. Golf was going to be our way to have better things. When we moved to Arizona, it was right before his second birthday."

Cassie sees J.C. Wright as Uncle Advice. "He would ask, 'What do you think of this?' or 'What about this?' That mentoring without trying has guided me, without forcing me down one path or another. It was solid advice. My grandad and my dad and J.C. ... all of us trying to figure it out together."

Often the stories of Native Americans in golf are beautifully woven together, with family members and mentees helping the new generation to bigger achievements and better positions and opportunities. But the significant challenge has been being a woman in a largely male-dominated industry.

Cassie explained, "I've been on my own in Texas, and I've had to figure out the industry as a young female. That's been my biggest struggle. That is my goal to keep breaking these barriers. Young women of color. It hasn't been a walk in the park. Golf is a male-dominated industry. ... I've applied for many jobs and heard things like, 'We're not ready for a female pro here.' You get that backlash, and you have to push through. There are a couple of sexist things you have to work through. It goes hand-in-hand in industries like this."

The barriers have been there, but have been knocked

back again and again. Oscar Bunn played in the U.S. Open before he could vote or be declared a citizen of the United States. Frank Dufina once insisted that the press take his heritage out of the story. And from Orville Moody to Rod Curl taking the Colonial flag, from Althea Gibson to Gabby Lemieux on the LPGA tour, Jason and Cassie and J.C., the history of Native Americans in golf is a varied tapestry of barrier breakers and—with gaming and golf resorts—now a story of economic recovery and reverse migration, stories that hold out hope for a more inclusive future. Cassie is "for sure" the first woman from the Lakota to find her way in professional golf. With her father's spirit looking on from the cosmos, and with J.C. Wright on her team, she expects to continue to succeed where others have stumbled.

It was hard to leave the warm personalities and the sunny and 75-degree weather of the Southwest. I was also leaving

An old photo of Joe Prue, little Landon Prue, and Cassie Prue.

with my slice intact. Neither J.C. nor Cassie had been able to shake their operational duties to give me a lesson, and that would be why I was off to a lesson with another legend in the Now-Time: Steve McDonald.

Beaman Wisdom had mentioned Steve, as had J.C. Wright. And further discovered him first through The Native American Athletic Hall of Fame and the First Nations Tour. From there, I had traced his travels to the Cape Club of Palm City on the Treasure Coast, where he was a teaching pro.

"Come on down," Steve called out when I reached him on the phone. His sunny personality was apparent at the start. And just as I had with my lesson with Mr. Curl, I'd be returning to the Sunshine State to try to learn— once and for all— the perfect swing.

Chapter 18

A ROUND OF GOLF WITH THE McDONALDS

The Sunshine State. Again. Land of the panther and pythons. Native and intruders. In some ways, the Gray, alligator state is where I began. Two years prior to my date with Steve McDonald, I had travelled to the River of Grass to speak with the Miccosukee. I had gone up the Sun Coast for a meet up with Rod Curl, who had pointed out the 36 (or was it 37?) things wrong with my swing. Now, I was returning to the Treasure Coast and a lesson that would confirm what many already knew:

"You need a miracle," Steve McDonald said. A miracle? We were standing on fairway of the third hole, three holes into a six-hole match on the pristine, undulating grounds of the Cape Club of Palm City outside of Stuart, Florida. And I needed a miracle even after being smudged!

"Have you been smudged before?" Steve asked. While I knew about sage sticks, I had never been smudged, but was more than willing with a kindly, good-natured spirit like Steve McDonald. On the third hole, we paused our match, and he produced a sage stick and feather from his golf bag. He had me take up a handful of earth, and he placed a sacred branch in my other hand. Then he had me face east and asked me to think pure thoughts. He lit a sage stick and began a prayer in a humming language. Anishinabek words mix with English, and with each pause, he has me turn—to the south, to the west, and to the north, and then return to the east—and he fans the smoke around me. With each turn, he issues a new cleansing prayer: that our work together be successful, that this history reach empathic ears, that Native cultures find the means to heal and honor the earth as it should be honored.

I might have been cleansed, but when we returned to our drives, I was still 2-Down with four holes to play, and 190 yards from an elevated pin at the Cape Club of Palm City, Florida. Would a smudging help my game?

"You need a miracle," he had said. With that, I hit my best shot of the day. From about 190, with a 3-wood, I laced one headed just left of the flag. The ball bounced up—over the lip of the Augusta-white sand bunker—onto the green and ran at the hole. Steve smiled.

Steve McDonald is not one to gloat, and he immediately reminds me, in so many words, of something he had written to me: "Golf is about enjoying the beauty of what the Creator of All Things has laid out in front of you: the rolling fairways, the blue majestic sky, the flowers, bushes and trees, the life water, the crisp moving and unpredictable wind that comes from every direction, the amazing sun, early morning tee times and late evening sunset practice sessions, the tranquility of it all."

Researching the First People in the game of golf, there are a lot of claims to be first. As we've seen throughout our stories, we might say "one of the first," but without a doubt, Steve McDonald is among the first Native American PGA professionals. In 1987, when he became a PGA member, one hand could count that number. Even today, only about 70 of the 30,000 PGA members are Native, but that number is growing—thanks to Steve McDonald, who lit the path at a time when the larger world was not as welcoming.

While golf is far from being decolonized, and despite those challenges, Steve's playing and teaching have spanned decades and influenced many different walks of life. In 2022, he was awarded the Deacon Palmer Award from the PGA of America, and in 2023 McDonald was elected into the North American Indigenous Sports Hall of Fame. His greatest joy is teaching, especially young people, who are the future of golf. As he told me repeatedly, "It doesn't matter what color you are: the ball doesn't know your age, your size, tall or short, your background, what nationality you are, if you're male or female. The golf ball just responds to the way it is struck."

Sure, but the question crossed my mind: How does a tribal member of the Prairie Band Potawatomi and a highly decorated golfer have perhaps the most Scottish surname in history?

McDonald laughs his genuine laugh and smiles. "My grandfather Henry Charles McDonald was adopted, and that is where the family story in golf begins."

Henry Charles McDonald (Ojibwe/Chippewa) had five sons with Alice Shipshee, a Prairie Band Potawatomi. He had been adopted by a family named McDonald from White Earth, Minnesota. Alice and Henry had met at the Haskell boarding school in Lawrence, Kansas, where 60 years later their grandson Steve would become a four-sport letterman now called Haskell Indian Nations University). Henry taught his sons sports, football, baseball, but mostly his favorite sport: boxing. And he saw something in his younger boys John and Frank and introduced them to golf. Like a lot of their peers, they served in the Korean War. John met a high-ranked officer who sparked his interest in golf and, like Orville Moody, had been relegated to special duties.

When John's tour was over in the late 1950s, he decided to chase the professional golf—as a caddie. While Steve was still an infant, learning to crawl, then walk, then golf, John caddied on the tour from 1959 to 1961 for the likes of Frank Beard, Doug Saunders, and Joe Campbell. Shortly after his two-year stint, he moved to Fort Worth, Texas, and landed a job through a high-ranking Army officer as caddiemaster at Colonial Country Club. This is where he met and caddied for a fellow by the name of Ben Hogan.

"All those stories about Mr. Ben Hogan," Steve says, "those are in the roots of our golf history."

Steve McDonald keeps his waist-length ponytail tucked into his shirt. Tall and lean, his swing is smooth with spectacular tempo. It reminds me of the Shivas Irons advice to "let the nothingness into yer shots." His rhythm and balance are modeled after Hogan, and there's a certain nothingness that comes before and after the click of a ball being flushed. And like many a golfer, Steve is a natural-born teacher who offers unsolicited advice. When he saw my stabbing putting stroke, he taught me a dancer's exercise he did with his children: "Make a gravity stroke, let gravity be your friend—no need to fight it or force it. Hold the putter like a feather. Soft, not crushed."

I mention that I had received a lesson from Rod Curl. Steve launches into a story: "Won Colonial in 1974. Beat Jack Nicklaus by a shot! Amazing! Especially on the same track my father had worked at some 10 years before."

Steve met and played with Rod Curl in 2006. They were paired in a First Nations Golf Association tournament together at Black Bear Golf Course, owned by the Fond du Lac Band of Lake Superior Chippewa, two hours north of the Twin Cities. Playing beside Rod, Steve set the course record that day: 5-under 67 and sees that round as completing a full circle for tribe and family. He is enormously proud of his Native heritage. It's completely fine that our conversation on the Darren Clarke-designed golf course veers into Steve's riffs on Indigenous dance.

"In the grass dance, the grass dancers," Steve says, as he bows down and sways from side to side, "they dance for the people who can't dance. That is their mindset, their mentality, their inner spirit. The people whose legs and feet are hurt, or a diabetic with a heart condition, or our elders who can no longer dance. And that is why I golf. When I step on the grass, it's for the people who cannot."

"Look," he grabs my shoulder warmly, "Our ancestors are right here, with us on this ground, in the trees on the wind, they sacrificed so much, worked so hard that you and I can be here and enjoy the Creator's work, to have this life." He offers a fist bump, and it's hard not to agree on a spectacular sunny day, on the grounds of a gated community's golf links—Cape Club of Palm City.

On the third hole of our match, he explains how he uses distance knowledge to his advantage: "In terms of scoring, learn to hit the ball pin high. Play to a number you're comfortable with that you have confidence in and know that you can hit repeatedly. I have a 95-yard club, 82-yard club, and 70-yard-and-below scoring clubs." He aims for those distances when laying up or hitting off the tee. With that, after my 3-wood got me on to the green, he softly lands a 90-yard shot to about 12 feet—pin high. Three down with three to play. Yes, a miracle would be nice.

From 1986 to 1996, Steve McDonald was one of the best in the Midwest Section of the PGA region, and he dominated the First Nations Golf Tour from 2005 to 2009. The First Nations Tour was a series of events spoken of in reverent tones by those who were there, one of the first efforts to organize Native golf. Steve took top honors over 40 times in these years. From picking up broken tees beside his father at the Colonial—Hogan's alley—Steve has lived out the dream of golf that includes triumphs but with tinges with sadness and disappointment as well.

"I broke my dad's heart a few times," Steve admits. "He had a desire for me to play the tour. I felt like I could do it all, get married, start a family and play the tour. Become a PGA professional first and then back-door it onto the tour. But I didn't want to risk losing her. I started working 25 hours in the shop, lessons, the range. Play with the members. Junior golf. Run the ladies' golf. And yes, I won the sectional match play championship in 1987. But injuries happened, and the rigors of work versus travel, and the reality of juggling the two and raising a family took over."

And McDonald, as for many Native Americans, thinking of the dead in the spirit world includes elements of magic.

When thinking about his father, he tells the story of his last day on this side of paradise: "There was a huge snowstorm in Topeka," Steve recalled. "I was at the Mirage, you see. I had finished my round in Phoenix at 1 pm. I saw that I didn't make the cut. My flight didn't leave Phoenix right away, so I jumped a plane to Vegas, and I'm in the Mirage and over the loudspeaker I hear: 'Would a guest by the name of Steve McDonald report to the front desk?'"

Then, over the phone, his wife told him his father passed away about an hour before. Steve was shocked by the sadness of losing the man who taught him the Native ways and how to love unconditionally. He was also shocked by the circumstances.

"Get this," Steve says, again grabbing my shoulder. "His native name was Sin-ya, which means 'Cold.' The day he died, December 14, 1989, was one of the coldest days ever recorded."

Steve McDonald's Native name is Cook-te-ya ("Spirit of the Dawn"). Man of the early morning. When he tells me the story of his father's death, it is done in the way the First People see the living world and the world of the dead as connected. His father's spirit—embodied by his name—was in keeping with the natural turns of our world. Any sadness has been driven out by the joy of knowing the cycle of life is as it was meant to be.

And he can move from his sadness at his father's passing to one of his fondest memories: serving as the commissioner of golf and *chief de mission* for Team Kansas at the 2006 Indigenous Games held in Denver. "The opening ceremonies were incredible, over 800 Native athletes singing, dancing, and slow-rolling into Mile High Stadium with families and elders looking on! Truly an inspiration!"

He helped develop a private golf course in Eleuthera Bahamas: Jacks Bay. The one and only Jack Nicklaus/Tiger Woods golf course collaboration in the world. McDonald started "Green Castle Youth for a Change," a youth golf program directed toward the youth of Green Castle, Eleuthera

Bahamas to instill the importance of physical, mental, social, environmental, financial and spiritual positive change through the great game of golf.

Steve is proud of his many roles in golf and says, "I've been rest assured by Sir Franklin Wilson and the honorable O.A.T. Turnquest that I'll always be an honorary golf professional at Jacks Bay for my contributions on and off the golf course."

In 2022, the South Florida Section of the PGA of America honored him with the Deacon Palmer Award, given to "the person who personally displays outstanding integrity, character, and leadership, in the effort to overcome a major obstacle in their life." In Steve's case, that obstacle was two separate battles with cancer stemming from over-exposure to the sun and not wearing sunglasses. After a series of surgeries and procedures, Steve was given a clean bill of health and started working at the First Tee of the Shanee County and the Palm Beaches as a golf instructor, developing youth golfers and instilling the core values of golf in young people. He showed me the Deacon Palmer plaque on the wall of the club with great pride.

Taking a lesson and getting the story from one of the greats was a better education than sitting in any classroom, and I still had a lot to learn. On the 3rd green, my ball had trickled to the back of the fringe, and when I failed to chip in, Steve showed me how to accelerate through the ball. His expertise was specific and extensive. On the next tee, he picked out an issue and was focused on my hands at the top of the backswing. I was cupping my hands.

Steve took my club and hands and guided me to the top of my swing.

"Hogan would slightly cup at the top and then bow at impact. Not a lot of players can do that," he said, pointing out that I was over-cupping and needed to flatten out my left wrist at the top of my swing. "Not everyone can do it. I wouldn't try it." On my next swing, I hit a duck hook into some heavy foliage. Still 3-Down with three to play, and my drive was in the schmutz.

The list of Steve McDonald's many students runs deep—and includes the great Native golfer Gene Webster Jr.—but none are closer than his own children: Two of his three are in the golf industry, and all three of them tell me the same story when I speak with them.

In the birthing room, Papa Steve had a sawed-off mallet putter and would put that club in their tiny hands moments after birth, just after they had opened their eyes. "Born with a golf club in their hands." That was the family legend. That's how education began for Danielle, Emily, and Alex McDonald, fourth-generation Potawatomi, and fourth-generation golfers. Before long, he would regale them with tales of their grandfather caddying for Ben Hogan at Colonial, and he'd take them through what anyone would consider a trophy case that long ago burst at the seams.

And that tiny putter seems to have worked. Emily and Alex have jobs in the golf industry. Danielle is the best putter among the three, though she chose youth education as a career field and is a professional photographer. In all, from caddying for Hogan to dominating the First Nations tour, to having jobs in the golf industry, the McDonald family—Prairie Band Natives with the most Scottish name in all of history—have thrived and been recognized.

Emily won the Native American Junior and back-to-back city championships. All-State Kansas. All-City. A teaching professional, she won. And Alex, who caddies at Seminole, can not only play but is also a good storyteller. Alex talks about the great people he's met while looping for his dad and watching and playing in PGA Midwest Sectional tournaments. At eight and nine years old, Alex learned to rake sand and read greens.

"I've caddied for so many great people," Alex begins, mentioning former major league pitcher David Wells and John Hand (a famed caddie from Seminole). And like all the caddies I have met, Alex has a favorite story he could recite as if it were a memorized poem: "We had the pro-junior sectional. The format was one pro and three juniors. My dad was our pro, with me and my sister Emily, and one of our good friends. We were tied with another team at the conclusion of regulation play, and so we went into a sudden victory playoff with another pro and his team. I was about 12, but I could tell there was some tension between this pro and my dad for some reason. We faced him in the playoff hole. ... I shoved my drive into the tall stuff on the right but still had a shot and swing. Chased it up to six feet and drained the birdie putt. The other pro missed his putt, and we won. I was just so happy we won."

When Emily speaks to these family memories, she is cradling her six-week-old daughter, and her two sons rush about in the background. Yes, they all know the "born with a golf club in your hand" story. For Emily, golf and her Native heritage are one.

"The game is special and sacred," Emily shares. "That's always been a such an important part of being Indigenous. Respecting land. Golf is one of those rare sports where you can be out there. For four hours. Walking the land, a deeper part of it than just 'this is my sport.' We've always known the importance of the four directions and the grandfather rocks. All the things that you grow up praying about, thanking the Creator for, and when you see such beautiful landscapes—what can be done with the earth, to play on it, to utilize it in that way—I have always found this so incredible. When you think about all the amazing courses out there. The earth is our sanctuary. The best of everything that the Creator had to offer you on that land, especially in America. It's yours. Your ancestors walked it. You're able to play a sport that honors all that time."

Alex has a similar take. "Everything in golf comes easy for me, because I've been around golf all my life," he says. "We've seen the golf industry and the people since we were three and four years old. I've seen clubs brought up from sticks and stones. Clubhouse and course design. The back office."

With a one-year-old son, he sees himself sticking it out in the industry. "Being native and playing the game of golf," Alex says, "I feel like you get a low-key kick out of it at times when you look back at it. You got a game that was dominated by White, Anglo-Saxon culture and brought to America, and to have that and be a professional in that environment and with that history ... to be Native, play a White man's game and be good at it, it's sort of like leveling the field of play."

Alex strikes a melody that sounds like the song of many who've come before. His goals include to honor the Creator and be a good father and husband.

"Golf teaches us things that make these things possible," he says. "Wherever your shot leads you, you must accept it and deal with the consequences, either good or not so good, eventually reaching your end goal/target. Once there, reset and do it again. Tackle another challenge, repeat the process until you reach the end."

As Alex speaks, I hear his father's storytelling ability as well. When we stood on the range at Cape Club of Palm City, Steve taught in a way that raised the specter of how golf relates to life: "If anyone needed a reminder that we are the top model of Mother Earth's existence and food chain, imagine the long-extended buffalo hunts, imagine riding that paint at full speed. No bridle, no stirrups, no reins, no saddle, just the strength of the legs and core to keep you upright, with one hand on the mane to keep from falling . ... And then to pull an arrow from the quiver, to ride no-handed, to place the arrow in the bow, to pull the sling back and take a shot, calculating the speed, the wind, the distance that the arrow must cover to precisely strike the scared one in its softest spot—the eye—with your family's survival in the balance and on the line."

I recall Michelle Moody's story of her father putting one between the legs of a noisy pelican. For Steve McDonald, too, golf is an extension of these ancestral challenges and what he passes on to his own. When I finally hit a good drive on the 5th hole, he says with a smile, "That dog will hunt."

As our match comes to an inevitable end on the next hole, Steve tells me, "As the sun sets on my career, will you be asked what great golf courses did you work at? Or were you a great dad? I chose being a great dad, teacher, coach, friend, and grandfather serving those willing to learn. That will be my legacy."

Then Steve reminded me of the stakes of our match. I owed him a dollar bill, signed by me, in acceptance of my defeat. When I hand it over, he says, "Fast pay makes fast friends."

A life in golf has filled Steve's quiver with a unique and colorful vocabulary, as well as trick shots and a shoot-your-number accuracy with the sticks. The marquee with his name on it would not only mention his victories and course records, but his work with the children of Southern Utes, Mississippi Band of Choctaws, Kick-a-poos, Pueblos, Navajos, Ojibwe, Sioux, Chippewa, Oneidas, Salish, Creek, Osage, Winnebago, Cherokee, Seminoles, and Potawatomi. It would also speak to and for his understanding of the world, of how nature and human life blend in a way that makes way for the young and acknowledges the dreams of those who had gone before.

"If more people played golf, the world would be a better place," Steve said, as we rode toward the clubhouse. Like Walter Hopper and Frank Dufina, like Curl and Bunn, like Gibson and Lemieux, Steve is a transformative individual who sees golf is a microcosm of the cosmos. Much more than a game.

Portrait of Alex, Danielle, and Emily McDonald by David Bunn Martine.

And it's a way to continue the Native tradition of giving gifts out of respect and awareness. And it doesn't end there. Golf connects me to my father and my first swings with my grandmother's hickory sticks she'd abandoned in the tool shed. Golf allowed us to tell the truth about our lives.

As we pulled up to the cart plaza and patio, Steve's next lesson was waiting in the cart. When I'd slung my clubs onto my back, in the cool shade of Cape Club's clubhouse, which had been modelled on Augusta's, Steve touched my shoulder warmly, as he had a dozen times. He handed me the smudged turkey feather he had used, now wrapped with brown leather story bands. (I had more work to do for my eagle feathers.)

In Native storytelling, as with a talking stick or the story lance, you pass the feather, and as you hold the band, you tell a story, a story for each one. Walking to my rental car, under the shade of stately palms, I counted the bands—15. And while I couldn't be entirely sure, after two years of running down the history our First People in golf, I felt I had at least 15 tales, and not just tales, but the stories and memories, and the struggles that the greats had overcome. Time's fist had unclenched. The elders—living and dead -had shared their memories. And I climbed into the front seat knowing my Southern Swing was over, and two things had been confirmed: I had 37 things wrong with my swing and would need a miracle. I'd be turning north with my slice intact, where golf season was still a winter's daydream.

But there was hope: spring was near, and I had plans to return to new friends where this journey all began: Shinnecock, a word that had begun to mean much more than "people of the stony shore."

Portrait of Steve McDonald by David Bunn Martine

Chapter 19

SWEET SHOT

Home is where one starts from. As we grow older
The world becomes stranger, the pattern more
complicated
Of dead and living. Not the intense moment
Isolated, with no before and after
But a lifetime burning in every moment ...
—T.S. Eliot, from "Four Quartets"

As I again drove up the familiar black ribbon of Tuckahoe Road, which cuts across Shinnecock Hills Golf Club and up to the west gate of the Shinnecock Nation reservation, I tried to trace back to where I first got the idea that burial sites were the foundation of civilization. It had to be from my mother, as she used to give me books. Sometimes the books were from her friendship reading group—Cheever's *The Falconer*, or Morrison's *Beloved*. But sometimes the titles were more directional, works she thought would shape me, like Richard Leakey's *Origins*. I believe that is the book where I first came across the idea that civilization was determined by burial sites. Lake Turkana, was it? 60,000-70,000 years ago? With fire pits and burial sites, there was evidence that humans had become reflective: someone had a name, had a favorite pet, and had been buried with a knife they carved. Our ancestors were cared for and would be missed.

I wanted to find Oscar Bunn's grave and pay my respects.

The Southampton town historian, Julie Greene, had given us what records exist. We do know that after Oscar Bunn's untimely death, local undertaker E.C. Peterson would have overseen his burial on Shinnecock Reservation on January 27, 1918. The weather in Southampton that day was clear. That year, the nearest newspaper of record—the *New York Times*—would be almost entirely focused on the war, and there would be no mention of the proceedings up Little Beach Road to Cemetery Road where Oscar would be laid in a beautiful bone orchard of Shinnecock Nation. But the newspaper did report a clear and cold sky, and we can imagine that flat land and swamps and kettle ponds were guarded by the hills where Oscar learned his trade. The grass tufts would look like little smoke clouds in the gray and purple. And the day I returned, the distant high grounds of Sugarloaf and Shinnecock Hills would have looked like the tops of the heads of giants emerging from the sea clouds.

Southampton could be said to be highly civilized early. The town cemetery opened in 1885, and is the resting place of Oscar Bunn's brother, Charles, and his family. Charles Bunn's family lot is marked by a granite "B," and while it's noteworthy that they chose to be buried off the res, it makes sense, too. Charles straddled the Native and White summering communities in a different way than Oscar. Charles was a hunting and fishing guide for the wealthy New Yorkers who came out to hunt fowl in the wetlands. He'd taught the Roosevelts and Vanderbilts, among others, how to hunt fowl and shorebirds. Charles' hand-carved decoys—today valued as museum pieces—would be the prize of the annual outdoors shows at Madison Square Garden. He took a spot in the town lot, also the resting place of Seth Raynor and Charles Blair Macdonald, whose genius in design had shaped the courses that rolled between Shinnecock and Peconic Bays—the National Golf Links of America, and Shinnecock Hills, and Raynor's solo design of the neighboring Southampton Golf Club.

Needless to say, Shinnecock Nation's rituals of burial would pre-date 1885 by many centuries, before there were time zones, and the tribe had selected the finest plots of land for miles to honor their dead: the high grounds, to be closer to the spirit world, to have watch over the catch and guide the whalers home. Sugarloaf Hill and Shinnecock Hills, where the tribe buried their dead before "contact and discovery," would have given the ancestors a vantage over land and seas and brought them closer to the unfathomable heavens.

The restless dead of Shinnecock Hills and the First Nation—from Charley Thom to Elmer Smith—may be seen to still be watching over the finest golf course in all the land, but also be guiding the generations through these unresolved matters. When the course was expanded to 18 holes in 1895, the Shinnecock Nation's burials grounds were moved to what should be considered the next best and finest plot of land within the known universe. Well before 1918, the year Oscar died, the old burial grounds would have moved off the highlands and would come to occupy a south facing plot that runs up gently from the dark-blue waters of Shinnecock Bay. Across the water is the highest point out east—Sugarloaf Hill—which has its own history in relation to Shinnecock Nation and their dead. That story would have to wait for another day.

As it was, Mike and Dave and I made our way to the tribal grounds that include Lubin Hunter, Mary Della Bunn, Dondi Williams Sr., Elmer and Peter Smith, Roland Eleazer, and many of the Shinnecock who had built and developed the relationship between the famed golf course and the first inhabits of the nicest piece of land on earth.

Not surprisingly, Oscar is laid next to the ten men who died on the Circassian ship in 1876, which included his father, David Waikus Bunn. The Circassian Ten are all buried in a horseshoe-shaped mound under a red oak and share a marker noting the shipwreck; the names include four other members of the Bunn family.

Standing with family near the memorial, I couldn't help but be moved, moved to silence and wonder. For two years prior, the name of Oscar Smith Bunn had come on my radar.

And as David Bunn Martine had noted: Oscar aimed much, much higher than the cards he and his tribes' folk were dealt. Like a lot of the folks I'd met and heard about, he'd beaten some steep odds. To elevate him in the pantheon of golf history would be a worthwhile endeavor. He became my spirit guide for the past two years as I traversed the country and heard the tales of both suffering and triumph, despair and recovery. For this, and on that early spring day, I felt the thin membrane separating the world of the living from the dead press down on Mike and David and me in a solemn quiet.

In the near distance, the wrinkled sea kept Forever Time, while the silence of the bone orchard reminded me of the Keres words carved in the tuff at Cochiti: "Where they once were, we are now. And where we are now, you will be." What William Butler Yeats had said about the Irish could easily be applied to golfers: "The Irishman [golfer] sustains himself during brief periods of joy by the knowledge that tragedy is just around the corner [the next shot]." Oscar had lived the joy of golf between tragedies—one, the shipwreck that took his father and, two, the wicked flu that took Oscar down that fall and winter. We can't know for sure his brief moments of joy between those events, but surely flushing shots and representing his nation would have been among them, not to mention piano dance parties at the Bunn family house.

We were where he once was, and I was moved.

And that was it. Or so I thought. After my two guides headed off for lunch, because the sun was still high, I went off to walk a few holes at Shinnecock, if only to take in those storied hills and catch my breath. To breathe the deep breath that attends the end of a journey. Perhaps I'd catch a glimpse of the spirits of the place, so I slipped between the aluminum rails of a side entrance along St. Andrews Road and walked alongside the 15 hole: named Sebonac, a 409-yard par four. I was accompanied by the sound of some children laughing and playing in the Southampton Montessori School, and while I didn't have my clubs—and being quite expert at errant golf balls—I began a quick search in the oomska at the edge of the fairway for a souvenir.

Sure enough, I soon found a monogrammed Pro V1 ("LGM": I found your ball.) And shortly after that, I saw something more curious in the dirt: just beneath some sort of gorse bush, the top of a ball peeking out of the grass and mud. At first just the size of a dime, and I could make out the muddied dimples. Out of curiosity, I began to dig around it. More of a job than I expected, the thing was packed into the muddy earth like an old stone. Not to be discouraged, I took to it with my heel, then dug with my hand. After that brief struggle, and taking on farmer's fingernails, I pulled that dirty sphere out of the ground. I cleaned it off and did a little research with my phone: I had found a ball from from the 1940s. No brand name. Just a red number 2 and the words on both side of the ball, in a black cursive—"Sweet Shot." Sweet shot! It wasn't my eagle feathers, but I now held in my hand what in all my golfing life I'd longed for! A finer souvenir than a flask or a bone.

I looked up and saw I was alone and had no witness, at least in the short term. And of course I took this to be a message from the spirit world. Was it Oscar? Elmer? Charley? The Dunns? I had yet to earn my headress, so perhaps it was too forward of me to know what spirit had left that 80-year-old ball there for me to find. At the same time, that dirty sphere had been witness to at least four U.S. Opens and a thousand-thousand hacker's rounds. If I put it to my ear, what story would it tell me?

I am sure my readers will forgive me for thinking that ball had the ancestor's handiwork all over it. And Oscar's. Along with the lemonade and hot dogs he'd bought for his niece, along with his hard work building Shinnecock Hills, and his patience in teaching the least violent and most difficult game in human history, in the Adirondacks and in Florida, in Connecticut and Argentina, he'd become my hero and spirit guide, his family and his people my friends.

Oscar was the ancestor who guided me as I studied the

history of our First People in golf, and as I dusted off that ball, I began to think of the whole spirit of the place to be infused with his sweet will, and—with deference to Downtown Freddie Brown—I have begun to refer to him in my internal dialogues as Oscar "Sweet Shot" Bunn.

It's fairly well known that many traditions of our First people say we form as a spirit first, as an essence, before taking a form on earth, whether that form be eagle or crow, turtle or coyote, human or tree. I flipped Sweet Shot up in the air a few times and laughed: When we pass from this world, we return to the essence, to something better, or something more powerful and more loving.

No one has ever come back from the spirit world to confirm any of this, but our First People have a way of seeing the world that allows us to live in the uncertainty of these concepts, to stand in the I-Don't-Know as a way to honor the living and the dead. The things that cannot be deciphered, the lifetimes burning in every moment, these may be the spirit world, pressing into our living world, all within the continuum of memory, and of escape from the great sorrowing river of history, and as an entry into a certain awakening of a greater understanding. Where it's never not beautiful, let Oscar walk among the unforgotten.

Golf is just one way to understand the past and present, the land and sky, this world and what lies beyond, each other and ourselves. The memories and voices—these oral histories—they are offered here as a means to simply tell the truth about the past. And if the gossamer strings of the universe are real—if life and light and ideas drift through space along invisible webs and vibrations—it makes sense the story of golf in our nation begins Out East and with our First People.

However ironic that the first golf pro and clubmaker born in this beautiful land was a Brown man who played in two opens before he could even be considered a citizen of the U.S., let it make sense that it ends with a Sweet Shot.

Oscar's story and spirit have steered me to the voices and

stories and histories contained here. And that shot of sweetness from our First People is for all of us who love history and golf, to have the hope that the better angels of our nature will prevail in all things, all in good time.

Part 4

GOLFING ON TURTLE ISLAND

A GUIDE TO NATIVE-OWNED COURSES

> "You can hardly call us wealthy," a Cow Creek Band attorney offered. "But before the advent of gaming, you certainly could call us destitute. Now, we're just in a position where we feel like maybe we've got a chance."
>
> "It's about our dignity. Regardless of what our tribe does upon recognition, it will never be all about gaming. ... We know who we are, and we will never be less than that."
> —Walter Vickers, Hassanamisco Nipmuc Nation

Impossible? Just a matter of time

The 8th hole at Blackstone National in Sutton, Massachusetts is both fetching and vexing. The elevated, scallop-shaped tee boxes, from red to black, sit under some stately oaks and pines. The high view of this Rees Jones design (1999) takes in the native forest of maples and oaks and pines down to a red maple swamp. A golfer could be forgiven for admiring the surroundings and taking a breather before attempting a drive. A reasonable player will aim straight out, skirting the fairway trap on the right that also sets the elbow of the dogleg. Beyond the trap, the hole features a sharp dogleg right. The riskier player may try to cut the corner with a cloud-scraper, over the sand trap and a stand of maple and oak. To land on a narrow strip of fairway anywhere between 180 and 120 yards from a well-guarded hole, it can be done, though it's also a good example of a golf hole that proves Pete Dye's assertion: the woods are filled with long drivers.

In September 2022, two Holy Cross collegiate golfers took the risk on the 8th at Blackstone. Christian Emmerich—a senior—went first and pumped his drive over the trap and trees, landing 180 yards from a two-tiered green. Owen Egan—a sophomore—followed and after a mammoth drive up and over the forested corner, Egan had just 120 yards for his approach.

In a stunning moment of golf history, both Emmerich and Egan holed out on back-to-back shots—two double eagles on the same hole on back-to-back shots! Up to this point, there was no existing record in golf history of back-to-back double eagles.

If you had come out of those woods that September day and declared to your mates that, on the dogleg right, 500-yard par five, two teenage golfers had back-to-back albatrosses, your mates might call for the wagon to take you away. You'd be like the character of Pip, the tambourine boy on the ill-fated Pequod in Melville's *Moby Dick*. Pip falls into the deeps and there saw—among many other wonders and vastness—God's foot on the treadle of the universe's loom. When he got back to the ship after his tour of the deep, his ship mates thought he'd gone mad.

Alas for Pip, visions of the divine will always be contended; Christian and Owen have merely done what has never before been recorded and seem to have proven again that the impossible is just what shall be done. A lot of sports remind us of this—seemingly impossible events made possible. The perfect game. Back-to-back no hitters. The sub-two-hour marathon. We are able to conceive, describe, and sometimes even achieve impossibilities.

Getting home in 54? Just a matter of time.

For those of us who have been through basic training, you learn the training slogan of the Ordnance Department of the Army before tossing a grenade and setting a claymore: "The possible we do immediately. The impossible will take a little longer." Not in any way shape or form original, the slogan is drawn from a long history that appears to have begun in 18th-century French literature, and it's as fine an expression of hope as human fancy gets: the impossible is something that can and shall be done.

Our knowledge of possible worlds is often based on notions of safety or sensitivities, the appearance of reasonableness. The problem with this is that dwelling in these notions of the possible means we are living our limitations. Most of us have been schooled on the phrases like, "not gonna happen" and "it'll never fly, Gulliver." In the possible world, back-to-back double eagles will never happen. We stay in the safety of possibilities and avoid the logical complexities of imagining the Impossible.

On the other hand, Impossible Worlds is a concept that suggests this instinct for limitations is temporary, a kind of conceptual blindness to the future. Imagining Impossible Worlds is a useful tool of hope and future discovery. Think: Jetsons video phone. Think a surgeon in New York City operating remotely on a child for life saving surgery 5,000 miles away. In sport and technology and television shows, maybe even in our longing for peace and prosperity in a warring world, The Impossible is only a matter of time, and our imaginations are—in Einstein's most famous quote—more important than knowledge.

Knowledge is limited. Imagination engenders new worlds. Of course, the theory of relativity explains a larger world than the world of golf does, but the point is that there are numerous positives to imagining a parallel reality where back-to-back double eagles—or, for that matter a hole-in-one worth $10,000—are possibilities. To live there is to live in an enchanted world, separate from the limiting stories we tell ourselves about the world.

While recovery of our First People might seem like a similar impossibility, on a much larger scale than back-to-back double eagles, we have begun to see a shift in epistemes, changes in culture and economy, and golf is a part of that. In 1992, Oneida Nation of Wisconsin (Laura Kellogg's ancestral tribe) announced it employed more workers in Green Bay County than the Green Bay Packers. By 2017, a St. Norbert College study determined the tribe's overall impact on the economy in Brown and Outagamie Counties estimated the Oneida tribe's businesses, events and members—which include the magnificent Thornberry golf course—directly contribute $494 million and sustain 3,616 jobs annually. When indirect spending is factored in, the totals rise to $744 million and 5,465 jobs.

The Indian Gaming Regulatory Act (IGRA), passed by the US Congress in 1988, was the earthquake, the watershed in the history of policymaking directed toward reservation-resident American Indians. IGRA set the stage for tribal government-owned gaming facilities. It also shaped how this new industry would develop and how tribal governments would invest gaming revenues. Since then, Indian gaming (the casinos and bingo halls owned by tribal governments in the United States are also sometimes referred to as tribal gaming or tribal government gaming) has approached commercial, state-licensed gaming in total revenues.

While the courts have long held that Indians have a right under the Constitution to govern themselves—from Laura Kellogg to today—having that right without adequate economic resources has been a hollow dream. The golf industry has been part of that change. Before golf became part of indigenous culture, you would never have seen a quote like this one from Notah Begay lll: "That's my message to young kids: you don't have to choose one or the other. You can still maintain your culture and identity as American Indian—your practices, your beliefs, your faith—and be successful in the modern business world. It's not a one-or-the-other choice."

As of year-end 2013, one commercial directory identified 468 open Indian gambling establishments in 31 states. Indian gaming has allowed marked improvements in several important dimensions of reservation life and the joys and suffering of golf is part of that. Annual Indian gaming revenues increased from about $100 million in 1988 to $28 billion dollars in 2013. Among the most successful of these endeavors, at the end of 2017, the Mashantucket Pequot Reservation (MPTN) employed 9,702 people as follows: Foxwoods and other tribal enterprises such as the Rees Jones designed Lake of Isles Golf Courses employed 6,772. An additional 2,386 people worked in non-tribal retail stores and restaurants on the reservation. If it were a single entity, the combined employment—of MPTN government operations, Foxwoods and other tribal enterprises, and the other businesses located at Foxwoods—would rank 8th in Connecticut, between the University of Connecticut and Wal-Mart.

Jonathan Taylor runs the Harvard Project on American Indian Economic Development. His many studies underscore this finding: "Economic development spurred by gaming revenue has for some tribes resulted in return migration and economic and civic resurgence."

Annual Indian gaming revenues increased from about $100 million in 1988 to $28 billion in 2013 (National Indian Gaming Commission 2014; Senate Committee on Indian Affairs, 1988). The number of tribal gaming operations swelled from fewer than 30 to about 450, across 31 states. In this same time frame, the number of Native-owned golf courses has grown from zero to +/- 55. Our First People are getting in on a very big game.

One Economic Impact Study, commissioned by the American Golf Industry Coalition and conducted by the National

Golf Foundation in 2022, notes that in addition to the almost $102 billion in direct impact on the U.S. economy, golf's indirect and secondary impacts bring that total to over $226 billion. The game of golf enables over 1.65 million jobs, including more than one million directly tied to the industry.

As one example among many, it should come as no surprise that one of the most economically successful tribes in American history—the Shakopee Mdewakanton Sioux Community—purchased Lone Pine Country Club in 2002. The course was completely remodeled, and then reopened in late summer 2005 as The Meadows at Mystic Lake. The golf course has since drawn numerous awards and recognitions. While the course might be seen as a loss leader, being that in Minnesota golf is a five-month season, this arrangement points to success stories that speak to what is to come. Golf has woven its way into Native culture, and the result has been a new generation of golfers, teachers, and golf industry workers among our First People.

If you recall, at that first Society of American Indians in 1911, Laura Kellogg said, "I am not the new Indian; I am the old Indian adjusted to new conditions." She saw as early as 1911 that cultural continuity, not removal or assimilation or forced schooling, would be essential for survival. Political and economic adaptation might help ravaged reservation communities, and that is certainly shown to be the case with Indian Gaming and Golf Resorts.

What follows is a glossary of Native-owned courses on reservations. As of this writing, no one alive has played them all. But let's imagine for a moment a world in which a tourism company announces a package: Golfing on Turtle Island—Play the Trail of No Tears—where all time and money and efforts go toward honoring the tribes and playing their courses. (In addition to finally losing the slice.)

Impossible? It's just a matter of time.

THE SOUTHWEST

Talking Stick Golf Club
Salt River Pima-Maricopa Indian Community
Scottsdale, AZ
talkingstickgolfclub.com

Bill Coore cannot answer the question about what is the most timeless of his course design work with Ben Crenshaw. "People ask us all the time," he says. "There is no answer. We've had such wonderful opportunities. But then I think about it. Talking Stick had the least potential of any site we've worked on. Zero qualities for golf, and yes, there's now two courses. Parking lot is full every day. There's a huge amount of repeat play. When you look at that, well, if you consider it that way, when you start with zero potential and then, that garners consideration."

Coore and Crenshaw have done two courses for tribal communities. Bill Coore is careful to point out that they worked primarily with construction firms, and not directly with the tribes, but that the idea of land as sacred came through at both sites.

"Land is such a part of their heritage. ... It seems to be that no matter which tribe we worked with, to protect the sacredness of the land, that's not just a perspective, that was to be part of the operations of the golf course. That's been the case in our designs."

Salt River Pima Maricopa community consists of two tribes, the Pima and Maricopa and they are proud of their ancient practices with water, including an intricate canal irrigation system, this would feature prominently in bringing desert golf to fruition at Talking Stick.

"Talking Stick was a giant, sand parking lot," he notes. So

as far as transformation of a site, Talking Stick is not only a source of pride, but also destination golf and more.

"We get kidded about doing elite courses, but we've done a bit of public-access golf. Talking Stick gets a lot of repeat play. The parking lot is always full, and it's local folks as well."

Roy Smith, GM at Talking Stick, makes a similar point, including the fact that the Salt River Pima-Maricopa Indian community members have their own league as well, with as many as 60 tribe members taking part.

Smith is currently overseeing a renovation of the clubhouse, which will feature an event space and a permanent exhibition of the tribal philosophies, which will include this statement: "The O'oodahm and Piipash have called this land home since time immemorial. Our ancestors created an intricate system and welcomed visitors from all directions and taught settlers how to live off the land. The Salt River Indian Community continues to thrive and the inspirations for its decisions are its young and its elders."

Bill Coore was thankful that the Salt River community let them do their work.

"There was never a directive. ... The primary focus was never real estate and development was never a consider-

Talking Stick (Courtesy Arnold Palmer Golf)

ation. The idea was to bring interesting golf that our hotel and casino customers would come for. My personal sense is that Talking Stick through the years has become so appealing for different reasons, to local citizens as well as the tourists. ... In both instances [Talking Stick and nearby We-Ko-Pa], the tribal communities allowed us to focus on the golf. "

The club is also one of the Valley's top locations for golf instruction. The First Tee of Phoenix has a chapter at the club—the first of its kind on tribal land in Arizona and only the second in the entire U.S. The club is also home to Vision54, the golf instructional company whose method is based on two sets of fundamentals: the technical and the human.

Cocopah RV and Golf Resort
The River People
Yuma, Arizona
cocopahrv.com

The Cocopah are also called the River People and have lived along the lower Colorado River for centuries. Unlike many of the tribes during the forced removal era, the Cocopah persevered in place, though not without surrendering land during the rapid growth in the west between 1865 and 1925, when railroads and homesteads and towns popped up and confined Native peoples to bounded reservations. Cocopah has existed since 1917, now covering approximately 6,500 acres with about 1,000 tribal members living and working there.

Situated along the Colorado River near Yuma, Arizona, the Cocopah Golf Course rests on a gentle lay of land and is considered an easy walk for golfers. The course is narrow and demands accuracy, but is also fair and rewarding to players of all levels. Water and bunkers are blended with doglegs and narrow fairways, and the course's three par threes are some of the best in the southwest. The par-73, 18-hole course measures 5,731 yards from the back tees. Three sets of tees are available to accommodate varying levels of play. The signature hole is the par-five 18th, a 502-yard hole that requires the utmost accuracy, as it is guarded by water on the right and boundary limits on the left.

Here's some advice, from local players: "Golf course tricks and turns are the exception at Cocopah, where straight and narrow fairways are signature. The back nine offers more of a challenge both in length and shot selection, with two finishing holes that can make or break a round."

Inn of the Mountain Gods Golf Course

Mescalero Apache Tribe

Mescalero, NM

innofthemountaingods.com

The Mescalero Apache Tribe were once nomadic hunters and gatherers, excelling in guerrilla warfare and horseback riding. But as the Era of Contact and Discovery reached New Mexico, the tribe's mountainous lands provided cover.

James S. Calhoun was appointed as the first territorial governor of New Mexico and the first Indian agent in 1849. In the census of 1850, he bemoaned the task of having to oversee various tribes, including the Navajos, Apache, Utes, Comanches, and peaceful Pueblo and Hopi Indians. The Mescalero Apache had no interest in surrendering their lands. They now claim one of the most picturesque golf courses in the U.S. The course is located in the Lincoln National Forest, a destination surrounded by pine, cottonwood, and aspen trees, designed by golf course architect Ted Robinson.

While it has received numerous accolades such as *Golf Digest*'s Top 40 Casino Courses and *Golfweek*'s Top Courses You Can Play, Inn of the Mountain Gods Championship Golf Course is accessible for all skill levels. Open from early April through late October, the course can be played for much of the year, in one of the most spectacular parts of the country.

Isleta Golf Club

Pueblo of Isleta
Albuquerque, NM
isleta.com/golf

In 1599, Spanish Conquistador Juan de Onate wrote, "It would be an endless story to attempt to describe in detail each one of the many things that are found there." The Pueblo Peoples have a reputation for diversity, resourcefulness, and peacefulness, though de Onate would organize a massacre and create the conditions that would lead to the Pueblo Revolt of 1680: a moment in history still spoken of today. Thankfully, the Pueblo reservations have been peaceful, with golf occupying many pieces of land.

Isleta Golf Club is a 27-hole resort course designed and built by William Phillips in 1996. Each nine—Mesa, Lakes, and Arroyo—is designed around the clubhouse and sit west of the Isleta Resort and Casino.

Sandia Golf Club

Pueblo of Sandia
Albuquerque, NM
sandiacasino.com/golf

The Pueblo Relief Bill (1933) and the Indian Reorganization Act (1934) were laws drafted by New Dealers in the 1930s—John Collier in particular—which would shift land policies and validate land claims throughout the country. In particular, the Fee-to-Trust regulations implement a provision in the 1934 Indian Reorganization Act (IRA) that allows the Secretary of the Interior to take lands into trust on behalf of federally recognized tribes or individual Indians. The Final Rule governs four types of land acquisitions that regulations will govern: 1) on-reservation; 2) contiguous; 3) off-reservation; and 4) initial acquisitions. Collier and others more than likely would not foresee this as benefitting the game of golf, but there it is: these Fee-to-Trust programs have enabled some tribes to get land back without lengthy court proceedings. In fact, the new Fee-to-Trust Rule that was published in the Federal Register and took effect on January 11, 2024 promises to speed the process by which tribes, bands, and nations can regain land.

Sandia, Santa Ana, Twin Warrior, and Cochiti are some of the golf courses that now populate the Black Mesa and the majestic Sandia Mountains.

Sandia was designed by Scott Miller in 2005 and offers 7,772 yards of grassy knolls, sparkling waterfalls, and landscapes of native plants and trees. Long-range views of surrounding mountains include the Sandia, which turns a watermelon hue for about 15 minutes every evening.

Sewailo Golf Club
Pascua Yaqui Tribe
Tucson, AZ
casinodelsol.com/sewailo-golf-club

Designed by Notah Begay III, Sewailo blends tribal wisdom with the natural beauty of the Sonoran Desert. Respect for the land was a consistent theme at the groundbreaking. "You cannot just come in, fire up a bunch of bulldozers and start changing the landscape. You have to be able to first talk to the land and ask for permission," says tribal chairman Peter Yucupicio. "We ask our Creator and the ground, the trees, the rocks—God put you here for a reason and we're going to change you a little bit, but all the things we're doing here are for everyone's benefit—the tribe, all of Tucson, all of Southern Arizona."

When the course opened in late 2012, Begay was on hand for a deer dancer, who came out of nearby desert shrubbery to dance and bless the grounds. This is Begay's third golf course design, about which he said, "These projects start from the standpoint of culture, and it's important we maintain and respect the culture and traditions of the communities we work with. As with all projects I work on, based on the teachings of my mother and grandmother, I ask for guidance from our Creator as we shape these holes."

We-Ko-Pa Golf Club
(Saguaro, Cholla)
Fort McDowell Yavapai Nation
Fort McDowell, AZ
wekopa.com

As Bill Coore has noted, he and his partner Ben Crenshaw have worked on two golf courses on Native land. He notes that, even before he had put a shovel in the ground, We-Ko-Pa possessed all the gifts that nature could bestow. For this, We-Ko-Pa is more a tourist destination golf course than, for instance, Talking Stick, which has a steady stream of local players. *We-Ko-Pa* is the Yavapai word for "Four Peaks Mountain," which rises to create an imposing skyline to the northeast.

Coore and Ben Crenshaw designed We-Ko-Pa's second 18, the Saguaro golf course. It opened in December 2006 and featured design elements not commonly found in the desert southwest. Saguaro is much like the older more traditional courses found on the east coast, where greens are close to tees and the course follows the natural movement of the land making walking easy and enjoyable.

A stunning natural beauty appears on all of the holes, which are routed around tall seguaro cacti. Throughout one's round, players are greeted with all sorts of amazing light displays, as the shadows that are cast by the interplay of sun and mountains approach the artistic. At sunset, the colors and textures approach the surreal.

The Cholla course, designed by Scott Miller, offers a fun test, with wide fairways, where one always knows where the danger lies. The contouring is a bit more pronounced on this course, giving players options in surrounding green areas.

Both courses at We-Ko-Pa are routinely recognized among the best public courses in Arizona.

Ak-Chin Southern Dunes
Ak-Chin
Maricopa, AZ
akchinsoutherndunes.com

You would be forgiven if you snickered a bit driving down the John Wayne Memorial Highway toward Ak-Chin Southern Dunes, a Brian Curley work of art in the desert outside Maricopa. You'd also be forgiven if you skipped the trip to The Duke, a course with a logo containing gun handles and with clubhouse walls that contained pictures of Hollywood star John Wayne, shooting what look to be American Indians.

At one point, Troon Golf considered purchasing The Duke, though they thought better. "It would need a bit of re-branding," Brady Wilson says with an understated smile.

Wilson is the GM at Ak-Chin, which is run by the Troon Golf organization. He notes that Ak-Chin Southern Dunes is more the varsity course in Maricopa. "The Duke Course, he noted, is more junior varsity."

The course has a somewhat curious story, and is unique among Native American courses, as the Ak-Chin tribe did not build the course, but rather purchased it after its sputtering start. Private interests built as an all-male club for the sports stars in the Phoenix area. They didn't even have women employees, and brought in John Daly, among others, to the opening of what they thought would resemble other all-male golf clubs. It changed hands four times between 2001 and 2010, when Troon and the tribe worked together to secure a Fee-to-Trust (FTT) land acquisition, also called "land into trust" transfer: a land title to be held in trust for the benefit of an Indigenous individual or tribe. Bingo. In 2010, this Brian Curley course was saved.

Wilson hails the working relationship between Troon

and the tribe, and says its success is due to consistency and longevity in leadership. The course has a staff of 88, selected from the 1,000 members of the Ak-Chin reservation. Known for being one of the more challenging courses in the southwest desert, it hosts the PGA Q-School every year, the University of Wyoming tournaments, the Copper Cup between the University of Arizona and Arizona State University, and many other events. Wilson notes that Curley's design has the 9th and 18th greens come in to meet the 1st and the 10th tees. The design makes for smooth flow of tournament golf.

Santa Ana Golf Club
Santa Ana Pueblo
Santa Ana Pueblo, NM
mynewmexicogolf.com

This course was designed by Ken Killian and Ken Green and opened in 1991. Visiting Santa Ana for the Native American Open, sitting on a patio with Jay Garcia and Larry Pasqual, I asked about competition from the other nearby Pueblo resorts.

"We are the standard," Mr. Garcia said. And given the Native American Open for the past four years, there's a reason Santa Ana Golf Club can make that claim.

And then there is nearby Twin Warriors Golf Course, designed by Gary Panks. The inhabitants of Santa Ana Pueblo have long believed their ancestors were visited by Twin Warriors who showed them the path to the Upper World along the banks of the Rio Grande. Here the tribe has remained, endured, and added golf in the new century. The Twin Warriors are invoked before competitions, such as the 2022 Senior PGA Professional Championship, and the second Women's PGA Cup—a prestigious international event—that was also contested there in 2022. The 2023 PGA Professional Championship was held here in May 2023, and the inaugural National Car Rental 17-and-under PGA Junior League Championship in November 2023.

Both courses offer desert golf, where the ball carries farther and the visuals alone are worth the trip.

Pueblo Cochiti Golf Club
Cochiti Pueblo
Cochiti Lake, NM
cochitigolfclub.com

One of Robert Trent Jones II's earliest high desert designs, Pueblo de Cochiti Golf Course is an 18-hole public golf course located in Cochiti Lake, New Mexico. Being conveniently located between Albuquerque and Santa Fe, it makes for a must play. The Pueblo de Cochiti Golf Course is consistently ranked as one of the best golf courses in the state. To go along with the fantastic layout of the course, it's nestled in the beautiful high desert terrain of northern New Mexico. After your round, take in the views at the Stone Kiva Bar and Grill. It's not hard to see why this place is called "Heaven with a Zip Code."

Cochiti in New Mexico (courtesy of Robert Trent Jones II Golf)

THE SOUTHEAST

Oscar Smith Bunn and John Shippen played in the first U.S. Open held south of the Mason-Dixon line, at Roland Park in Baltimore in 1899. Neither finished in the money, though the Park family was there in the person of James Park, and somewhere along the line, Oscar would form a working relationship with Mungo Park ll. They would sail together to Argentina to build one of its first golf courses, near Buenos Aires. Shippen, as we know, became a golf pro in New Jersey. He played in five U.S. Opens, and after his start in 1913, no man—Black or Native—played in the U.S. Open until Ted Rhodes in 1948.

For this and many other reasons, the South plays a key role in our golf history. In 1899, when Bunn and Shippen played in Baltimore, no one could have predicted what the golf gods had in store for the southlands. Pinehurst was still a pine barren in 1899, and the long pains of Reconstruction and the implementation of Jim Crow laws would have been fresh. Nevertheless, by the 1940s and '50s, hundreds of thousands of Americans would be moving to warmer climes and would drive interest in year-round play of the most difficult—and least violent—game in human history. Our First People would follow suit in time by building some of the finest courses in the country in places that, like Oscar Bunn's Shinnecock, were also some of the nicest places to live.

Sequoyah National Golf Club
Eastern Band of Cherokee
Whittier, NC
sequoyahnational.com

In 1838, the Cherokee—along with the Seminoles, Creeks, Chickasaw, and Choctaw—were marched along the aptly named but also misnamed Trail of Tears to Tahlequah, Oklahoma. The word tears is correct, but there was more than one trail, and, as noted, some of the tribes resisted and remained. Some made it to Oklahoma and then walked back home. Others are descended from Cherokee who managed to keep land they owned and did not march west. Sequoyah National Golf Club occupies a kind of hinge of land where history live and where most of the routes of the Trail of Tears converged, if only briefly. Here the Eastern Band of the Cherokee—the one of three Cherokee tribes—had managed to purchase land. (The other two Bands occupy reservation land in Oklahoma.)

And as witnessed by Shinnecock Hills, We-Ko-Pa, and many other Native owned courses, the EBCI selected some of the finest places on earth to build their course. Oak- and fir-filled and flowered valleys in the heart of the Great Smoky Mountains make up their forever home. To this they added a Robert Trent Jones II design.

Sequoyah National Golf Club in North Carolina

"Golf course design is an artform," Jones II had said. "There are so little rules. I mean, there are the five elements of defense. Length-width, vertical-horizontal. Fine tuning around short game. Compositional mode. All those are in a structural sense. My drawings have arrows, and I am showing the shape of how I want them to drain. But I don't use a formulaic approach."

Jones feels that the greats—his father among them—were great because of their routing, and Tillinghast was the best of all on how to use land in a sequence.

"He makes you look forward to the next hole. Great golf courses are collaborative: the land, the golfer's eye, the designer. A composition and collaboration, like an orchestra that is playing the land." Robert Trent Jones II continues: "I walk the land, feel it through the soles of my feet. The land itself is teaching me as a walk it. I feel it through a golfer's prism. Using all the senses, six senses."

This relation to the land might explain why the Eastern Band of the Cherokee have embraced the course and the sport.

According to Brad Adams of Kemper Sports, the organization that runs the facility, Cherokee members here have been playing golf for decades, maybe half a century. Sequoyah did not open until 2009, so most played at Lake Junaluska's course and perhaps Maggie Valley.

The course is used heavily by members of the tribe, with a tribal specific membership, and heavily discounted rounds for any card-carrying EBCI member. Three of the area high school golf teams practice here (Cherokee, Swain County, and Smoky Mountain High). There are usually a few tribal members that attend the latter two. The junior camps and clinics work with organizations like the Cherokee Children's' Home, and the course regularly hosts fundraisers for EBCI causes, where many members of the community gather at the course for a day.

Some of the tribes walked on. The Eastern Band of the Cherokee knew home when they saw it. The result includes the stunning Sequoyah National.

Dancing Rabbit
Mississippi Band of Choctaw Indians
Philadelphia, MS
dancingrabbitgolf.com

Long before Tiger Woods, legendary golf writer Bernard Darwin had said, "It is today an accepted principle of golfing architecture that the tiger should be teased and trapped and tested, while the rabbit should be left to peace, since he can make his own hell for himself."

What then to make of Dancing Rabbit?

Built upon the ancestral lands of the Mississippi Band of Choctaw Indians, Dancing Rabbit Golf Club, which includes two 18-hole courses, The Azaleas and The Oaks, is a celebration of their rich culture, as well as their perseverance. A masterpiece from renowned course creators, Tom Fazio, and former tour pro Jerry Pate, Dancing Rabbit Golf Club features two championship golf courses: The Azaleas and The Oaks. Both stunning courses are 7,000-yard masterpieces carved out of the dramatic valleys, ancient pines, and hardwoods that define an ecological wonderland.

Featuring many elevation changes with greens that are

Waterfalls on the Azealea course, at Dancing Rabbit in Mississippi.

large, undulating and fast, the challenging Oaks Course has proven to be a favorite among golfers of all skill levels. Its beauty is cradled in the same rustic landscape as The Azaleas, but The Oaks offers golfers a completely different look. The fairways cut through the pine forest and several holes require players to carry over water.

Dancing Rabbit Golf Club commemorates one of the most popular assembly grounds on the ancient Choctaw tribal lands. It is named for its location on the banks of the Big and Little Dancing Rabbit Creeks not many miles distant from the clubhouse. In the Choctaw language it is Bok Chukfi Ahithac ("the creek where rabbits dance"). It was like a well-tended park–beautiful, spacious–beneath a canopy of mature trees.

It is ironic that in September 1830, the tribe was stripped of its dominion over its ancestral land by a treaty that was forced on them at the site. The old Choctaw nation was removed to Indian Territory, now Oklahoma, from which favorite son Orville Moody would win the U.S. Open in 1969.

Koasati Pines at Coushatta

Coushatta Tribe of Louisiana

Kinder, LA

coushattacasinoresort.com/golf

When Maddison Long and Zachary BlueEyes travelled to Koasati Pines in Fall 2023, the name of Notah Begay was their guide and support, along with their parents. Maddison's mother, Kristi notes that that support began with her father.

"We hold our elders in high regard. They are the ones who persevered so we can be here." This writer has heard those words several times while travelling to many Native-owned courses, and nowhere is this more apparent than with the rise of a youth movement in Native golfers.

That type of parental support followed Maddison to Koasati Pines and Coushatta Casino Resort, which partnered with Notah Begay III to host the Inaugural Junior Golf National Championship. This prestigious tournament, held annually in November, features the nation's best junior golfers.

This is fitting in many ways. Despite Hollywood depictions, many of our First People sought to avoid warfare and maintain a position of peaceful warriors, with the family at the center of their cultures. Such is the case of the Koasati. In the late 18th century, the Coushatta chief Stilapihkachatta, or "Red Shoes," led a group of followers to Spanish Louisiana and, in the spring of 1804, another group of 450 Coushattas joined them in the territory. Over the next several decades, the Coushattas moved their villages from place to place, crossing the Red, Sabine, and Trinity rivers: tributaries of the mighty Mississippi.

The serenity of gently rolling terrain and 65 acres of looking-glass lakes submerge players in a relaxing, yet challenging, golf experience. Immaculate greens extend a velvet invitation that is impossible to ignore. At 7,617 yards from the championship tees, it is one of the longest public courses in Louisiana.

Kristi Daniels-Long was there when Maddison competed in the Junior Golf National Championship. She had this to say: "My Pop's always taught me that when I am playing sports, I am representing my family, tribe and all Native people. I have instilled this also in my children. It is hard being a minority playing golf, and I told my girls that someone is always watching so there is no crying in golf, until you get to the car or at home. I am hoping that what I have been taught through my traditions that my kids will teach their kids."

Tamahka Trails Golf Club

The Tunica-Biloxi Tribe

Marksville, LA

tamahkatrails.com

Named after the Tunica-Biloxi word for "alligator," the Steve Smyers-designed golf course sits on a beautiful 230-

acre tract of rolling terrain. It has hosted U.S. Open qualifiers three times. The tribe's interests extend beyond recreation as well.

The Tunica-Biloxi Tribe of Louisiana is well known for an annual pow-wow, held on the Tunica-Biloxi reservation in Marksville, one that welcomes various regional Indigenous tribes to celebrate culture through vibrant craft displays, music performances, dance presentations, and cultural exhibits. An assortment of interactive events and live performances throughout the weekend aim to highlight the history and traditions of the tribe. Not only does this cultural event celebrate the traditions of the Tunica-Biloxi Tribe, but also neighboring tribes from across the region, who are invited to share their own culture and heritage alongside Tunica-Biloxi citizens.

2024's rendition of the pow-wow also celebrates advancements by the tribe. This past year, the Tunica-Biloxi Tribe hosted U.S. Department of the Interior Secretary Deb Haaland to its reservation; was also awarded a $6.4 million grant to provide new, affordable housing for tribal families; and members of tribal leadership were selected to serve on numerous federally appointed boards and committees with the hopes of amplifying the Tunica-Biloxi mission and the goals of Indian Country nationwide.

Miccosukee Golf and Country Club
Miccosukee Tribe
Miami, FL
miccosukeegolf.com

The Miccosukee Tribe in Florida has run Miccosukee Golf and Country Club (formerly Kendall Lakes Golf Course) since 2001. Speaking with Curtis Osceola, the chief of staff of tribal government, he acknowledges the Miccosukee were among the first in other areas, including U.S. government recognition.

"It is a unique story," Mr. Osceola begins. "The U.S. government did not want to recognize the tribe. They thought we were subdivision of Seminole. But we are and always have been a separate, distinct tribe. In 1961, our leader, Buffalo Tiger, flew down to Cuba just after the revolution and met with [Fidel] Castro and Che [Guevara]. We recognized their government, and they recognize us as a sovereign nation. It was an interesting political maneuver."

"Interesting" might be a understatement. When Buffalo Tiger and his entourage returned, the federal government recognized the Miccosukee tribe under two conditions: 1) Buffalo Tiger will never go back to Cuba, and 2) you can never set foot in the White House.

"That is a sort of a tribal legend," Mr. Osceola harumphs as he continues. "We were a disenfranchised community. A small and discreet minority, and we had to do something bold. So, yes, it is a source of pride ... for the sheer brass it took."

That brass can be seen in other ways. The tribe is known for having resisted the Trail of Tears and made a culture for itself in the sawgrass rivers and swamps called The Everglades,: one of the fiercest environments on the planet. Miccosukee adapted to living in small groups in camps on cypress tree islands. In this fashion, they kept to themselves for 100 years, resisting assimilation. From the pride of their recognition and their surviving in such an environment, the Miccosukee's deep history shapes their culture today.

In 2001, the tribe bought the Kendall Lakes Golf Courses. "Thank God the Miccosukee bought it," Jon Mahannah exclaims. "They put money into it." The course was designed by Jon's grandfather, Mark, whose journey as an architect began when he found his way onto the construction crew for William Flynn's project in Boca Raton. He was no snow bird. Born in Fort Lauderdale, after working on Flynn's projects, Mahannah would move on to become lead architect at Miami Biltmore Country Club, which he was hired to redesign. He moved to full-time practice in the early 1950s. During his time as a golf course architect, he learned to add style and drama to flat sites and integrate water as both a beautiful landscape and magnetic hazard. Mahannah would have been 68 when Miccosukee opened (originally Kendall Lakes Golf and Country Club), a late design considered by many to be his masterpiece.

THE MIDWEST

"Impossible worlds have no borders."
—Bertrand Russell

As noted earlier, Congress passed the Indian Reorganization Act in 1934, led by John Collier among others. This act formally affirmed Indian tribal self-governance and was intended to restore Indian self-determination and tribal culture. Perhaps not surprisingly, the U.S. government also adopted the Indian Termination and Indian Relocation policies, and this Janus-faced history stunted the practice of Indian self-government. In the 1950s, a number of strong leaders among the Ojibwe (i.e., Fred Jones and Jerry Martin of the Mille Lacs Band) courageously laid the groundwork for a modern era of successful tribal government. The upper Midwest would continue to provide models of both resistance to termination and relocation, as well as economic development, and this includes some of the country's finest golf courses.

Firekeeper Golf Course
Prairie Band Potawatomi Nation
Mayetta, KS
prairieband.com/golf/

If there is only one, why not make it the best? Along with Dancing Rabbit and Circling Raven, Firekeeper may be in the hunt for best name for an 18-hole loop. The organization, Everything Good about Kansas, is found here, and it's planning on adding a short course designed by Christine Fraser.

The current 18-hole layout by Jeff Brauer, former president of the ASGCA (1995-96), along with Notah Begay III, sits an hour west of Kansas City and 20 minutes north of Topeka.

Architect Jeff Brauer considers Firekeeper his best work,

noting the course traverses three distinct environments while creating minimal disturbance to the existing land. The course, which opened in 2012, is an endeavor of the Prairie Band Potawatomi Nation, and the tribe was very interested in preserving the character of the land, which Brauer feels he and Begay III managed. "But [the tribe's] main goal was to build a course that stands with the best in Kansas, which it seems most people think we also did, making it a very successful project for my firm."

Michael Powell, the professional who has been at Firekeeper since Day 1, suggests the course has generated a clientele that has changed the perceptions of the area and its tribal cultures.

"Gaming has been a source of financial resources to take care of each tribe's people," said Powell. A member of the Osage Nation, he also notes that Firekeeper sits on land toward the end of the Trail of Tears, and started as a bingo hall in the '90s. "A lot of tribes got shoved off into the middle of nowhere. Well, nowhere is now this beautiful golf course. A lot of nations have taken advantage of building top-tier resorts, and changing attitudes and the living conditions of our native people." The course added a 10-acre wildflower-pollinator garden, and are planning on adding the short course to better teach the game.

Firekeeper Golf Course, in Kansas. (courtesy of the Prairie Band of the Potawatomi)

Firekeeper joins 55+ tribal-owned courses, made possible in part by gaming. In addition to golf facilities such as Rees Jones' design at Dakota Ridge (the Lakota), and Lakes of Isles (the Mashantucket Pequot), Powell notes the Potawatomi nation in Kansas now includes a Boys and Girls Club, early childhood education center, a senior center, a functioning government, and a course that "sneaks up on you, how good it is."

He continues, "It's nice being part of the operation that invests in continuing to be great. I mean, let's face it, Reservations were not selected for deeds of access and prime real estate. But we've made something great. And we are fortunate that we are within a short drive of major metro areas, pulling from several populations there."

"When we first built, people viewed it as 'the Indian Casino.' There were negative connotations of the reservation, but then people came to see our property, and they saw how unique it is. In 13 years, the perception has changed considerably. And there're no houses around the course, and it will stay this way. The resort funds a lot of operations of a normal functioning government and culture."

Land with a capital 'L' is deeply embedded in Native cultures. Powell sees his role as golf operations, but also to be an ambassador for the community. "I want our course and staff to represent every tribal member. We strive to save on resources, to be more sustainable and responsible. When I hand it off, I want to say that I have been a good steward. The land is going to outlive us."

Dakota Winds Golf Course

Sisseton-Wahpeton Oyate Band

Hankinson, ND

dakotamagic.com/golf

As has been standard for this book, the word legend comes up in relation to folks that the golf world has yet to fully understand. Joe Prue, Orville and Michelle Moody, and to this list we should add Joel Goldstrand. Like fellow golf course architect Geoffrey Cornish, Goldstrand was known to work on a budget and was renowned for his feel for the land. And like Robert Trent Jones II, Goldstrand was known to love a lone tree as a part of the course's defense.

A vision for a course would appear in his head as he walked the land. Only later, he would put it on paper for others to see what he felt. Not fond of Macdonald-Raynor templates, he would get up on the machines himself. He worked in rural communities with the intension of growing a game for everyone.

The two courses at Dakota Winds—Sisseton and Wahpeton—are a reversible design adjacent to the Dakota Magic Casino & Resort. Golfers can play 18 holes one day and the next day play a different layout on the back nine. The course is affordable and fun to play.

Cherokee Hills Golf Club

Cherokee Nation

Catoosa, OK

hardrockcasinotulsa.com/golf

Perry Maxwell's name comes up in our story of Walter Acey Junior Hopper in Chapter 8. Maxwell was likely hired by the Osage during the Reign of Terror and designed a now-defunct course in Pawhuska, which featured sand greens.

Designed by Perry Maxwell in 1924, Cherokee Hills Golf Club is still very much alive and was renovated by Tripp Davis, who is known for his attention to the environmental impact of golf courses. The course has nurtured a tremendous array of golf talent, including many members of the tribe. Nearly forty percent of the 24,000 average annual rounds of golf played there are by members, and Cherokee Nation oversees golf operations.

The 18-hole course preserves Maxwell's trademark bunkering style and four of his original holes, as well as his uniquely placed tee boxes.

Cherokee Springs Golf Club
Cherokee Nation
Tahlequah, OK
cherokeecasino.com/tahlequah

Purchased by the Cherokee Nation in December 2012, Cherokee Springs Golf Club features 18 holes, as well as a driving range, putting green, pro shop, and on-site restaurant. The course's most famous hole is the par-five 6th, which requires two shots over ponds to reach the green. But that's not the only chance to get wet here: Cherokee Springs is littered with water hazards.

Cherokee Trails Golf Club
Cherokee Nation
Tahlequah, OK
cherokeecasino.com/tahlequah/

Every golf course has a story. This course was one of the first designs by a young Tripp Davis, who cites legendary Oklahoman golf course architect Perry Maxwell as a source of inspiration and ideas. And his story might sound familiar: After Davis was an NCAA All-American in 1989 on the University of Oklahoma golf team, he thought he could play professionally. But then, he writes, "I injured my shoulder, and it was a blessing in that I realized I really love to play the game, but making a living is another matter." That matter was golf course design. The most impactful courses for Davis have been Prairie Dunes, Winged Foot, and Pine Valley. You could call Cherokee Trails a diamond in the rough, except it is very much in the heart of Cherokee country, right beside Cherokee Casino in Tahlequah.

Eagle Creek Golf Club

Quapaw Tribe

Joplin, MO

downstreamcasino.com

The word Quapaw means "downstream," and the tribe has a long and complex history in relation to the vast river systems of the heartland. There are still many questions about the origins and migration patterns of the tribe. While these debates might not be resolved, the river and water play key roles: some archaeological evidence suggests the Quapaw are descended from the people of Pacaha and possibly the people of Casqui, both of whom claim immigration of their ancestors from the Ohio River Valley to the Arkansas River Valley.

And like the Seminole and Miccosukee, the Quapaw's nimble history seems to suggest they avoided the large nations and bands that walked the Trail of Tears and kept their camps. Quapaw's casino is in Oklahoma and their golf course is in Joplin, Missouri.

In 2008, building the Downstream Casino, the tribe also purchased Loma Linda Golf Course, which they renamed Eagle Creek. The original courses were designed by Tom Sturemen and first opened in 1989. Not surprisingly, water factors into 11 holes, with a creek trailing through the front nine. On the back nine, golfers reach higher ground with mature, tree-lined fairways.

It was Mark Twain who said that "golf is a good walk spoiled." We can only imagine he would forego the golf and head straight for the Downstream Casino Resort to try his hand at fortune (spoiler alert: he had terrible luck).

FireLake Golf Course

Shawnee Tribe

Shawnee, OK

firelakegolf.com

Water is a main player on defense at FireLake Golf course. The course is almost 33 years old; the tribe began its second phase of renovation in January 2016. Much is done to protect the 11 beautiful lakes and natural creek that cuts through the middle of the course. An endeavor of the Citizen Potawatomi Nation, which also runs a truck stop, two gas stations, two smoke shops, a bingo hall, two tribal casinos, FireLake Discount Foods in Shawnee, and First National Bank and Trust. Their estimated economic impact is $422.4 million.

FireLake Golf Course was originally designed by Donald Ray Sechrest, who designed more than 90 golf courses, mostly in the Midwest. He was a star at Oklahoma State University and played briefly on the PGA Tour.

WinStar Golf Course

Chickasaw Nation

Thackerville, OK

winstarworldcasino.com/golf

Chickasaw Nation runs a First American Youth program for any Chickasaw between 10-18 years of age, who has a citizenship card or CDIB card. The tournament is also a qualifying competition for the Team Chickasaw golf team. These tribe-specific programs play out on a course designed by Champions Tour player D.A. Weibring, and WinStar's 27-hole layout stretches across 280 acres of vast green in the Red River Valley.

Many of us will remember the song which originated from the Red River Rebellion of 1870. A Metis Native girl falls in love with an Anglo solider who comes to suppress the rebellion. Love knows no bounds.

The river is one of the few north-flowing streams on the North American continent, which would seem to be a real-world metaphor for the unique tribe that occupies its valley.

Our friend Beaman Wisdom plans a big Native golf tournament to go along with the tribe's nearby WinStar World Casino and Resort, which is the world's largest casino.

Dacotah Ridge Golf Club
Lower Sioux Indian Community
Morton, MN
dacotahridge.com

If my math is correct, the Jones boys— Robert Trent Jones II and Rees Jones—account for 10% of the designs of our First People's courses. Dacotah is Rees' layout, which its website brags is "far removed from the hustle and bustle of everyday life."

"Anything I can do to help the tribes, I'm willing to do," Rees Jones has said, noting that Dacotah Ridge and Lake of Isles are two of his designs at the heart of economic endeavors of First People.

The club hosts many Native golf events, including Pow-Wow Scramble and the Vet Pow-Wow Scramble each June. The course is cut into rugged prairieland, and Jones notes that its native fescue grasses were left to dance in the wind. Once renowned as "the Open doctor" for making corrections to major championship golf courses, Jones' Dacotah Ridge is a destination course for historians.

As far as the contest for best named casino? Hands down winner is the Lower Sioux's casino, Jackpot Junction. You may want to hit the tables before your round.

Grand National Golf Club

Mille Lacs Band of Ojibwe
Hinckley, MN
grandnationalgolf.com

The Mille Lacs Band of the Ojibwe call themselves the non-removable Mille Lacs Band. And from their website, it appears that golf will remain part of their culture when they post some of the happiest words in creation: "nine holes—walking: $22." This is not the land of the $170 round.

The Mille Lacs Band purchased the course in 2006. Originally a Joel Goldstrand design, the Band hired Herfort Norby in 2010 to complete the preparation of a master plan. Their motto of "Make Golf Fun Again" would seem a perfect phrase for the philosophy of Goldstrand as well. Grand National hugs ponds, marshes, and creeks just 90 minutes northwest of St. Paul.

The intrepid golf tourist will also want to see Norby's re-routing of Golden Valley, just outside St. Paul.

The Meadows at Mystic Lake

Shakopee Mdewakanton Sioux Community
Prior Lake, MN
golfthemeadows.com

The Shakopee Mdewakanton Sioux Community purchased Lone Pine Country Club in 2002. In 2003, the course was completely remodeled, and then reopened in late summer 2005 as The Meadows at Mystic Lake. The tribe selected the golf course architecture firm Paul Miller Design, based in Northfield, Minnesota, for the project.

Tribal Chair Keith Anderson said at the time: "Surrounded by acres of wildflowers and prairie plants with water on 13 holes, the Meadows is already a high-caliber golf course, and the design and maintenance of our course are second to none. We have an opportunity with these improvements to make our course even more unique and are excited to see these concepts realized."

Phil Wogan once said his course design work "combined a love of the land with empathy for those who would eventually play on it." The Meadows at Mystic Lake is a public golf course designed by Garrett Gill and Paul Miller that embodies Wogan's statement well. The duo of Gill and Miller addressed several environmental issues and reflected the cultural values of the local tribal community in preservation, protection, and enhancement of land, including the protection and preservation of surrounding wetlands. Mystic Lake opened 12 holes in 1970. Prospective members were offered a deal: bring back loose rocks (in a provided bag) and they can play for free.

Gill is a member of the American Society of Golf Course Architects (ASCGA), the American Society of Landscape Architects (ASLA), and the Tillinghast Association. (In 2024, he is renovating Indian Hills Golf Club.)

Paul Miller is known for many innovative designs, none more than his Snoopy Hole at Highland Park National Golf Course in St. Paul: a hole that pays homage to Charles Schultz, who caddied and learned to play golf at Highland National.

Mount Frontenac Golf Course
Prairie Island Indian Community
Frontenac, MN
mountfrontenac.com

Mount Frontenac was designed by George Emerson and opened in 1985. Prairie Island Indian Community purchased the course in March 2000, joining many other community enterprises. And herein lies a mystery for those who like to drop down rabbit holes: George Emerson was a dentist who eschewed the best practice of hiring a trained, experienced golf course architect and instead designed a compelling course of his own along the Mississippi River Bluffs and Lake Pepin. Overall, he designed 14 courses in the Minneapolis area. If he has a philosophy of design, this writer cannot find it. And yet, Mount Frontenac offers a challenging yet playable golf course, spectacular views, and friendly service. It is a must-see on our stops of Native-owned courses.

The Wilderness at Fortune Bay
Bois Forte Band of Chippewa
Tower, MN
golfthewilderness.com

The Bois Forte Band of Chippewa (also referred to as Ojibwe) has lived in northern Minnesota for centuries, though they could be called a restless tribe, or a tribe forced out of its own land more than once. Their people are traced to the east coast up the Saint Lawrence River, around the Great Lakes, where they followed rivers and lakes inland. The Bois Forte Band first entered into a treaty with the U.S. government in 1854 that set aside "an undefined region" around Lake Vermilion as its reservation. This has since been defined, and in 1997, the Band assumed sovereignty.

Golf course architect Jeffrey Brauer invests in how a tribe's heritage is interested in preserving the character of the land. The Wilderness at Fortune Bay joins a gaming operation as part of the tribe's portfolio of enterprises.

Brauer's work at Firekeeper is complimented by his work for the Chippewa at The Wilderness, which has the alluring tag, "Golf the Wilderness." And it includes a famous hole: the short par-four 13th, where long hitters might take a go at driving the green. Brauer is an architect who seems to know he is designing for mere mortals.

The Band holds an Annual Indian Summer Classic, a fundraising tournament for educational scholarships. Since its inception in 2004, the course has garnished several national awards and is known as one of the best in Minnesota.

Grand National Golf Club

Mille Lacs Band of Ojibwe

Hinckley, MN

grandcasinomn.com/amenities/grand-national-golf-club

Like many of the tribes in the northern Midwest, the Ojibwe began migrating west from the Atlantic coast due to colonial expansion. Mille Lacs Lake is the place "where the food grows on water." By the mid-1700s, the Ojibwe had established themselves in the region around Mille Lacs Lake in what is today East Central Minnesota.

In 2006, it was purchased by the Mille Lacs Band as an added amenity to Grand Casino Hinckley. In 2010, Herfort Norby completed a long-range master plan to maximize the playability of the course, which included a redesign of two holes and regrassing of the fairways.

Grand National surrounds a wildlife habitat that has been created for the golf club. While the fairways and greens are manufactured and manicured, parts of the Grand National Golf Club provide shelter for wildlife. More than 20 of the 170 acres feature tall native grasses, ponds, marshes, and creeks where ground-nesting birds and animals live.

Lac Vieux Desert Golf Course

Lac Vieux Desert Band of Lake Superior Indians

Watersmeet, MI

northernwaterscasino.com

Five ponds spread throughout the course, two of which are involved with area restocking programs for trout and walleye. There is also a seasonal creek system running through four of the fairways. These ponds and streams add beauty and challenge for the pleasure of the golfer. With woodlands guarding many of the course corridors, there is always a possibility of animal visitors, which can include birds, squirrels, deer, and bears, reminding any golfer they are in the heart of the northwoods.

Sweetgrass Golf Club
Sage Run Golf Club
Hannahville Indian Community
Harris, MI
Island Resort and Casino
islandresortgolf.com

The original Hannahville settlement is thought to have been along the mouth of the Big Cedar River, on Lake Michigan. The Hannahville are descendants of those who refused to leave Michigan in 1834 during the Great Indian Removal. They lived with the Menominee in northern Wisconsin, and with the Ojibwe and Ottawa people in Canada. In 1853, some of these people began returning to Michigan, including to the Peninsula. It was at this time they settled along the Big Cedar River, about a two hours' drive today north of Green Bay.

Sweetgrass was designed by Paul Albanese, who is the director of golf course architecture at the Edinburgh College of Art in Scotland, which is one of the only graduate-level golf course architecture programs in the world. The course opened in 2009 and was named one of the best new courses in the country by both *Golf Digest* and *Golfweek*. It features rumpled fairways framed with native grasses, and a few template holes, including a Redan, Island, and Biarritz.

In 2018, Island Resort & Casino opened a second golf course, Sage Run, which, was also designed by Albanese. The Sage Run and Sweetgrass courses are studies in contrast, with Sage Run a more rugged terrain with hardwoods, open areas, and a massive ridge/drumlin and bunkers that Albanese likened to Royal County Down, a Northern Ireland golf course rated among the world's finest.

Wild Bluff Golf Course
Bay Mills Indian Community
Brimley, MI
wildbluff.com

Designed by Michigan architect Mike Husby, the course features five sets of tees, which allow players to choose how challenging or playable their round will be. The website claims Wild Bluff is "a green haven with emerald fairways and looking-glass lakes."

Wild Bluff Golf Course also hosted a PGA Canada tournament for four years, in the early 2000s. Legendary player Michelle Wie made national news in 2003 when she competed here against the men, at the young age of 13.

Tatanka Golf Club
Santee Sioux
Niobrara, NE
golftatanka.com

In 2015, Scottish architect Paul Albanese designed Tatanka, a Dakota word that translates to buffalo, the animal that so defines and sustains the historic culture in northeast Nebraska, just south of the Missouri River and the South Dakota border. The name is apt, as buffalo roam the adjacent property to the course, meaning players may come within 40 feet of these beautiful beasts. The course takes advantage of rolling hills and sizeable ridges to offer intriguing land movement to many of the holes. The Santee Sioux Nation plans for Tatanka to become synonymous with great golf there as well. Golf Digest's former architecture editor Ron Whitten described the course as "Nebraska's Sandhills with trees."

Spotted Tail Golf Club

Rosebud Sioux

Rosebud, SD

rosebudsiouxtribe-nsn.gov

This course figures into this book prominently: it's the home course of legendary Joseph Prue, and where his daughter Cassie learned to play. Spotted Tail is also the course on which J.C. Wright honed his skills before taking to golf and Indian Country in the Southwest.

Joe Prue first played at age 12, proudly parring his opening hole. He carried a scratch handicap for 30 years, competing in Native American Golf Association (NAGA) events across the country. Cassie learned early how much golf meant to her father, and how much Spotted Tail meant to the tribe.

The course is still managed by tribal volunteers on the Rosebud Sioux Reservation.

Thornberry Creek at Oneida

Oneida Nation

Hobart, WI

golfthornberry.com

If Laura Cornelius Kellogg were alive to see the golf course just outside of Green Bay, in northeast Wisconsin, she'd be both impressed and also inspired to continue the struggle to regain the integrity of the Oneida Tribe. Thornberry Creek at Oneida is 27 holes of championship golf. Once the site of a multiyear partnership with the LPGA, the courses sit on one of the highest peaks in Brown County. Thornberry is the official golf course of the Green Bay Packers.

Tsiˀ niyukwalihotʌ is the Oneida word for "our ways." Golf has become an integral part of the resurgence of the Oneida, one of the primary tribes in the Iroquois Nation. Rick Jacob designed two golf courses here: the Legends and the Iroquois, and you will need to plan your trip here in advance.

All of this year's leagues are sold out early, and tee times are needed to play your way through these Northwood prairies and meadows.

Pine Hills Golf & Supper Club

Stockbridge Munsee Community Mohican Nation

Greshman, WI

pinehillsgolf.net

At every turn, with every tribe and its course, a new view of history emerges. Pushed out of the East, the Stockbridge Munsee Tribe was presented a Bible by the then Prince of Wales and later-to-be King George III. Dispossessed of most of their land in Massachusetts by the 1780s, the Stockbridge Mohicans headed west to establish themselves first in New Stockbridge, New York, before they were pushed farther west to Wisconsin.

A model of the post-1988 Native recovery, Pine Hills is just minutes away from North Star Mohican Casino Resort, just an hour northwest of Green Bay, Wisconsin. Its short season does not keep golfers from making the journey to play behind a curtain of towering pines in Wisconsin's Northwoods. From the clubhouse, situated on the highest point of the course, overlooking the 1st tee and the 18th green, visitors can gaze at awe-inspiring sunrises and sunsets. (Not to be confused with Pine Hills Country Club, in Sheboygan.)

THE WEST

"The land teaches me to walk"
—Robert Trent Jones II

Eagle Falls Golf Club
Cabazon Band of Cahuilla Indians
Indio, CA
fantasyspringsresort.com

Among the vaunted names in golf course architecture, Clive Clark may not be a household name, though this English golfer and onetime Walker Cup player has designed 33 golf courses both in America and Europe. His most recent is Dumbarnie Links, a genuine links course on the western

The 11th at Eagle Falls. (courtesy of Clive Clark)

coast of Scotland, near St Andrews. Clark's portfolio includes what many who have been there call a masterpiece, Eagle Falls.

"The initial site at Fantasy Springs Casino was flat desert," Clark says, "with the only vegetation being tumbleweed. It was therefore necessary to move around 600,000 cubic yards of sand. This was particularly applicable to the two holes running parallel to the southern border of the site, which abutted the I-10 freeway. Substantial dunes were created to eliminate both the sight of traffic as well as to subdue any freeway traffic noise. At the northern end of the site sits the short par-four 11th hole—I love introducing risk-and-reward- holes, and this is one of my best. One takes the risk of attempting to drive the green, or you lay up to the fairway to the right and play a half wedge for your second shot."

Clark uses a technique that this writer finds on many a great golf course: privacy between holes. Clark continues, "Nearly all the holes are individual holes which means that generally a golfer will not see players on other nearby fairways because of the sand dunes we created. ... As a climax to the final hole of the golf course, a large waterfall was constructed to the left of the 18th green which, when running at full pace, has a thunderous dramatic roar."

Like Talking Stick, this is both a destination course and a course that locals play repeatedly.

"To lift the profile of the course, we introduced wildflowers on the dunes which were largely a colorful variety known as Gazania. Occasionally, as a different kind of highlight, we introduced some patches of annual flowers, being largely Petunia."

"It is also very popular for many locals who are used to playing golf here in the Coachella Valley on courses surrounded by homes on every hole. At Eagle Falls they are instead able to enjoy the beauty of the surrounding rugged desert together with magnificent mountains."

Privacy may also be gotten by sound. Clark notes that, as a climax to the final hole of the golf course, a large waterfall was constructed to the left of the 18th green.

The Cahuilla Band of Mission Indians did their homework. As they prepared to get into the golf game, they travelled with Clive Clark to The Hideaway Golf Club here in La Quinta. "By the time they had seen the first two or three holes, they likened it to Steve Wynn's golf course in Las Vegas called Shadow Creek (designed by Tom Fazio)—this was certainly a very nice compliment. This Hideaway Tour enthused them to start their own golf course as soon as possible!"

As noted throughout our study, our First People seem to have selected some of the finest places in the world to live. Nestled against the backdrop of two breathtaking mountain ranges, this 18-hole championship course is within walking distance of the property and can easily be accessed by visitors coming from either direction on Interstate 10.

Circling Raven Golf Club

Coeur d'Alene Tribe

Worley, ID

cdacasino.com/golf

When finishing Circling Raven—widely viewed as a masterpiece—Gene Bates and the Coeur d'Alene, named each hole. The par-four 9th is called Qine, and the course guide explains that it means "Grandmother. She is the teacher, the lesson giver. Pay attention here, or the lesson is harsh."

Owned and operated by the Coeur d'Alene Tribe, Circling Raven is in the scenic Northern Idaho panhandle approximately 55 minutes from Spokane International Airport (GEG). Measuring 7,189 yards from the rear tees, the 18-hole, Gene Bates-designed layout sprawls magnificently through 620 acres of woodlands, wetlands, and Palouse grasses. Its gleaming white sand bunkers are large and strategically placed, and its variety of holes is tremendous.

Circling Raven is named in honor of an important tribal Chief, and paying homage to ancestors and tradition are involved in everything found at the award-winning golf club. This includes a nationally honored retail shop which has twice won Merchandiser of the Year honors in the Resort Category by PGA of America. The excellent Twisted Earth Grill offers great food and drink, as well as indoor and outdoor seating.

The layout has garnered numerous best-in-kind honors since opening, including being rated a Top-100 Resort Course, Best in State, and a Top U.S. Casino Course. In 2021-23, it was the host venue for the Circling Raven Championship, an Epson "#Road2LPGA" Tour event which included many of the world's top women players.

Other Coeur d'Alene Casino Resort amenities and activities include the superb casino; expansive, rejuvenating Spa Ssakwa'q'n; an array of hotel rooms and suites, multiple bars, restaurants, lounges, and eateries; cultural immersion activities; fitness center, bingo, entertainment showroom, and more.

Discerning golfers care about great playing conditions, wonderful course designs, setting, service, and the satisfaction derived from money well spent at places that move

3rd hole at Circling Raven in Idaho.

them. Circling Raven Golf Club checks all those boxes and then some. An amenity of the Coeur d'Alene Casino Resort Hotel in the Idaho panhandle, the Gene Bates-designed course winds through 620 acres of Palouse Region terrain. That's a vast amount of land compared to most courses globally, and it ensures that the land unfurls naturally, as the Creator intended. And it's an ideal, serene place to play the deeply satisfying game amid pristine beauty in the perfect social-distancing environment. Named for a seminal Chief who guided the tribe through some of its most difficult times, Circling Raven has garnered many honors since opening.

Eagle Springs Golf & Country Club
Table Mountain Rancheria
Friant, CA
eaglespringsgcc.com

Table Mountain Rancheria purchased the 18-hole, Johnny Miller signature design formerly known as Brighton Crest, in January 2010. Founded in 1916, the Table Mountain Rancheria measures 61 acres and is located in Fresno County, near Friant, California. The reservation population is approximately 11 people, with 34 tribal members living in the general area. The course offers equal amounts of challenge and fun, with dramatic land movement and stunning views of the surrounding area.

Indian Canyons Golf Resort
Agua Caliente Band of Cahuilla Indians
Palm Springs, CA
indiancanyonsgolf.com

Indian Canyons Golf Resort has been the jewel of Palm Springs and the Coachella Valley since 1961. Originally opened on New Year's Eve as the Canyon Country Club, the site comprised a 550-acre tract of land owned by several different tribal members of the Agua Caliente Band of Cahuilla Indians. After many years of complex negotiations, Harold Simon, a Palm Springs attorney, drafted the country's largest Indian land lease in history, for what would become the Indian Canyons Golf Resort. This may be the first Native-owned course in the country.

The names of the famous who have played here include Frank Sinatra, Bob Hope, and Jackie Gleason. Former U.S. presidents Dwight Eisenhower, Lyndon Johnson, and Ronald Reagan. The course is set on 550 acres on the Agua Caliente Indian Reservation.

The course is popular among women players, such that LPGA hall-of-famer Amy Alcott was brought in as a design consultant to Casey O'Callaghan during the 2004 renovation. Alcott leads her own Santa Monica, California-based event consulting and course design company.

Journey at Pechanga

Pechanga Band of Luiseño Indians

Temecula, CA

pechanga.com/indulge/journey

The "traditionalist" philosophy of Arthur Hills shapes Journey at Pechanga, which opened in 2008, and has since become known for treating the land as a living, breathing, and life-giving entity, just as the Pechanga people had been treating it for many years before. The Temecula Valley and the Pechanga original lands have sustained the Pechanga people since the beginning of life on earth. According to their website, Journey operates with 30-percent less grass than the California average of about 120 acres. The water used in irrigating the course is reclaimed and recycled water, much of it from the two lakes at holes 5 and 15.

Morongo Golf Club at Tukwet Canyon
Morongo Band of Mission Indians
Beaumont, CA
tukwetcanyon.com

Tukwet Canyon is located about 30 minutes west of Palm Springs. The resort features two courses: The Champions and The Legends. Lee Schmidt and Brian Curley (of Ak-Chin Southern Dunes fame) designed both courses, and both opened in 2000. Schmidt-Curley's philosophy is to "push the envelope of design, keeping a fresh approach while avoiding redundant styles and balancing the owner's desires." Curley grew up caddying at Pebble Beach and spent time with the Landmark Land Company, working alongside Pete Dye on numerous courses. Some holes feature Dye's concepts of large bunkering and visual deception off the tee.

Morongo has hosted the Symetra Tour IOA Championship for the past five years, and has also hosted the Champions Tour National Qualifying Finals, the PGA Tour Qualifying School, the Southern California PGA Professional Championship, and the NCAA Division III National Championships.

Singing Hills Golf Resort
(Oak Glen, Willow Glen, and Pine Glen)
Sycuan Band of the Kumeyaay Nation
El Cajon, CA
singinghillsgolfresort.com

Singing Hills Golf Club at Sycuan features 36 holes designed by Ted Robinson. On the ASCGA page, under philosophy of design, Ted Robinson's page begins: "The golfer attacks, the designer defends. He is considered one of the first to begin to use water hazards as part of that defense, incorporating waterfalls and other large green-side water features in his designs." This work led to his nickname of the King of Waterscapes. Every picture of the courses—located in the serene Dehesa Valley, just 30 minutes east of San Diego airport—includes water. So bring your waders. Run by the Sycuan Band of the Kumeyaay, one of the Mission Indian tribes, the course is associated with the many tribes in the Southern California Tribal Chairmen's Association.

Soboba Springs Golf Course

Soboba Band of Luiseño Indians

San Jacinto, CA

soboba.com/golf

This village was originally settled in 1780, when the Soboba Band of Luiseño Indians were first controlled by the San Juan Capistrano Mission. Back then, California was still a Mexican territory. The area was blessed with a large river, two streams, and many springs, which allowed the Soboba Band to be independent farmers. The tribe were recognized as an established community by Spanish and Mexican rule, and they used Luiseño labor at nearby cattle ranches.

Located less than 90 minutes east of Los Angeles, the Soboba Resort is nestled among the San Jacinto mountains. The course is routed to take advantage of stunning mountain views. Desmond Muirhead designed the course, which opened in 1966, and it was renovated by Cary Bickler in 2006 and 2018. Water comes into play on 11 of the 18 holes. The course has hosted several Nationwide Tour events, as well as the California State Open.

Teleli Golf Club

Tuolumne Band of Me-Wuk Indians

Tuolumne, CA

teleligolfclub.com

Just about two hours east of Oakland, California, the Black Oak Resort is located in the old gold-rush town of Senora. In

2019, the Tuolumne Band of Me-Wuk Indians purchased this Robert Muir Graves-designed golf course as a resort amenity to the Black Oak Casino. The name Teleli is from the Me-Wuk language and translates to "Black Oak." The course is routed among the Sierra Nevada foothills and offers a natural feel. Graves is well known for his minimalist approach to landscapes. In 2002, Graves and his good friend Geoffrey Cornish published a book called *Classic Golf Hole Design: Using the Greatest Holes as Inspiration for Modern Courses*.

Temecula Creek Golf Club
Pechanga Band of Luiseño Indians
Temecula, CA
temeculacreekinn.com

Originally built in 1969, the 305-acre Arthur Hills designed Temecula Creek borders the Pechanga Reservation in southern Temecula. Using the aforementioned Fee To Trust programs, the Pechanga Band of Luiseño Indians—a federally recognized Indian tribe that has called the Temecula Valley in Southern California home for centuries—purchased the Temecula Creek Inn Golf Resort. It is roughly equidistant from Los Angeles and San Diego.

There are 27 holes here, designed by Dick Rossen & Ted Robinson. The three nines—Creek, Oaks, and Stone House—offer a good amount of variety. Creek and Oaks are a bit more friendly, while Stone House offers a great deal of challenge over dramatic elevation changes and among large rock outcroppings.

Whitney Oaks Golf Club
United Auburn Indian Community
Rocklin, CA
whitneyoaksgolf.com

It was Richard Nixon, who—in 1971—finally declared the policy of termination a failure. This set the stage in 1976 for a new federal policy entitled Indian Self-Determination. Ned Blackhawk and other historians view the so-called period of "Self-Determination" as the one we are in, and this would lead to the Indian gaming policy which has spurred economic recovery and in some cases reverse migration.

In 2018, The United Auburn Indian Community (UAIC) purchased Whitney Oaks Golf Club for $3.95 million. The course was originally designed by Johnny Miller and Santa Rosa architect Fred Bliss. Located just 6.3 miles away from its Thunder Valley Casino in Lincoln, the golf operations follows the course of others in the business: golf is added as a lure for out-of-town guests to the casino, but also serves as a destination for golf aficionados.

Yocha Dehe Golf Club
Yocha Dehe Wintun Nation
Brooks, CA
yochadehegolfclub.com

Managed by Troon Golf, Yocha Dehe ("Home by the Spring Waters") is designed by former PGA Tour pro Brad Bell, who made sure to safeguard any sacred or burial grounds. Bell worked with Tribal Council members to create hole names in the native Patwin language, starting with "Sul Sah" (Eagle Eye), aptly named, as the tee box is perched 160 feet above the fairway. Wildlife is the prevalent theme on the majority of holes, with names such as "Watak Kewe" (Frog's House), "Tiwidl" (Rattlesnake), "Sedeo" (Coyote), "Pehtino Hoya" (Animal Gathering Place), and finally "Selai" (Bear) for the 18th hole, the second most difficult hole on the course. The course opened in 2008, and has, like many others, been experiencing a boon through the Covid-19 pandemic.

Volcano Golf Club
Kamehameha Schools Trust
Volcano, HI
volcanogc.com

There's a type of flowering tree on the Hawaiian islands, a gorgeous, seemingly fragile red flower—*'ohi'a'lehua*—but don't be fooled. The tree only grows on the harsh lava rock flows of volcanoes, and might have something to teach us about how the 110-year-old Volcano Golf Club survives on the edge of Kilauea crater, where new earth emerges in fire, smoke and black slag.

Volcano Golf Club sits at 4,000 feet above sea level and began as a three-hole attraction beside the Volcano House, a spot founded in the 1890s for tourists traveling to see the earth make more earth. The golf club went through various iterations until 1968-69, when Jack Snyder—the architect who "brought golf to Hawaii"—created a layout in the shadow of the island's two major, volcanic peaks: Mauna Loa and Mauna Kea. Snyder is also known for four words: "Golf should be fun." Volcano GC had a twilight rate of $30 walking. We played until dark, getting in a full 18. And Jack Snyder's philosophy was readily at work—long fours, long threes and reachable fives.

Like anything 110 years old, Volcano GC has a storied history: the land for Volcano Golf Club and the Volcano National Park were deeded by Princess Bernice Pauahi Bishop, heir to the royal family of King Kamehameha, the chieftain who had united the archipelago nation through diplomacy in 1812. The Princess died in 1884 and dedicated her lands to the establishment of the trust forming the Bishop Estate and the subsequent Kamehameha Schools, the golf course, and also the National Park. In addition to golf, these lands help the schools to support the memory and persistence of Hawaiian culture, supplanted when the United States annexed the islands in 1893. (Hawaii became a state in 1959).

The beauty of Snyder's design is both its playability and its subtlety. The course begins and ends on the land's high point, and the 18 holes are tucked into a northwest-facing slope that has stunning views of the two volcanos—Mauna Loa and Mauna Kea—where the locals believe the goddess Pele the Creator lives. The golfer strolls through the newest of living earth, in a delicious thin air, looking to capitalize on the reachable fives, and stay close on the long threes.

Las Vegas Paiute Golf Resort
Las Vegas Paiute Tribe
Las Vegas, NV
lvpaiutegolf.com

Herbert Warren Wind wrote that "While a man's battle against himself is undoubtedly at the heart of golf's abiding appeal, the setting in which it is played is, for most golfers, one of the most wonderful things about it."

Paiute Golf Resort would appear to be one of our First People's masterworks. Three Pete Dye courses here all present challenge and fun, with the Wolf Course (*Kwetoo-Unuv*) offering the highest difficulty to battle one's self.

On December 30, 1911, ranch owner Helen J. Stewart deeded 10 acres of her land in downtown Las Vegas to the Paiutes, establishing the Las Vegas Paiute Colony. The Indian Reorganization Act of June 18, 1934, in conjunction with the Las Vegas Paiute Tribal Constitution, approved on July 22, 1970, recognized the Tribe as a sovereign nation.

The gaming tsunami would put the Paiute Tribe front and center in Las Vegas's Sin City aura, though golf would be one way to avoid the more damning sins. Head to the first tee rather than the brothel or casino.

One of the best golf course architects of his generation, Pete Dye was known for his humor, and, on completing LV Paiute, is quoted as saying, "One-of-a-kind can now come in threes." He also said, "Golf is not a fair game, so why build a fair course?" The two Paiute courses offer a great escape from the lights of Las Vegas.

Mojave Resort Golf Club
Fort Mojave Indian Tribe
Laughlin, NV
mojavegolf.com

Lee Schmidt and Brian Curly are well known in the Southwest for their bold, original designs. The Mojave Resort course, on the banks of the Colorado River, is now complimented by the Huukan Golf Club, an 18-hole course designed by Robert L. Baldock and Bob E. Baldock in 1989 and now going through a change of ownership to the Fort Mojave Tribe.

As has been noted, Native Americans are the more bullish of communities investing and expanding and growing the game. The two courses span two states, just 15 minutes apart.

Chinook Winds Golf Resort
Chinook Indian Nation
Lincoln City, OR
chinookwindscasino.com/golf

Chinook is a challenging course located just north of the casino. This seems to be a working model: golf as a lure for folks looking to try their luck.

Even so, what' we've found is the tribal communities have done their homework on who they bring in. Casey O'Callahan started his business in 1993, after a soul-searching trip, about which he says, "When I got back from the trip I started interviewing with different design firms. Oddly enough, I met someone on a golf course who knew Cal Olson. I got an interview with Cal and got hired."

O'Callahan notes the increase in renovation projects and how the pandemic has introduced new people to the golf scene. His design principles focus on fun and playability, and he considers the dreaded 7,000-yard golf course a trend that has hurt the game.

Ocean Dunes Golf Links
Coos, Lower Umpqua, and Siuslaw Indians
Florence, OR
threeriverscasino.com/golf

Herbert Warren Wind famously wrote, "No golfer has completed his education until he has played and studied Royal Dornoch." That might be a tip of the cap to the way wind plays into the game. Nae Wind, Nae Rain, Nae Golf. In other words, Golf is best when the weather is bad. When it's blowing, and the rain is falling, the real golfers come out to play.

Ocean Dunes Golf Links will test these truisms. William Robinson, who interned with Robert Trent Jones Sr. and was a full partner with Geoffrey Cornish, has built a lasting beauty and destination course on Oregon's central coast.

Kaha-Nee-Ta Golf Course
Confederated Tribes of Warm Springs
Warm Springs, OR
kahneeta.com/golf

The Kah-Nee-Ta hot springs were removed from communal ownership sometime after the passage of the Dawes Act, also known as the General Allotment Act of 1887. In 1935, F.B. Freeland, a physician from Portland purchased the 320 acres surrounding the mineral springs for $35,000 and quickly developed a small-scale resort. The tribe bought this back in 1961. They added golf in the 1970s.

Designed in the 1970s by William Bell (front nine); Gene "Bunny" Mason (back nine), Kaha-Nee-Ta Golf Course is operated by the Confederated Tribes of Warm Springs. They also operate the spa, which makes for a New Old World.

Golf Course at Birch Creek

The Confederated Tribes of the Umatilla Indian Reservation

Pendleton, OR

birchcreekgolfcourse.com

There appears to be some deep history to the Golf Course at Birch Creek that needs a golf sleuth to pursue: A local paper claims that a golf tournament happened here in November 1902, but the first annual tournament of the Pendleton Golf Club was played in May 1903. The Club purchased the property in 1919, and in 1929 the course went through a remodel with Shirley G. Stone as the architect. Not much can be found about Shirley Stone, though she is listed as having designed four other courses in Oregon and Washington.

The tribe purchased Birch Creek Golf Course in 2019. It is no longer a country club for members, but is now open for public play and membership privileges. They also own Wildhorse.

Wildhorse Resort & Casino Golf Course

Confederated Tribes of the Umatilla Indian Reservation

Pendleton, OR

wildhorseresort.com/golf

John Steidel's history in design runs through Robert Muir Graves, among others, and his portfolio includes Coeur d'Alene. Wildhorse claims 5 lakes and 66 sand bunkers, all the in the shadows of the foothills of Oregon's Blue Mountains. *Golf Digest* created a category called "top casino golf courses," though the author thinks this category should directly reference the tribes that have purchased, restored, and renovated—as well as built—many top-flight courses.

Cedars at Dungeness
Jamestown S'Klallam Tribe
Sequim, WA
7cedars.com/golf

Designed by Jack Reimer and Mark Miller, the Cedars golf course opened in 1969, The Cedars may be the first tribe casino-owned course in the state, setting a trend that would be repeated across Washington. The Jamestown S'Klallam Tribe purchased the property in 2007, and the 122-acre Sequim course has become a top spot not just for local golfers but across western Washington. The Cedars claims to be playable for about 300 days per year.

When the tribe purchased the course, they wanted to bring in not just a "tribal feel," but the philosophy that everything should be built to last for 100 years, to be something their ancestors will be proud of.

The Cedars has another historical reference. One of its spokespeople is Sonny Sixkiller, the standout quarterback for the University of Washington Huskies in the early 1970s.

Loomis Trail Golf Course
Lummi Nation
Blaine, WA
golfloomis.com

In what might sound like a familiar script, in 2018, the Lummi Nation purchased "the crown jewel of the Washington golfing community," Loomis Trail Golf Course. The Nation took the private course public and opened it to the entire golfing public as a public course. The course is within—St'l'el-nep—ancient grounds or the primary village pf the tribe. Reclaiming these areas honor the ancestors and the history of tribe.

Designed by the Canadian Golf Hall-of-Fame golfer Graham Cooke, Loomis Trail accents harmony with the environment. While designing environmentally sound golf courses, Cooke emphasizes natural features by making them an intricate part of the aesthetic experience. The course continues to be listed as among the best in the state of Washington.

Salish Cliffs Golf Club

Squaxin Island Tribe
Shelton, WA
salish-cliffs.com

Salish Cliffs is the first Salmon-Safe certified golf course in the world, awarded in 2012. The Salmon-Safe Golf Course Certification program is an offshoot of the Northwest eco-label for agricultural and vineyard practices, administered in Washington by the Seattle-based non-profit Stewardship Partners.

Dave Lopeman—the tribe's council chair at the time—said, "When we decided to build Salish Cliffs, we vowed to uphold our Tribal mission to nurture our people and our land and ensure both thrive for generations to come. Creating and maintaining an eco-sensitive course from site planning through ongoing operation was essential to us and the people of Western Washington."

Designed by Gene Bates (Circling Raven, among others) Bates noted a double tee on the eighth and 16th holes. That came about, Bates said, because he wanted to lengthen the eighth to more than 600 yards.

"There's a certain wow factor to having a 600-yard hole," said Bates, adding that today's good players can easily manage that distance as well. Ouch.

White Horse Golf Club
Suquamish Tribe
Kingston, WA
whitehorsegolf.com

White Horse is the first design of Cynthia Dye McGarey, yes, niece of Pete and Alice Dye. Cynthia became the only woman to ever solo design a course that won *Golf Digest*'s Best New Course Award, which was accomplished with White Horse in 2007.

When the Suquamish Tribe purchased the course in 2010, they bought it out of bankruptcy. With resources from their gaming operation—Clearwater Casino and Resort—they have saved a gem with pedigree. Not only the Dye family, but Lee Elder—the first African American to play in the Masters Tournament (1975)—made a habit of playing White Horse once or twice a week for an extended period when he lived in the area.

And there is another turn worth noting: Cynthia Dye McGarey's original design included waist high fescue close to the greens and cart paths and 156 bunkers—not good for business.

The tribe hired Tacoma's John Harbottle to soften the course in 2012 and spent $700,000 removing about 200 trees and over 90 bunkers (leaving only 62), cutting back the fescue and adding a new, shorter set of tees. The course has since thrived.

THE NORTHEAST

"Our Mother sang to us so deep
We sleep as children do
Dreaming of where the buffalo roam
We are that dream. We are that home."
—Robert Trent Jones II

Lake of Isles

Mashantucke-Pequot Nation
North Stonington, CT
lakeofisles.com

Lake of Isles sits on 1,000 acres of stony scarp and wetland. "A dramatic piece of land," according to Rees Jones, the decorated architect who, beginning in 2002, designed and built 36 holes here that dance through what once was and is now again Mashantucket Pequot tribal territory.

"Anything that would help the tribes, I am happy to do,"

Lake of Isles. The turtle-shaped bunker left.

said Jones, noting that his family supports efforts to make life better for America's indigenous people. They are not alone in the desire to right the profound wrongs that have been done.

Mashantucket Pequot Tribal Nation was officially recognized in October 1983 when President Ronald Reagan signed the Mashantucket Pequot Indian Claims Settlement Act, an act of Congress that provided the tribe federal recognition as well as funds to repurchase over 800 acres of stolen tribal land. Today the reservation encompasses 1,637 acres and is the longest continually occupied reservation in American history.

According to Lori Potter, public affairs director at Mashantucket Pequot Tribal Nation: "We are a people of precedent. We are the first genocidal massacre survivors in what would become the continental U.S. The tribe occupies the first Indian reservation, the first tribal casino and the first tribal gaming commission."

Historically known as the Fox People, the Pequots prospered for thousands of years on their traditional lands—roughly 250 square miles—on what is currently known as Connecticut and Rhode Island.

By 1991, the Mashantucket Pequot Tribal Council had expanded its bingo hall into a casino known as Foxwoods, now the one of the largest casinos in the U.S. The gaming and entertainment venues were successful enough that the tribe built and operates an award-winning museum and research center. And in 2002, the tribe secured 1,000 acres from the state and hired Jones.

Jones's portfolio includes two of the 55 Native American-owned courses in the country. In addition to Lake of Isles, he has worked on Dacotah Ridge for Lakota.

About Lake of Isles, Jones says: "It was a difficult site—a newbie would have been stifled. The daily work required consulting with the tribal council and archaeologists to ensure that sacred sites were protected." He also notes holes are carved around wetlands, carved around the lake, and he designed for a vast amount of conservation land.

"We studied the topo more than the land. We cleared

what was pretty dense forest, then we had rock problems. We would put in a hole, but then had to reset a lot of them due to various concerns." One of those concerns was the tribe's heritage.

In addition to archaeological surveys and respect for sacred sites, seashell and turtle symbols were both worked into the design. The turtle and seashell symbols are worked into bunkers on both the North and South courses—recognition of the turtle, the spirit animal of the tribe, and the seashell for the aquatic economy by which the tribe thrived before European contact.

"We worked with the tribe considering their background and history and what was essential to them," says Jones. "We understood what was important to them and included that in our approach."

While the issue of reparation for slavery continues to roil our national dialogue, a number of studies show casinos, entertainment venues, and golf have reversed social and economic decline for tribes nationwide. Lori Potter says, "Being able to provide jobs, housing, healthcare, pharmaceuticals, cultural and educational opportunities, and a secure community are among our highest priorities as a tribe."

For Jones, that golf can play a role is second nature. "Giving them the land to control their own destinies?" he asks rhetorically. "Why did America decide to take care of these people whose land they took away? It's a self-determining ability to be able to build... venues. It's beneficial to the tribes to have these opportunities to build courses."

Even for non-golfers, golf courses can give people a place to go, says Jones. "Look at Torrey Pines and Bethpage," he says. "People go there whether they are playing golf or not. Look at Wellman [in South Carolina, where Jones is currently restoring a public course], Dacotah Ridge... for the tribes, the courses become social centers as well as golf centers."

That the game of golf has aided in the process is not a surprise to historians of a sport which, by its nature, requires truth-telling, humility, and a love of the land.

Mohegan Sun Golf Club
Mohegan Tribe
Baltic, CT
mohegansungolfclub.com

The name of Geoffrey Cornish is one that will last as long as the game of golf is played. Though not a player himself—once his design work became a Piccadilly Circus he left his clubs in the attic—he was a tireless promoter of golf for the people. As his friend Ron Whitten wrote, "His were mostly low-budget public ones, easy to maintain, easy to play, ones that made money. No, Geoff was a great golf course architect because he was more interested in spreading the game than in making a name for himself."

One of those low budget affairs was Pautipaug in Baltic, Connecticut. In 2007 Mohegan Tribal Gaming Authority acquired and renamed the course Mohegan Sun Golf Club. The gaming authorities have an interest in player Development. In other words, they want to attract high rollers who come and lose money. But they have a gem of a course that has all of Cornish's values in play.

Pautipaug is a Nipmuck word for "miry land." Basically, a bog with rocks. Cornish, who designed more courses in New England than any other, built Pautipaug in 1960 at the behest of a group of local doctors. He has said about design: "We make golf courses too damned hard." His "design triangle" accented playability, maintenance, and aesthetics. Impeccable greens—when the ball does what your read says it should do—aid in this process of making the game more accessible.

Cornish passed in 2012 at the age of 97. His courses live on.

Turning Stone Golf Club
(Atunyote, Kaluhyat, Shenandoah, Sandstone Hollow, Pleasant Knolls)
Oneida Indian Nation
Verona, NY
turningstone.com/golf

Atunyote is an 18-hole layout designed by Tom Fazio. It opened in 2004. *Atunyote* is the Oneida word for "eagle." Atunyote also is the site of the Notah Begay III Foundation Challenge.

Kaluhyat is another 18-hole course here, designed by Robert Trent Jones II, which opened in 2003. *Kaluhyat* is the Oneida word for "the other side of the sky."

Designed by Rick Smith in 2000, Shenandoah is the third 18-hole offering here. Smith redesigned the course in 2016.

There are two nine-hole routings here as well. Sandstone Hollow is a par-three course designed with the busy golfer in mind. Designed by Rick Smith, it opened in 1999. The second is Pleasant Knolls, a country nine first designed in 1950.

Golfweek noted that coming out of the turn of the century, there was one group in the golf industry bullish on new course work: Oneida Indian Nation might be said to be the lead bull. Their five courses in and around Verona, New York include work by Robert Trent Jones II, Tom Fazio, and Rick Smith. While Fazio and Joes are household names, Rick Smith's design at Shenandoah comes in for discussion as the finest of the three. Robert Mercer Deruntz is quoted as saying, "I think the Shenandoah course is by far the best course at Turning Stone. ... Every hole is angled so that where a drive ends up makes the approach easier or harder depending on pin location, etc.—it is not enough to be in the amply wide fairways. High handicappers can play this course while the pro can be very well challenged. It has yet to be really shot up despite awesome quality putting surfaces!"

On Smith's website, there is a picture of him with Robert Trent Jones Sr, with the caption, "It All Started With Robert

Trent Jones, Sr." Course design appears secondary to Smith's teaching, as Smith notes that he was a swing coach of some the greats of the game, including Nicklaus and Palmer.

As noted throughout this book, the twists and turns in golf history are many, and Rick Smith is an impresario with three golf academies to go with his design work. Speaking of Arnie, Smith has said, "I noticed the unique swings early in my career and studied them. And I mean in depth study. I was able to separate what should be left alone (your uniqueness) and what should be taught and improved."

Seneca Hickory Stick
Seneca Nation of Indians
Lewiston, NY
senecahickorystick.com

Akin to Foxwoods, the Seneca Casino rises out of the northern forests in an Oz-like way. It's so dramatically out of character that it has a certain enchantment. Seneca's Hickory Stick Golf Course shares that same allure.

Like Geoffrey Cornish, the name of Jones in relation to course design is as close to eternal as life on Earth gets. Robert Trent Jones II considers design an artform, a type of musical compositions made from earth and rock and water. He aims to have his courses "appear to have been shaped by the same forces that created the surrounding landforms." The effort required to shape a course to look like it landed there might be said to be herculean, or of the post-bulldozer era.

A lover of history, Jones II noted that the Seneca were part of the original five nations of the Iroquois League. In addition to noting how music figured into Lincoln's declaration about the first thanksgiving, he noted in our interview how Senator Daniel Inouye accepted the invitation by the Onondaga Nation to discuss the role of the Six Nations and the Great Law of Peace in the creation of the principles of the United States government. The acknowledgement came in time for the Constitution's 200th anniversary. It was in 1987 when a

Native historian by the name of Faithkeeper Oren Lyons explained to Senator Inouye the Great Law of the Iroquois and the Haudenosaunee's influence on the founding of the United States.

"Not only did the Senator write about the influences of the Haudenosaunee in setting up the United States government," Oren Lyons wrote, "but also reaffirmed the government-to-government relations between us and the United States." The resolution that passed the Senate stated: "Whereas the original framers of the Constitution, including most notably, George Washington and Benjamin Franklin, are known to have greatly admired the concepts, principles and governmental practices of the Six Nations of the Iroquois Confederacy."

Leave it to Jones II to connect the founding of American democracy with our First People and the game of golf. We cannot tell the story of America—or golf—without our First People. Aho.

Author's Note

Born in Paterson, New Jersey, on the ancestral lands of the Lenne Lenapae, an area named Lenapehoking, Dr. Mark Wagner is the fourth child of eight born to Jack and Pat (Coyle) Wagner. From Irish grandparents on their maternal side and German on their paternal side, The Wagner clan were brought into the world in the great river of DNA and blood lines that streamed into this country in the late nineteenth and twentieth century. Mark's father—writer, community leader, consultant—had many jobs throughout his life, while his mother's job—for most of her life and lucky for all—was loving the eight kids she pushed into the world. She raised us on the banks of a turtle pond in Northern New Jersey, from which we have many happy memories and from which we have all scattered.

In 2021, as he explored the history of golf and golf architecture, Dr. Mark began to realize there were many firsts among our First People in the ancient club and ball game, a game he has loved since his childhood outings with his family to the Adirondacks. Part of summer vacations were spent learning some of Algonquian (Mohawk) words—like Adirondack (Tree Eater). We would hike those hills and live out fantasies of being Natty Bumpbo and Chingachgook. We also had fantasies about learning golf, about which Frank Dufina would quip: The first hundred years are the hardest.

Back Nine Press's motto—"Golf Books for Everyone"—seemed like a good place to begin to push back on this idea that golf is an elite, White-man's sport. In an attempt to give a suitable history of those First among Firsts, *Native Links* is a kind of travelogue and oral history about and by our Indigenous people who have shaped and played the game, as well as the tribes that have hired the finest designers to build magnificent courses.

From the 1896 U.S. Open at Shinnecock Hills to the 2023 Native American Open at Santa Ana, *Native Links* collects stories meant to broaden our understanding of Indigenous culture, as well as how the game we love plays a part of that history. These stories make us, and these stories may also remake us. Stories that are retold or that need to be told can reshape the past, can acknowledge the ancestors who paved the way for us, and may make a new and better way for those who are to come.